W9-DEO-905

THE CULTURAL CONSTRUCTION OF
POLITICS IN ASIA

THE CULTURAL CONSTRUCTION OF POLITICS IN ASIA

Edited by Hans Antlöv and
Tak-Wing Ngo

ST. MARTIN'S PRESS
NEW YORK

#464075

St. Martin's Press, Scholarly and Reference Division
175 Fifth Avenue, New York, NY 10010

First published in the United States of America in 2000
Printed and bound in Great Britain by
TJ International Ltd, Padstow, Cornwall

ISBN: 0-312-22828-7

Library of Congress Cataloging-in-Publication Data

The cultural construction of politics in Asia / edited by Hans Antlöv
and Tak-Wing Ngo.
      p   cm.
Includes bibliographical references and index.
ISBN 0-312-22828-7 (cloth)
      1. Politics and culture--Asia. 2. Political anthropology--Asia.
3. Democracy--Asia. 4. Asia--Politics and government.
I. Antlöv, Hans. II. Ngo, Tak-Wing, 1962-
JQ36.C85 1999 2000   99-37896
306'.095--dc21   CIP

CONTENTS

List of Figures

PREFACE

This volume originated from a conference on 'Democracy in Asia', held at the Nordic Institute of Asian Studies (NIAS) in Copenhagen on 26–29 October 1995. The central theme of the conference was the controversy over the issue of the development of political systems in Asia which claimed to be Asian variants of democracy. The conference elicited great response, reflecting the growing interest in the issue. A wide range of topics were discussed, including the notion of an Asian concept of democracy, the discursive struggle between rulers and the ruled, the democratization process, the role of social movements and the construction/maintenance of political order under different types of regimes. Among these topics, one theme surfaced repeatedly during the heated debates: the relationship between culture and politics in Asia. Positions were divided between those who offered a culturalistic explanation of political behaviour and those who emphasized non-cultural determinants of the body politic.

We decided, therefore, to take up this controversial topic and develop it into a book. The aim of this volume is to explore the relationship between the normative/moral order and the actual political order. Instead of focusing on what we believe to be a futile debate as to whether Asian culture is suitable for democracy or whether there is an Asian democracy, this book looks at how certain values are mobilised and articulated in a way that sustains, produces, or modifies a particular political system. It also examines how these values and systems are interpreted as being 'democratic' in a specific sense in different countries.

Papers that suited the theme were selected for this volume, while new ones were commissioned to fill in the gaps. The case studies include countries from East Asia, South Asia and Southeast Asia, covering a variety of regimes ranging from praetorian politics to authoritarian regimes to Western-style liberal democracies. All the contributors to this volume have revised their original papers substantially in order to take up the quest. Although individual chapters highlight different factors in their country analyses (historical legacies, institutional artifice, social norms, political indoctrination, ethnic conflicts, class cleavages, etc.), the volume as a whole gives a dialectical view on culture and politics: both are seen as mutually constitutive in the sense that cultural norms are politically sanctioned as much as political acts are evaluated by use of culturally perceived categories.

The project received generous support from various institutions and persons. Financial support for the conference came from the International Institute for Asian Studies in Leiden, the Nordic Institute of Asian Studies in Copenhagen, and the Centre for East and Southeast Asian Studies in Göteborg. We are grateful for the input of all the conference participants, especially the keynote speakers Richard Robison, Stein Tønnesson, Olle Törnquist and Laurence Whitehead. Their valuable suggestions helped to put the project in perspective. During the copy-editing and production process, we have been extremely fortunate to have work done professionally by Liz Bramsen and Gerald Jackson at NIAS. Finally, our home institutes have provided the essential support and space for our task. To all the above-mentioned, we give our grateful acknowledgement.

Hans Antlöv, Jakarta
Tak-Wing Ngo, Leiden
September 1999

1 POLITICS, CULTURE, AND DEMOCRACY IN ASIA

Hans Antlöv and Tak-Wing Ngo

The focus of this volume is the relationship between culture and politics in Asia, mediated by the contentious issue of democracy. The concept of a certain type of democracy based on so-called Asian values has aroused increasing global attention not only because it represents a challenge to the liberal democracy orthodoxy, but also because it compels us to rethink the assumptions of the long-existing modernization paradigm. The different paths of Asian countries in achieving economic development and in organizing political order provide at least prima facie evidence for an alternative understanding of the historical trajectories to modernity.

Notwithstanding the importance of the Asian case, the debate over Asian democracy – as well as that over liberal democracy – has been mingled with emotional, rhetorical, and ungrounded generalizations. This is understandable, given the far-fetched implications of the notion of Asian democracy in *realpolitik*, so that politicians and academics alike are keen to register their own interpretations of the concept. However, the domination of polemics over genuine scholarly exchange have so far only sidelined the opportunity to reflect on our existing understanding of human history, culture, and politics; and it may turn the critical concept into a new ideological dogma used either to justify or to attack an existing regime. In order to avoid this, we need to differentiate carefully the critical aspects of the concept from its polemic overtones.

Political development in Asia, of both a democratic and authoritarian nature, has forced social scientists to refine their instruments of analysis

1

and general theories. The democratization process in several Asian countries provides fascinating insights into new paths of achieving democracy; while the resilience of other authoritarian regimes challenges the modernization paradigm. The chapters in this book focus on the specificity of democracy and authoritarianism in Asia. They do so by putting history and culture into the national political framework. Although the individual chapters do not portray a single one-to-one relationship between history, culture and politics, they argue that it is also impossible to understand present day development only as a result of contemporary global processes such as a third wave of democratization. We need to contextualize political change. The purpose of this introduction is to make explicit some of the major underlying assumptions in the current debates about the nature of Asian polity, and clear the ground for more fruitful academic debates.

The Background of the Debate

The rise of Asia and the debate over 'Asian democracy' pose an important challenge to the influential modernization paradigm that upholds a view of history as progressing from traditional towards modernity, characterized by the establishment of a capitalist market and liberal democracy. The once sacrosanct principle of liberal democracy as the yardstick of modernity and human rights is being questioned as representing no more than the imposition of Western values and standards over developing nations. This challenge arises at a time when Asia emerges as an increasingly powerful economic player in the post-Cold War international order. Before we look more closely at the debate, it is useful to have a brief overview of the context in which the debate arises.

The earlier faith in the modernization paradigm is reflected in the enthusiastic establishment of modern republics and the introduction of parliamentarism for newly independent nations after the Second World War. In Vietnam, Ho Chi Minh referred to the American and French constitutions in the nation's declaration of independence in 1945. In Indonesia, leaders laid their claim for national sovereignty on the Atlantic Charter. In India and Sri Lanka, parliamentary politics and the principle of trias politica were introduced. However, subsequent development shows that liberal democracy has far from taken root in most parts of Asia: the military came to power in Thailand and Korea, Indonesia declared martial law and practised the so-called 'Guided Democracy', Burma and Vietnam emerged as one-party dictatorships, while Sri Lanka underwent dramatic political decay and eventually turned into civil war. Only a few countries, notably Japan and India, and to a certain extent Malaysia and Singapore, have maintained some degree of parliamentary order in the subsequent decades (ironically, it was the democratically elected prime minister of India, Nehru, who first used the concept of Asian Values, at the Asia–Africa conference in Bandung in 1957). Yet, until only very recently, even these countries have been dominated by one strong party in every election, and hence are often criticized by Western observers as far from genuine democracies.

First, it must be noted that the last decade has seen democratization in a number of Asian countries. In Thailand, a military coup failed to oust the elected government in 1992. In the Philippines, parliamentary and electoral politics have been gradually normalized. In Cambodia a new government was voted to power under UN-supervised elections in 1993. In South Korea, a peaceful transition from martial-law rule has been completed. In Taiwan, the parliamentary bodies and the president were fully elected for the first time in 1995 and 1996. Indonesia is taking its first step toward a democracy with the 1999 election. And last but not the least, Nepal, Pakistan and Bangladesh have all returned to democracy.

However, while observers are still debating whether this wave of democratization represents a landmark towards the victory of liberal democracy or merely a historical conjuncture expecting another backlash,[1] some leaders in Asia, who were once close allies of Europe and the US, have begun to criticize the use of the Western standard of democracy to measure the political progress of their countries. Among the most vocal critics of Western democracy are Malaysian Prime Minister Mahathir and former Singaporean Prime Minister Lee Kuan Yew, who have engineered de facto one-party democracies. In response to Western accusations about the illiberal nature of their polity, they criticize the West for claiming its values as universal, and attempting to set a global standard for evaluating other political systems that are fundamentally different in historical, economic, and cultural terms. The endeavour to impose such Western views is, for these Asian critics, not merely ethno-centric arrogance but also a political intrusion of sovereignty. In the words of Mahathir:

> It is clearly dangerous to make a religion of an ideology. … As much as the communists were intolerant, the democrats, particularly the liberal democrats, are intolerant … challenge democracy and you will be branded a heretic, an unbeliever, a renegade.[2]

Echoing this view, several Asian leaders have argued that each country has the right to choose its political system – or what they called an Asian style of democracy – according to its own cultural and historical conditions. They see the attempts of Western countries to press for political liberalization and democratization in non-Western countries as running counter to the principle of non-interference in domestic affairs of other sovereign states. For them, the rhetoric of Western-style democracy has become an instrument for the continuation of Western hegemony.

The criticism over liberal democracy and the proclamation of an Asian alternative arise out of a specific historical conjuncture in the international political economy. Several interrelated trends can be delineated. The first is the demise of the Cold War. Nations become more independent from Cold War politics, resulting in more willingness on their part to openly address their disagreement with US ideas.

The second trend is the rising economic power of Asia as a region. Some parts of Asia, notably Japan and the East Asian industrialized economies, have modernized at a remarkable speed. Notwithstanding the recent financial crisis, these nations have succeeded in economic development without adopting the Western model of liberal democracy. The rest of Asia (and perhaps even the world) can now look to them as a model of development.[3]

With the increase of Asia's economic power in the international arena, Asian leaders are now much more confident in condemning the hypocrisy of Western interference in the developing world in the name of human rights and democracy. For these Asian leaders, criticizing the universality of liberal democracy has become part of a nationalist project.

Linking the critique of liberal democracy to nationalism has made the debate rather emotional and rhetorical. The issue is then closely connected with such normative questions of human rights, national sovereignty, and East-West relations. For instance, in response to the criticism of Western hegemony, sceptics argue that Asian leaders' challenge of liberal democracy is nothing more than an excuse to defend their violation of civil and human rights, and a justification for the continuation of their authoritarian rule. This kind of debate leads sometimes to a polarized view that a political system can only be either a liberal democratic one or a non-Western one, corresponding to totally different civilizations. As we mentioned earlier, this runs the danger of over-generalization. While one can criticize the hegemonic Western view about the universal applicability of democratic practices, one cannot jump to the conclusion that therefore an anti-hegemonic stand is equivalent to the adoption of authoritarian politics. This kind of either–or generalization confuses rhetoric with serious debate. Worse still, such a simplified view of polarization can be used as evidence of a potential clash of civilizations, thus injecting further emotional and ideological dimensions into existing international relations.

Notwithstanding the unfortunate over-generalization and simplified polarization, the debate over Asian democracy, we believe, does raise serious issues that deserve attention. These issues include the relationship between development and democracy, power politics and political culture, and ostensible values and actual practices. It is issues such as these raised by the Asian democracy debate, rather than the rhetoric, that will contribute to scholarship and learning. Let us look at them in the following discussion.

Development and Democracy

For decades, students of politics have been concerned with the presence or absence of democracy in developing countries. Series of comparative studies have been undertaken to throw light on the conditions, or requisites, of liberal democracy. The four-volume work *The Breakdown of Democratic Regimes*, edited by Linz and Stepan, attempts to study the transition to authoritarian rule from democracy in Europe and Latin America. This was followed by another four-volume study, *Transitions from Authoritarian Rule*, edited by O'Donnell, Schmitter and Whitehead. Another major project followed soon after, aimed at making a systematic comparison of country studies in Asia, Latin America, and Africa. The project resulted in a four-volume publication on *Democracy in Developing Countries,* edited by Diamond, Linz and Lipset.[4]

Despite their varying positions, these studies share one important moral assumption: liberal democracy is a desirable form of government. As the editors of one of the works stress, they study democracy because they value political democracy and liberalism as an end in itself.[5] This normative assumption has been criticized by advocates of Asian democracy, who see politics as no more than a means to other social goals: harmony, stability, growth. As Helgesen and Xing's chapter in this volume argues, a government can be 'authoritarian' from a procedural definition of power, and yet still considered to be 'just' from a native point of view because it ensures the well-being of its people. Subsistence and development, many Asian leaders emphasize, take precedence over civil rights and political freedom. Legitimation is based on growth and economic improvement for the nation as a whole, not on the protection of civil rights that can guarantee individual freedom. Bread-and-butter (or perhaps rice-and-tofu) issues are more important than choice and plurality.

In other words, Asian democracy assumes that the quest for development precedes the quest for political democracy. Furthermore, it is believed that development requires a concerted effort that is often undemocratic. The seminal study of Gerschenkron argues that late-comers to the world economy need a centralized approach to industrialization and economic growth.[6] 'Catching up' demands a more centralized mechanism for capital mobilization, industrial adjustment, and technology upgrading. The need for catch-up becomes an important argument for the non-liberal democratic form of rule in Asia. Gerschenkron's thesis has been picked up by state-led theorists who want to explain the economic success of the East Asian countries.[7] A 'strong' state that can overcome popular pressure becomes a requisite for rapid economic development. The economic success of Japan and the rapid industrialization and growth of Taiwan, South Korea and Singapore have been attributed to the presence of an interventionist government that puts economic development as its top priority. The ability of the government to do so, according to the statist literature, depends upon the high degree of political autonomy of the state from sectional interests and popular pressure, and the capacity of the state to implement develop-mental programmes effectively.[8] This autonomy and capacity in turn derive from the authoritarian nature of East Asian states, arisen from their historical processes of state formation.[9]

The East Asian experience becomes a role model for other Asian countries. Advocates of such an Asian model argue that economic devel-opment and liberal democracy are incompatible variables for developing countries. In addition, they see order and stability as the essential condition for economic development, constituting another social priority for developing countries. Adversarial politics – a form of political life that is often associated with liberal democracy – runs the danger of arousing internal conflicts and disorder; it is therefore seen as unsuitable for the developing Asian countries.

6

Even when one agrees with the above position, the issues of social and economic priority and the relationship between development and democracy have little association with being 'Asian'. It is an issue faced by many developing countries – Asian as well as Latin American and African. The position is in fact supported by some of the modernization literature, and is not very different from the experience of Europe and North America in the previous century. Various studies have found that the state-building process leading to economic modernization is characterized by a concentration of state power in terms of coercion, extraction, regulation and distribution.[10] Hence LaPalombara suggests that rapid economic change leading to industrialization can be effected without conforming to the Western patterns of governance. It may very well be more related to undemocratic systems.[11] In comparing the Eastern European and the Latin American situations, Przeworski concludes that there is an inherent dilemma in the course of democratization. Whereas political democracy hinges on co-operation, compromise and inclusion, economic reform is best undertaken by initial brutality and exclusion of social interests.[12] In the current debate, the issue of development is often mixed with the argument that Asian countries have a different set of social priorities informed by cultural heritage. Although the two are related, it may still be useful to distinguish the developmental issue (which has a more universal concern) from the Asian concern.

The chapter by Ngo in this volume, on Hong Kong under British rule, offers a good example. The primacy of economic growth and development was emphasized by the British colonial government without making reference to any Asian values. The colonial government of Hong Kong promoted wealth creation through policy measures such as low profit tax, limited social welfare provisions, minimal labour protection, free enterprise, and free capital inflow and outflow, all being done under an authoritarian political system. These measures were grouped under the label of 'laissez-faire' – a nineteenth-century Western economic doctrine which was virtually alien to the Chinese population in Hong Kong. Yet the doctrine enjoyed widespread support because it was correlated with growth and development, in stark contrast to the lack of it in socialist China. In other words, it is not Asian values but pragmatic adjustment to circumstances that counts. The pervasiveness of laissez-faire rested not so much on the idea itself but on the way it fitted existing perceptions of the people in contemporary circumstances, in which

7

economic rewards and political protection (from communist China across the border) were deemed more important than freedom and liberty.

Culture and Politics

Another central element in the current Asian democracy debate is the role of culture in politics. The question of culture has again come to the forefront of heated debate after Huntington proclaimed his controversial thesis about the clash of civilizations.[13] One does not have to agree to this thesis to accept the point that cultural differences are becoming politically relevant in world affairs and are increasingly seen as the basis of political cleavages.

The centrality of culture in politics and democracy is nothing new. The best-known formulation is perhaps Weber's notion of a Protestant ethic contributing to the rise in Europe of a capitalist political and economic system. In contemporary scholarship, the seminal work of Almond and Verba asserts that democracy requires a supportive civic culture: a set of attitudes and values towards politics shared by the citizenry and political elite concerning individual rights, public authority, and political power.[14] Subsequent writers have attributed the absence of a liberal democratic style of government and the existence of authoritarian practice in non-Western countries to the absence of such a civic culture. For instance, Pye argues that the paternalistic nature of Asian political culture – characterized by dependency on authority, avoidance of open conflict, emphasis on stability, etc. – makes democratic government an unlikely project.[15]

This cultural determinist view of politics rests upon what Emmerson calls 'ultra-Orientalism'.[16] It assumes the existence of a single set of values upheld by all the people in Asia, spreading across dozens of countries, speaking mutually unintelligible languages and believing in different religions. This is then contrasted to a single but different set of values supposedly held by an equally diverse population in the West. Cultural plurality and diversity are reduced to no more than two polar extremes: the East as the East and the West as the West.

The implication of the culture determinist argument can be far-fetched. The most extreme case can be found in the late-nineteenth- and early-twentieth-century China. During that time heated debate occurred among the intellectuals and the ruling elite on whether China should abandon its cultural heritage and opt for 'complete Westernization' in order to achieve modernization. The argument at that time was that 'science' and 'democracy' were the keys to modernity; and since the traditional Chinese culture was a hindrance to their development, China should move away from its own heritage and learn from the West. The debate, earmarked by the launching of a New Cultural Movement, had significant impact on the subsequent historical trajectory of modern China.[17]

The case of China illustrates the danger of marginalizing the cultural heritage of developing nations if we combine the logic of political culture argument to the modernization paradigm. Given that liberal democracy represents human progress from traditionality to modernity and given that liberal democracy can only exist under a civic culture which is absent in non-Western cultures, it follows that non-Western countries either have to abandon their own culture in order to achieve democracy, or they can never attain modernity if they maintain their own culture.

It is here that the notion of Asian democracy emerges as a critical response to the above claims. In resisting the imposition of a Western-turn-universal standard onto Asian politics, advocates of Asian democracy uphold the cultural determinist view of politics, but reject the supremacy of liberal democracy over other forms of political system. They argue instead that there are other ways of organizing power and authority that are more appropriate to indigenous culture and norms. By denying liberal democracy as the only desirable form of modern government, proponents of Asian democracy avoid falling prey to the claim that the inferiority of Asian culture is a hindrance to political modernization.

In contrast to the liberal democratic emphasis on individual rights, rule of law, procedural legitimation of rule, and impersonal authority, Asian polity, as argued by Helgesen and Xing in this volume on China and Korea, is said to be characterized by respect for authority and hierarchy, emphasis on leaders rather than on laws, the presence of a strong state vis-à-vis society, emphasis on communitarianism, and conformity to group interests over individual rights.[18] Based on a different conception of rights, authority, and legitimacy, the semi-official Commission for a New Asia criticizes liberal democracy as 'a highly imperfect form of government'.[19] The Commission proposes an alternative form of democracy: a strong and stable government, responsible media, and harmonious exchange and consensus in decision making. However, in order for the concept of Asian democracy to become a genuine alternative to Western universalism and liberal democracy, a number of gaps and missing links need to be filled and bridged, and this might also make the notion of Asian values untenable in the end. Let us take up some of these below.

Culture or Cultures?

The importance of cultural values in shaping everyday political activities is undeniable. Everyday practices of politics are filtered and constituted through cultural perceptions and historical experiences. Legitimate execution of power and authority depends to a large extent on the exercise of political symbols, rituals, customs, etc. Cultural representations provide the discursive language for understanding and evaluating politics. Cultural ideas, metaphors and semantic systems are used by the people to discuss public issues and to make sense of their lives. The expression of global conditions is mediated by local concerns, where political languages and symbols are often localized. The China chapter by Bakken is a case in point. Bakken identifies a particular Chinese notion of (s)election that relates more to good governance and efficient rule than to interests representation or checks and balances. Although this exercise is carried out under the universal notion of 'election', the actual meaning behind the act derives largely from local concerns.

Having said that, the critique of Western universalism nonetheless obliges us to go further. To do so it is necessary to distinguish dominant culture, minority values, ruling ideologies and so forth, from an undifferentiated notion of 'Asian Values', which rests on a similar ultra-universalist assumption as liberal democracy – an assumption, as mentioned earlier, that sees a single set of values as being upheld by all the people in Asia, and a single set of values upheld by all the people in one country. In saying so, it reifies the dynamic and diversified nature of culture. It is obvious that such an assumption is untenable on several grounds. From the outset, culture is not – and never was – a closed system of unchanging norms and values. Societies have co-existing cultural discourses and value systems, both traditional and modern. This is particularly so at a time when global capitalist culture is becoming more and more penetrative. The interaction between traditional and modern values, and that between global and local cultures, gives rise to cultural plurality and diversity, in the best sense of the words.

Besides the question of traditional versus modern, cultural values are mediated by power relations. Robotka's chapter on India reveals the

10

intimate relationship between power struggle and values. When democracy was introduced to India in the first half of this century, it took root not only after a struggle of values but also a struggle of power. It was a struggle between a relatively small number of highly educated, secularized, and Anglicized Indian elite, and the more grassroots oriented activists. The former saw the British system as a desirable form of government. They thought that India and its people should adapt themselves to that system and its underlying ideology. In contrast, the latter pleaded for a system that could accommodate traditional Indian political conduct. As Robotka argues in her chapter, the intellectuals who led the Indian national movement were far more influential than the lower class activists. At the end, India adopted a British parliamentary system instead of a sectarian system.

Like India, many Asian countries are characterized by differences in ethnic background, religion and language. One wonders whose values and cultures are being referred to when talking about Asian values. Is the culture of the majority more genuine than that of the minority? Antlöv's chapter is particularly clear about the co-existence of several sets of cultural values within a society. The ideas that prevail are the result of power domination, including coercion, rather than that of undisputed social norms. Likewise, cultural narratives can function as instruments of rule by strengthening the claims of aristocratic families, defending political closure, and maintaining prevailing authority and clientelist positions. In criticizing the hegemonic imposition of a Western cultural standard onto Asian countries, proponents of Asian democracy have to show that they are not imposing a monolithic national standard onto the multi-ethnic and cultural societies of Asia. Otherwise the culturalist view of politics becomes nothing but a replacement of the Western domination by a local domination of the ruling majority.

The Primacy of Culture?

In addition to the problem of multiple cultures, there is the question of the primacy of culture(s). In arguing for the centrality of culture in politics, one is obliged to assess the significance of culture vis-à-vis other factors. We can easily identify a range of factors affecting political behaviour, including ethnic relations, electoral system, colonial legacy, clientelist politics, etc. These are all being discussed in our chapters on Sri Lanka, Japan, India, Hong Kong, Malaysia, and Indonesia. However, these country cases do not always find culture to be the determining or the most important factor in shaping political order/disorder.

Sri Lanka is a case in point. It is a country that adopted constitutional democracy after independence. However, like many other Asian countries, the democratic system was short-lived. Political decay soon followed. In his chapter, Kloos explains this outcome not in cultural terms, but instead, he argues that the demise of the division of the executive, legislative and judicial powers (the *trias politica*) was due to a deep-seated ethnic conflict. The Sri Lankan government, being dominated by the Sinhalese majority, was responsible for the escalation of violence. It did so by marginalizing the Tamil minority through a majoritarian system. Under such a system, minority interests were being suppressed constitutionally. For the minorities, political violence aiming at changing the rules of the game became the only alternative. This made room for even more repression, violence and hence political decay. In this case, it can be said that the ethnic cleavages are culturally conditioned, but it would be wrong to conclude that the breakdown of the democratic system in Sri Lanka is due to its Asian values.

Similarly, one can argue that Asian authoritarianism is often a reaction to ethnic, religious, or regional conflicts rather than a result of cultural values. As shown by Shamsul's chapter on Malaysia and Antlöv's chapter on Indonesia, the authoritarian/semi-authoritarian system in the two countries offers a quite effective answer to the threats to political order: identity politics, religious separatism, mob rule, etc. Of course, this assumes that political and social order has a higher priority vis-à-vis individual freedom and rights. Here again we encounter the question of social priorities that we have discussed earlier. But there is an additional dimension in this regard: the emphasis on order and stability may have a cultural foundation, but it may also grow out of the contemporary reality as a response to acute social cleavages.

The strongest case against a culturalist explanation of politics comes perhaps from Japan. Japan is commonly seen as characterized by extreme consensual politics. It is said that this consensual politics leads to a long-standing one-party system typical of Asian democracy. However, as shown by Iwanaga in his chapter, this one-party democracy is deeply related to the electoral system. After World War II, Japan adopted an election system based on single, non-transferable votes. Under such a system, it takes four to five times as many votes to elect a representative in the densely populated urban districts as in the rural areas. This has led to a grossly unequal representation in which a relatively low overall percentage of votes spreading evenly in the countryside constitutes the parliamentary majority. For instance, in the 1993 election, the Liberal Democratic Party received 36 per cent of the national votes, but controlled 46 per cent of the seats in the House of Representatives. This system has clearly benefited the Liberal Democratic Party which has a fairly even distribution of votes over the country. Likewise, the dominance of the United Malays National Organization (UMNO) in Malaysian politics is related not to cultural factors but to ethnicity, as Shamsul's chapter argues. The UMNO is the main political party of the Malays, the largest ethnic group in the country. Nevertheless, unlike Sri Lanka, coalition rule has remained the main feature of the Malaysian system. It is through such coalitions that the process of peaceful ethnic bargaining becomes institutionalized in Malaysian politics. The effectiveness of the system leads even the opposition parties to adopt this model. Regardless of the merits and problems of the above mentioned arrangements of obtaining/ exercising political power, the point is clear that according cultural factor with primary status in explaining regime formation and change does not always match reality.

A Transitional Phase to Democracy?

A further controversial issue brought out by the Asian democracy debate is whether the 'developmental–authoritarian' rule is merely a transitional phase during economic catch up, or a fundamentally different historical trajectory compared with the West. The former view has a long tradition, which sees liberal democracy as the inevitable outcome of economic modernization. Economic development, it is said, nurtures the rise of a middle class that is capable of providing resources for independent activities against the state. This is widely seen as one of the social requisites of modern democracy. In his classic study, Schumpeter states that 'modern democracy is a product of the capitalist process'.[20] Capitalist society, according to Schumpeter, produces a bourgeoisie that limits the sphere of public authority. In a similar vein, Friedman argues that economic freedom under competitive capitalism promotes political freedom because it separates economic power from political power.[21] Lipset suggests that a competitive market economy is the best way to reduce the impact of nepotistic networks. The wider the scope of market forces, the less room there will be for unrestrained state actions.[22]

In this regard, one can compare the similarities and differences between nineteenth-century Europe and contemporary Asia. The European bourgeoisie, who were the main beneficiaries of the nineteenth-century economic expansion, were no more interested in democracy than their counterparts in contemporary Asia. It was liberalism – or more narrowly the freedom to pursue economic activity and wealth accumulation without state interference – that made liberal democracy a desirable form of government for the propertied classes. Liberal thinkers such as De Toqueville, Bentham and the Mills were sceptical about mass rule. John Stuart Mill thus argued that some members of the voting public should have more votes than the others. Such an argument has been echoed by Asian leaders such as Lee Kuan Yew, and has indeed been put into practice in the Hong Kong Special Administrative Region.

Some studies regard the recent democratization in South Korea and Taiwan as a confirmation of the conventional wisdom about the consequence of economic development: the formation of a strong middle class, the rise of political aspiration after decades of economic growth, the subsequent pressure for political participation, and the eventual onset of democratic reform.[23] Others, using Singapore and Malaysia as examples, doubt the generalization of a democratizing middle class by highlighting the resilient Southeast Asian rulers.[24] In general, the elites in many Asian countries do not, as did those in the West, view the state as a threat to their economic pursuits. On the contrary, many big businesses support the state and in return continue to enjoy state patronage. They may ask for changing the mode of state intervention and may even ask for liberalization, but not necessarily democratization. In fact, as the case of Taiwan shows, big business has been discontented with the rise of labour power during the liberalization process and once even threatened to launch an investment strike in protest against the 'weakened' state.[25] The case of Hong Kong tells the same story. The business class has been the main opponent of political reform during the transition to Chinese rule. They want to retain the authoritarian system under which they can exchange political support with economic patronage. The outcome is a system that gives them more votes than the others.[26]

Conclusion

With the serious gaps discussed above, the concept of 'Asian democracy' is both useful and not useful. It is useful insofar as it provides a powerful challenge to the hegemonic, teleological universalism of Western democracy. It forces us to rethink long taken-for-granted assumptions about liberal democracy. It is less useful in presenting itself as an alternative to liberal democracy since it embodies the same underlying universalist assumption that it sets out to refute. It ascribes common characteristics to countries that are in reality very different: dominant one-party electoral regimes in Singapore and Malaysia; one-party authoritarian regimes in China, Burma and Vietnam; multi-party countries such as Japan and India; disorderly regimes such as Sri Lanka, Cambodia, etc. However, notwithstanding this major problem, to dismiss the concept altogether runs the risk of throwing out the baby with the bath water.

One way to begin a meaningful debate is to drag the arguments about culture and politics from their high moral ground into a more sociological debate about the interpretation, understanding and explanation of empirical practices. Instead of relativizing cultural politics, the aim should be to contextualize values and practices. In other words, we suggest a middle way between seeing liberal democracy as a global moral norm and treating Asian democracy in terms of cultural relativism. To do so we need a careful examination of the historical, political, social and cultural practices of each individual country. Neither reference to a global norm nor to an Asian culture alone would explain the paramount differences between countries.

A good illustration about what we mean by contextualization is the case of elections. Taylor has argued forcefully that elections in Asia are specific, and must be understood contextually. Yet they are also a nearly universal institution, constituting an indispensable part of the modern political order. [27] In other words, it is a universal act that has a local meaning. For instance, in the case of both China and Vietnam, elections are not concerned about choosing governments. In Malaysia, Singapore, and Japan, elections have for a long time not caused a change in government. In Sri Lanka, elections as an institution do not solve the problem of distributing power, but are part of the problem itself. Yet ruling parties in Asia have never abandoned the idea of election for long and replaced it with sheer dictatorship. As Taylor points out, elections are not only held regularly, but they are taken seriously both by the ruling parties and the opposition groups. Massive amounts of money, a wide section of the population, and a lot of political attention have been mobilized and spent on electioneering. In these circumstances, nothing is more misleading than treating elections as a yardstick of democratic politics; and equally, it will not be less misleading to see elections as a mere cover-up for authoritarian rule. This ambiguity, or universal-specific complexity, provides an interesting starting point to look into the culture and politics of countries in Asia. The final chapter by Whitehead in this volume will attempt to probe into the areas in which meaningful comparisons can be made between Asia and the rest of the world in order to understand better the universality and specificity of democratic institutions.

Notes

1 See the discussion in Samuel Huntington, *The Third Wave: Democratization in the Late Twentieth Century*, Norman, OK: University of Oklahoma Press, 1991; Francis Fukuyama, *The End of History and the Last Man*, London: Hamish Hamilton, 1992; and Larry Diamond, Marc F. Plattner, Yun-han Chu, and Hung-mao Tien (eds), *Consolidating the Third Wave Democracies: Regional Challenges*, Baltimore: Johns Hopkins University Press, 1997.

2 *Straits Times*, Singapore, 2 October 1993.

3 See John Naisbitt, *Megatrends Asia. The Eight Asian Megatrends That Are Changing the World*, London: Nicholas Brealey, 1995.

4 Juan J. Linz and Alfred Stepan (eds,) *The Breakdown of Democratic Regimes*, 4 volumes, Baltimore: Johns Hopkins University Press, 1978; Guillermo O'Donnell, Philippe C. Schmitter and Laurence Whitehead (eds), *Transitions from Authoritarian Rule*, 4 volumes, Baltimore: Johns Hopkins University Press, 1986; Larry Diamond, Juan J. Linz and Seymour Martin Lipset (eds) *Democracy in Developing Countries*, 4 volumes, Boulder, Colorado: Lynne Rienner Publishers, 1989.

5 Larry Diamond, Juan J. Linz, and Seymour Martin Lipset, 'Preface', in *idem* (eds), *Democracy in Developing Countries: Asia*, Boulder, Colorado: Lynne Rienner Publishers, 1989, p. xxv.

6 Alexander Gerschenkron, *Economic Backwardness in Historical Perspective*, Cambridge: Cambridge University Press, 1962.

7 The pioneer work is Chalmers Johnson, *MITI and the Japanese Miracle*, Stanford: Stanford University Press, 1981.

8 See, for instance, Stephan Haggard, *Pathways from the Periphery: The Politics of Growth in the Newly Industrializing Countries*, Ithaca: Cornell University Press, 1990; and Robert Wade, *Governing the Market: Economic Theory and the Role of Government in East Asian Industrialization*, Princeton, NJ: Princeton University Press, 1990.

9 See Frederic C. Deyo (ed.), *The Political Economy of the New Asian Industrialism*, Ithaca: Cornell University Press, 1987.

10 See, for instance, Leonard Binder *et. al.*, *Crises and Sequences in Political Development*, Princeton, N.J.: Princeton University Press, 1971; and Charles Tilly (ed.) *The Formation of National States in Western Europe*, Princeton, N.J.: Princeton University Press, 1975.

11 Joseph LaPalombara, *Bureaucracy and Political Development*, Princeton, N.J.: Princeton University Press, 1963, p. 10.

12 Adam Przeworski, *Democracy and the Market: Political and Economic Reforms in East Europe and Latin America*, Cambridge: Cambridge University Press, 1991.

13 Samuel P. Huntington, 'The Clash of Civilizations', *Foreign Affairs*, Summer 1993, pp. 22–49.

14 Gabriel Almond and Sidney Verba, *Civic Culture: Political Attitudes and Democracy in Five Nations*, Princeton, N.J.: Princeton University Press, 1963.

15 Lucian W. Pye, with Mary W. Pye, *Asian Power and politics: The Cultural Dimensions of Authority*, Cambridge, Mass.: Harvard University Press, 1985.

16 Donald K. Emmerson, 'Singapore and the 'Asian Values' Debate', *Journal of Democracy* 6, No. 4, October 1995, p. 100.

17 See Chow Tse-tsung, *The May Fourth Movement: Intellectual Revolution in Modern China*, Cambridge, Mass.: Harvard University Press, 1960; and Wen-hsin Yeh, *The Alienated Academy: Culture and Politics in Republican China, 1919–1937*, Cambridge, Mass.: Council on East Asian Studies, Harvard University, 1990.

18 In addition to the above, Fukuyama adds that many Asian systems are characterized by the combination of a market-oriented economic system with a kind of paternalistic authoritarianism that persuades rather than coerces. Francis Fukuyama, 'Asia's Soft-Authoritarian Alternative', *New Perspectives Quarterly* 9, No. 2, Spring 1992, pp. 60–61.

19 Commission for a New Asia, *Towards a New Asia*, Kuala Lumpur: Commission for a New Asia, 1994, p. 32.

20 Joseph A. Schumpeter, *Capitalism, Socialism and Democracy*, 3rd. ed., London: George Allen & Unwin, 1950, p. 297.

21 Milton Friedman, *Capitalism and Freedom*, London: University of Chicago Press, 1962.

22 Seymour Martin Lipset, 'The Social Requisites of Democracy Revisited', *American Sociological Review* 59, No. 1, February 1994, p. 3.

23 See Edward Friedman (ed.), *The Politics of Democratization: Generalizing East Asian Experiences*, Boulder: Westview Press, 1994; and James W. Morley (ed.), *Driven by Growth: Political Change in the Asia-Pacific Region*, Armonk, N.Y.: M.E. Sharpe, 1993.

24 See Donald Emmersson, 'Region and Recalcitrance: Rethinking Democracy Through Southeast Asia', *Pacific Review* 8, No. 2, 1995, pp. 223–248.

25 See Tak-Wing Ngo, 'Civil Society and Political Liberalization in Taiwan', *Bulletin of Concerned Asian Scholars* 25, No. 1, January-March 1993, pp. 3–15; and *idem* 'Business Encirclement of Politics: Government-Business Relations Across the Taiwan Strait', *China Information* 10, No.2, Autumn 1995, pp. 1–18.

26 Tak-Wing Ngo, 'Changing Government-Business Relations and the Governance of Hong Kong', in *Hong Kong in Transition*, Robert Ash, Peter Ferdinand, Brian Hook and Robin Porter (eds), London: Macmillan, forthcoming.

27 R.H. Taylor, 'Delusion and Necessity: Elections and Politics in Southeast Asia', *Items* 48, No. 4, December 1994, p. 85.

2 DEMOCRACY, CIVIL WAR AND THE DEMISE OF THE *TRIAS POLITICA* IN SRI LANKA

Peter Kloos

Introduction

In 1947 Ceylon – as Sri Lanka was known at that time – seemed to have all that was needed to transform a largely cultivation-based society with a feudal, and later colonial, past into an independent democracy, with all the political and para-political safeguards democracy requires. It had already had an elected Parliament for more than a decade and a half – in fact, since 1931 (Ceylon had universal suffrage earlier than several European states). It had a high rate of literacy and also a newspaper tradition of a century and a half. It had a well-established, island-wide legal system and it had, inherited from the British colonial government, a Public Service – the Ceylon Civil Service – that was virtually free of corruption. It was, finally, one of the most affluent countries in Asia. Thanks to wares such as tea, rubber and coconut products, Ceylon enjoyed a comfortable income in terms of foreign currency. This made possible a welfare state with island-wide free medical care and free education.

Indeed, during the first years of independence, Ceylon was often seen as a model of Third-World democracy. Especially the fact that voters repeatedly voted a government out of office was seen as a not-to-be-mistaken sign of democratic maturity: in Ceylon the ballot ruled, not the bullet.

However, in 1988, 40 years after independence in 1948, Sri Lanka (as Ceylon had become in 1972) had an executive President with almost dictatorial powers, also in Parliament. The Parliament no longer controlled the cabinet. Politics had become an avenue to become rich and the Public Service had become thoroughly corrupt. Sri Lanka had become one of the low-income countries, with a huge foreign debt. It also had the dubious reputation of being one of the worst countries for the violation of human rights in the world. And last but not least, there was a war raging in the Tamil-dominated north and east of the island, and a revolt among the Sinhala in the southwest and central parts. Especially in the period 1987–1990 it seemed that the bullet ruled rather than the ballot. Still, even at that time, President Junius Jayewardena was succeeded by Ranasingha Premadasa on the basis of general elections. These elections probably were rigged to some extent, but still, succession to presidency was based on votes cast, not on the use of weapons.

Many, and perhaps the majority, of the former post-colonial states in Asia and in Africa share with Sri Lanka such features of dictatorship, corruption and violation of human rights, but few had a similar favourable point of departure when they started their career as independent states. How can we explain the transformation of the political arena in Ceylon from a promising democracy in the 1940s and 1950s, into an almost Hobbesian 'Warre of every one against every one' in the 1980s?[1] What has been the role of the state (or rather the government: the state, after all, is an abstraction, not an actor) in this process of transformation? I shall be brief about the escalation of violence as such, and concentrate on the role of the government and on the demise of the *trias politica*, the principle of the separation of powers, which in democratic politics is regarded as a safeguard against the abuse of power. My main point is that the Sri Lankan government has been a major agent in the escalation of violence and, once involved in a struggle of life and death with violent adversaries of its own making, began to blur the boundaries between executive, legislative and judicial power. This made room for even more violence.

Section two of this chapter is devoted to a brief discussion of the escalation of violence in Sri Lanka since the 1950s. Section three presents a notorious series of events, concentrated around one particular inspector of police, Mr Premadasa Udugampola. The Udugampola case illustrates in a down-to-earth manner the way executive power in Sri Lanka has encroached on legislative and judicial powers, thus opening the gate for more violence. This process of the blurring of boundaries between the three powers is described in the fourth section. The final section contains a few concluding remarks on democracy in Sri Lanka.

Escalation of Violence in a Democratic State

Because historical events invariably have antecedents, it is rather non-sensical to use the concept of 'beginning'. Yet for practical reasons one has to break into a historical process somewhere. Exactly where one breaks in betrays already one's perception of the process. Sinhala chauvinists are likely to begin the history of political violence some 25 centuries ago, when their ancestors are supposed to have arrived in Ceylon. They might take the epic war in the second century BC, between the Sinhala prince Dutugemunu and the Tamil king Elara of Anuradhapura, as their point of departure. Nationalists may prefer the colonial period, because in this period Sinhala and Tamil were incorporated into one political community. I prefer to begin my analysis in 1948: the year of Ceylon's independence, fully realizing the artificiality of my choice and the relevance of the early history for the present-day predicament of Sri Lanka.[2]

There is something striking about Sri Lanka's independence: it came peacefully, and at a moment when in Asia and Africa wars of independence were gaining momentum. Already in 1943, before the end of the Second World War, the so-called Soulbury Commission was flown to Ceylon 'in order to examine and discuss any proposals for constitutional reform in the Island'.[3] The Commission was supposed to effect an earlier promise of the British government to grant to Ceylon a full responsible government in all matters of internal civil administration – though still under the Crown in London.[4] The constitutional reform was effected in 1947. When the first post-war Parliament, elected in the same year, requested independence, the Crown in London in 1948 promptly granted it.

In the same year, however, and in 1949, the first seeds were sown by the new government of Ceylon that would bring about civil war within one generation. The independent state of Ceylon, territorially coinciding with the shoreline of the island, was very much a product of colonialism.

During pre-colonial times Ceylon was politically united only for one brief period in the fifteenth century. At the beginning of the colonial era, the early sixteenth century, there were three kingdoms, two Sinhala ones with their capitals in Kotte (near present-day Colombo) and Senkadagalle (present-day Kandy), and one Tamil, with its capital in present-day Jaffna. Ceylon was politically united for the second time in 1815, when the British occupied Kandy, the capital of the last Sinhala kingdom. The British exiled the king. Political unification was effectuated in the 1830s, as a result of the work of the Colebrooke–Cameron Commission.

In 1947, the Sinhala formed in this polity a clear majority of about 70 per cent. There was a politically and economically quite powerful minority of almost 23 per cent Tamils. Somewhat less than half of the Tamils were so-called Ceylon Tamils, who had lived in Ceylon for many centuries. They formed a majority in the north, in Jaffna in particular, and in the northeast. Somewhat more than half, however, were Indian Tamils, who as contract labourers had been brought from South India to Ceylon by the British in the nineteenth and early twentieth centuries. The Indian Tamils lived mainly in the mountainous interior, on or near the tea estates.

The Sinhala majority saw Ceylon as a Sinhala state. For them the Sinhala kingdom of Kandy was the predecessor of the modern state. This conception is symbolically expressed by the flag, depicting a yellow lion with a sword in its right paw, which was the Kandyan emblem (see De Silva and Wriggins for the issue of raising the flag at independence).[5] Already during the war the issue of national language was broached: that language should be Sinhala. The language issue was tabled for the time being, however, there being more pressing issues.[6]

The politics of independent Ceylon were based on general elections. The electoral system was similar to the British district system, each electorate supplying one member of Parliament. This implied that the ethnic composition of the population came forcefully to the fore, also in districts traditionally part of the Kandyan kingdom where the majority of the Indian Tamils lived.

Among the earliest acts passed by the House of Representatives were the Citizen Act (1948), the Indian and Pakistani Residents (Citizenship) Act (1949), and the Parliamentary Elections Amendment Act (1949). The first two acts denied citizenship to the majority of the Indian Tamils and the third one disenfranchised them. The political motive behind these Acts was fear of Sinhala leaders for the electoral strength that could be exercised by the Indian Tamils, especially in the Central Province, where they outnumbered the Sinhala in several districts like Nuwara Eliya, the centre of the tea plantations. Moreover, the Indian Tamils were suspected of sympathizing with the Trotskyist *Lanka Sama Samaya* Party (which in 1947, with 10 seats, was the second party in Parliament, after the UNP with 42 seats). These Acts caused a split in the Tamil political party, the Tamil Congress. Some Tamil politicians, hoping to be accepted by the Sinhala political elite, accepted the Acts.[7] Others remained loyal to the Indian Tamils and opposed. As a result the Federal Party was formed, led by S.J.V. Chelvanayakam.[8]

This absence of solidarity tells something about the late- and post-colonial political elite: it was an Anglicized and often Christian elite of Sinhala and Tamils who in many respects shared more with each other than with the Sinhala and Tamil population of the villages.

The leaders of independent Ceylon came from the same families as those in power in the late-colonial 1930s. These leaders 'became new drivers of the existing vehicle and all the contribution they made was to make the carriage go along' wrote Victor Ivan in order to emphasize the continuity.[9] Still, the acts referred to above indicate that these new drivers were not quite continuing the path on which their vehicle was going, and in the early 1950s they met serious obstruction on the road: an anti-English, anti-Christian, Sinhala–Buddhist platform, supported by Sinhala-speaking rural elites (village headmen, Sinhala teachers, ayurvedic physicians, etc.) and by the Buddhist *sangha* (the Buddhist monastic order). The first felt discriminated by a Civil Service, an education and medical system that were still monopolized by the English-educated late- and post-colonial elite. The *sangha* felt that Buddhism had suffered severely under Western rule and that it was time for redress. Rural elites and Buddhist monks had expected more of independence than the late- and post-colonial Anglophone elite was willing to grant. A convenient coincidence was that 1956 happened to be the year of the *Buddha Jayanthi*, the 2,500th anniversary of Buddhism.[10] On the rising waves of this belated nationalism, S.W.R.D. Bandaranaike won the 1956 elections.

The issue of language set Bandaranaike on a collision course with the Tamils. Teaching in native languages had been an issue from the early 1940s,[11] but the slogan which won the elections was not 'native languages' (*swabasha*) but 'Sinhala Only'. Because Buddhism and Sinhala were so interwoven, here for the first time Ceylon was explicitly conceived as a Sinhala–Buddhist state. In 1956, soon after the elections, the Official Language Act was introduced. It became known as the 'Sinhala Only' Act. Sinhala would be the official language of Sri Lanka. The Act was, curiously enough, not in agreement with the constitution of 1947, which explicitly forbade language discrimination! The Sinhala Only Act was a direct attack on an essential ingredient of Tamil identity: language and literature. It also greatly reduced the possibilities for Tamils to compete with Sinhala for administrative jobs.

The Act brought Tamil politicians, who had split as a result of the Citizenship Acts, together again. As a result of fierce protests, Bandaranaike retraced his steps. He began negotiations with the (Tamil) Federal Party, and reached an agreement with its leader Chelvanayakam, in the form of a certain degree of devolution of power on a regional basis. The Buddhist *sangha* especially, however, was very much opposed to this, and due to its pressure the agreement (the so-called Bandaranaike–Chelvanayakam Pact) was unilaterally revoked by Bandaranaike. Tamil opposition to the Sinhala Only Act led to counter-demonstrations in the Sinhala areas. The prime objective of these demonstrations was to oppose any concessions to the Tamil minority.[12] Tension erupted in the communal riots of May 1958 – the first of a series of Sinhala–Tamil riots throughout the country.[13] It was not the government which started using violence, but the riots were definitely induced by the Sinhala-dominated government that used its majority in Parliament to steam-roll over the Tamil-speaking population.

In the years that followed the idea of the Sinhala–Buddhist state remained the leading idea. Many strands of Sinhala–Buddhist nationalism came together in the 1972 constitution, which transformed Ceylon into *Sri* Lanka – a Sinhala qualification of Lanka, a designation used by both Sinhala and Tamil for Ceylon (which is, of course, a foreign designation). Tamil politicians were, given their numbers, unable to prevent Tamil interests being systematically put on a lower plane. As a result, young, often low-caste and unemployed Tamils were unwilling to participate any longer in what they saw as a lost struggle. When in 1972 the new constitution was adopted black flags were raised in Jaffna, and youth groups were formed with the aim of establishing an independent Tamil state. One of these groups, the Tamil New Tigers (TNT), was the forerunner of the *Liberation Tigers of Tamil Eelam* (LTTE). The TNT was the first group to use violence by assassinating the Tamil mayor of

Jaffna, A. Duraiappah, a member of the reigning Sri Lanka Freedom Party of Sirimavo Bandaranaike (S.W.R.D. Bandaranaike's widow), in 1975. This was the beginning of a guerilla war against representatives of the Sri Lankan state, both Tamil and Sinhala.[14]

When in 1977 the UNP government proscribed the LTTE, the latter went underground. Guerilla actions turned into a veritable civil war in July 1983, after the ambushing by the LTTE of 14 soldiers, killing 13, and the ensuing July pogrom in Colombo and elsewhere. Meanwhile the Sri Lankan government had become engaged in a second life-and-death struggle: an insurgency among the Sinhala themselves. Ceylon in the late 1940s and 1950s was a relatively affluent state with a definite welfare ideology. Part of the state income was spend on medical care and island-wide free education. This resulted in a fast-growing, relatively well-educated population. At the end of the 1960s a large part of the population consisted of young people who were educated – but also unemployed, because in the course of the 1960s foreign income went down due to lower prices on the world market for tea, rubber and coconut products, and stagnation had set in.[15] The elite tended to keep profitable jobs for themselves. Youth unrest resulted in the 1971 insurgency of the leftist *Janatha Vimukthi Peramuna* (JVP).[16]

The JVP radicalism turned into Sinhala chauvinism in the 1980s, when President Jayewardene in 1987 agreed to have the Indian army (in the form of the so-called Indian Peace Keeping Force) operate on Sri Lanka's soil in order to constrain Tamil militants. As a result, the Sri Lankan government became involved in a violent struggle on two fronts (see Figure 1).[17]

One struggle acquired ethnic aspects (although it had hardly anything to do with cultural differences between Sinhala and Tamil); the other was a struggle over scarce resources such as jobs and political influence between the established elite and educated, unemployed youth among both Sinhala and Tamils. Although logically unrelated both struggles were combined in the case of the struggle between Tamil secessionist groups and the Sri Lankan government, a struggle that on the Tamil side eventually came to be dominated by the LTTE: young Tamils were at the receiving end of both struggles.

The use of violence from the side of the government quickly began to influence the democratic process: the executive power, faced with a series of challenges from adversaries extremely hard to counter, began to violate

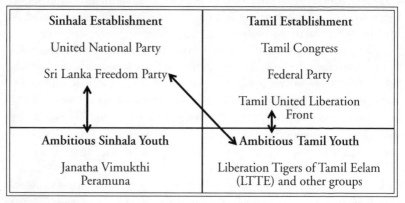

Sinhala Establishment	Tamil Establishment
United National Party	Tamil Congress
Sri Lanka Freedom Party	Federal Party
	Tamil United Liberation Front
Ambitious Sinhala Youth	**Ambitious Tamil Youth**
Janatha Vimukthi Peramuna	Liberation Tigers of Tamil Eelam (LTTE) and other groups

Figure 1: The two main dimensions and the major parties in the Sri Lankan post-independence struggle for power (Kloos 1997)

the privileges of the other powers – with the result that there were less and less checks on the use of violence by the executive. As a result, Sri Lanka found itself sucked into a maelstrom of violence – and into the political and moral crisis of the years 1987–1990. The events together forming the 'Udugampola case' are characteristic of the political, legislative and judiciary climate of that period.

The Udugampola Case

Premadasa Udugampola was a policeman who, as Deputy Inspector General of Police, had been in charge of the Southern Province, and later the North Central Province and the Central Province, during the turbulent years of the second JVP insurrection (1987–1989). He then became Head of the Bureau of Special Operations (BSO), a unit set up to suppress drug trade and gold smuggling and perhaps other activities as well. In January 1992, shortly before his expected retirement in April 1992, he was placed on leave.

At that moment he was already a man with a past. He had been one of the police officers who in 1978 had been promoted by the government after having been convicted by the Supreme Court in connection with human rights abuses. His name had also been mentioned in connection with the assassination of a lawyer involved in *habeas corpus* petitions. In fact, the *Status Report – Human Rights in Sri Lanka* (published in January 1992 by the Overseas Publicity Division of the Government Information Department) announcing the retirement of police officers accused of human rights violations brought his name again to public attention.

This Status Report lead to a newspaper interview.[18] In the interview Udugampola alluded to political killings by death squads called 'Black Cats' (*kalu pusa*) in the North Central and the Central Province of Sri Lanka during election time in 1988, and to efforts to cover up these killings by politicians (who may have been the instigators of the killings in the first place). Three days later the Prime Minister at the time, D.B.

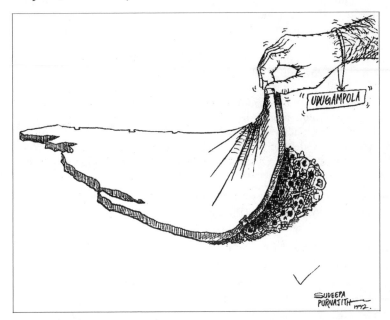

Figure 2: Cartoon published in *The Island*, 8 April 1992.

Wijetunga, using the government-controlled newspaper *Daily News* of 8 April 1992, stated that Udugampola's statements contained several falsehoods. According to Wijetunga, Udugampola was 'harbouring a malicious vengeance against the government' because his conduct was being investigated, his role in the fight against the JVP and in the BSO included. As to the first, 'Black Cats' had surfaced wherever Udugampola was stationed. As to the second, the BSO had failed to detect gold smuggling by Udugampola's own brother.

The same day, however, the newspaper *Aththa* quoted the following statement from an affidavit said to have been made by Udugampola:

> Former DIG Premadasa Udugampola states that in the past years of terror, over tens of thousands of persons have been massacred by the 'Black Cats' and that the concept of 'tire pyres' was born after these 'Black Cats' began their operation. According to what he says, the 'Black Cats', which was activated under the guidance of a powerful politician of the government, consisted of about one hundred persons. Over and above their monthly wages, they received a sum of Rs 3000 per month under the defence budget. They also had free use of state vehicles including those belonging to various government Departments, with free fuel. They were mostly allocated the use of Pajeros and Hiace vans. All of these vehicles operated without license plates, or with false ones ... Several senior Police officials were also members of this 'death squad'. During the period of terror, the Emergency Regulation 55 FF was utilized to cover up the massacres committed by the 'Black Cats'. Under this regulation, an Assistant Superintendent of Police or any other official senior to him could dispose of a corpse by cremation or burial without an inquest being held. This gang disposed of all their victims by burning the bodies without any such authorization. The numbers murdered in the North Central Province by this gang number close upon two thousand. Of them, most were members or supporters of the Sri Lanka Freedom Party.[19]

This statement was followed by the names of 95 persons presumably killed in the North Central Province in the period January 1988–March 1989 (a far longer list was printed in *Rajaliya* on 30 April 1992). The last line of the *Aththa* article just quoted turned the UNP government from accuser into accused.

The government responded swiftly: on 9 April 1989 the Attorney General filed two indictments in the High Court of Colombo, one against Udugampola, the other against the Editor of *Aththa*. They were charged under Emergency Regulations for causing hostility, ill-will, hatred and contempt of the government of Sri Lanka (Emergency Regulation 16a) and creating dissension and/or ill-feeling among citizens of Sri Lanka (Emergency Regulation 26e). The charges against Udugampola were based on an affidavit, affirmed before a Justice of Peace on 18 March 1992. In it he had confirmed that the 'Black Cats' were government-sponsored death squads. As a result of the Attorney General's quick move the debate was effectively stopped, both in public and in Parliament, because the case was now *sub judice*. Members of the opposition tried to discuss the case in Parliament because Udugampola had intimated that SLFP members and sympathizers had been the main victims of the 'Black Cats'. They did not succeed. Prime Minister Wijetunga stated in Parliament that it would be against the constitution and the order of the Parliament.

Udugampola refused to come to court and disappeared. Although a few journalists managed to interview him, the police at first failed to locate him, or so they said. When he finally was found, in June 1992, the policemen in charge could not arrest him because they had no detention order. Udugampola repeatedly challenged the government to appoint a committee of inquiry into his accusations but refused to come to courts himself. He said that his life was being threatened by powerful personalities. Scores of policemen were said to be in search of him but at the beginning of 1993 he was in Madras, South India. For a few months there was silence.

The Island of 19 June 1993 suddenly reported that 'Udugampola had spoken over the telephone to [now President] Wijetunga and obtained assurances that the charges would be dropped'. He in turn had promised not to pursue the allegations. Presumably as a result of this discussion between the President and Udugampola, the latter returned to Sri Lanka on 18 June 1993, on an ordinary flight from Madras to Katunayaka, Sri Lanka's international airport. Newspapers reported that the police were at the airport but, alas, the plane had been ahead of schedule and Udugampola had already left when the police arrived. The day after his arrival he went to court and was released on bail.

Early in July 1993 Udugampola officially withdrew the allegations he had made. In a new affidavit filed in the High Court of Colombo, he said, among other things:

> 9. The allegations contained in these documents [among others the affidavit published by *Aththa*] consist of those which had been made by me bona-fide but mistakenly on anonymous and unsubstantiated information ... All these allegations are erroneous and unfounded ...
> 10. I hereby withdraw all the allegations made by me. I deeply regret any embarrassment or inconvenience that I may have caused the Government or any other person.[20]

As a result, Udugampola was discharged. Colombo was alive with wild and unconfirmed rumours about what Udugampola had received as a reward for his withdrawal. A few weeks later the *Government Gazette* casually announced that one P. Udugampola had been appointed as vice-chairman (in fact: acting chairman) of the Sri Lanka Ports Authority.

After Udugampola had been discharged, the editor and the publisher of *Aththa*, who had published the first affidavit in which Udugampola had accused the government of complicity in Black Cat assassinations, were acquitted.

This brief review gives rise to numerous questions, some of them regarding details of 'what actually happened', others regarding the background of the events composing the case. Many questions will never be answered in any satisfactory way, if only because neither the Government (or the Attorney General) nor Udugampola are likely to completely open their files. Yet a few observations are in order. Many events can hardly be taken seriously, like policemen unable to find Udugampola, or arriving too late, and when they find him, not having a detention order. The final statement of Udugampola, that his allegations were based on unsubstantiated information, cannot be taken seriously either: as an experienced policeman he surely knew better.

More important here is the role of the Attorney General, who first of all speedily served the Government by indicting Udugampola, thereby preventing further debate in press and Parliament, and in the end discharged Udugampola on the basis of his July 1993 affidavit in which he had said that his allegations had been based on anonymous and unsubstantiated information. Both decisions resulted in severe criticism of the Attorney General. If the documents on the basis of which Udugampola was indicted were 'fabrications', the Attorney General had failed to check their authenticity. If the documents were authentic, the Attorney General should not have discharged Udugampola. In any case, it is hard to believe that an experienced police officer like Udugampola had based on hearsay his claim that the Premadasa government had ordered political killings. In both decisions the Attorney General seems to have acted as an instrument of specific Government interests to cover up extra-judicial killings rather than as an instrument of judicial wisdom.

Also interesting is the use that was made of Emergency Regulations, legislation never agreed upon in Parliament. The impotence of the opposition to put the issue on the agenda of the Parliament should be noted too.

The case shows, finally, how police officers as public servants can become enmeshed in a violent power struggle in which the Parliament is powerless, the administration of justice the victim, and the executive in the end dominates the arena. In short, the Udugampola case demonstrates many issues closely related to the blurring of the boundaries between three powers. It is to this process that I turn now: in a violent situation the blurring of boundaries created room for even more violence.

The Demise of the *Trias Politica*

The Soulbury Commission, visiting Ceylon in 1943 in order to discuss the constitutional reforms promised by the British government in 1941, had a Westminster form of democracy in mind. The blueprint for Ceylon's political system that was devised by the Soulbury Commission was based on the expectations of the Commission regarding the future of Ceylon (during its brief stay it therefore discussed numerous issues with leading Ceylonese), on the experiences of the British in England and, of course, on West European principles regarding democratic government. Some of these principles were formulated almost two hundred years earlier by Montesquieu in his *De l'esprit des lois* (1748).[21] In this influential political treatise Montesquieu argued against French absolutism of his time. He favoured the British system in which three governmental powers, executive, legislative and judicial, were separated from each other. This separation as a matter of principle but also as a condition for the freedom of citizens became known in political philosophy as the doctrine of the *trias politica* and

> [I]t became an axiom of republican theory that the concentration of these three kinds of power in a single centre was the very essence of tyranny and that they must therefore be located in separate institutions, each serving as a check on the others.[22]

The principle of the separation of powers became one of the cornerstones of the 1947 Constitution of Ceylon.[23] The 1978 constitution is explicit in this respect (see articles 4 (a)–(c)).

One of the implications of the separation of powers is that each serves as a check on the others. A corollary of this is that the demise of the separation of powers increases the risk that especially the executive in the execution of its policies may be seduced to liberally use the means of coercion that it, by its very nature, already possesses. The separation of the three powers does not mean that there are no relations between them. These relationships are necessarily present and they are of different kinds. For instance, judicial power presupposes legislation and also executive power; yet both judicial and legislation power both check the executive. Moreover, between executive and legislation and judicial power there are interfaces and interstitial institutions, like Parliament and the Attorney General. My point is that in Sri Lanka the executive power, in the face of serious challenges by violent antagonists like the JVP and the LTTE, tried to curtail and even neutralize the other powers. Because it succeeded, at least to some extent, it created for itself more room for violence in its struggle against its antagonists. Concrete Sri Lankans and their abstract human rights became the victims.

In Figure 2, I visualize the *trias politica* and the internal interfaces that I shall deal with in this chapter in order to demonstrate the blurring of the boundaries between the three powers.

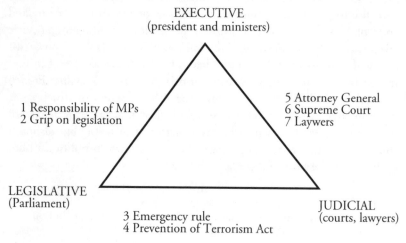

EXECUTIVE
(president and ministers)

1 Responsibility of MPs
2 Grip on legislation

5 Attorney General
6 Supreme Court
7 Laywers

LEGISLATIVE
(Parliament)

JUDICIAL
(courts, lawyers)

3 Emergency rule
4 Prevention of Terrorism Act

Figure 3: The *trias politica* and some of its internal interfaces

The expression 'blurring of boundaries between the three powers' covers a number of phenomena: one power (as a rule the executive) begins to dominate at the expense of the other(s), transgresses its or their rights and takes over prerogatives belonging to another power. In short, it tries to control other powers, making itself immune to their influence. In practice, the process does not deal with abstract 'powers', but with concrete individuals involved in a struggle for power. In a democracy based on regular elections the whole electorate is involved in this struggle – after all, democracy is simply one of the mechanisms dealing with conflicting interests and struggle. The involvement of the electorate is on the whole restricted to the election of representatives.

In practice, the struggle is most of the time carried out among elected representatives. I therefore begin with the responsibilities of the Members of Parliament, as controllers of the executive (the cabinet) and as legislators. The 1947 election system followed the British district model. Candidates who had won a seat in Parliament represented first of all the majority of a district. As a result they tended to become brokers between the central government – the cabinet – and the electorate. When an MP belonged to the majority party, which was also present in the cabinet, he or she had a fairly easy access to resources that could be utilized in his or her electorate. These resources were quickly used in the fierce election struggle between contesting candidates in the same electorate: MPs turned into patrons with many clients who helped them in the election campaign, and who had to be satisfied after a (successful) election campaign was over. Electoral success therefore depended heavily on personal networks within the electorate, on connections with top-level politicians, and on access to resources. Sri Lankan politics turned into what Bailey called 'machine style politics'.[24] Political patron–client relations were not an innovation brought by the British: the Westminster system was consistent with basic features of the Sinhala kingdom in which the king used land grants (land was the prime resource in the time of the kings) to ensure the services and the loyalties of his higher officers – who did the same with their subordinates.[25] Although the resources have changed over time, Sinhala politics has always had a strongly instrumental *do ut des* nature, on state and village level alike. There is not only a basic similarity between British and Sinhala feudalism in the past, but there is also a high degree of continuity between pre- and post-colonial politics in Sri Lanka.[26]

Entrepreneurial politics was already clearly there in the 1930s and 1940s. During those decades, however, parliamentary candidates used to belong to wealthy families, and many used part of their own resources to reach positions in the political arena. Campaigning was still relatively simple. In 1947 the elite candidates for the Parliament went to their home bases, and simply told local leaders like village headmen to see to it that the villagers under their authority would cast their votes for them! This changed in the 1950s, with the shift toward MPs also coming from local elites who did not initially possess the financial resources but saw an opportunity to acquire these via politics. These opportunities increased vastly when a veritable torrent of development funds flowed into the country. In this way the programmes and projects financed by development cooperation from foreign governments to the Sri Lankan government probably made it possible for politicians to tap money that could be used in the public political competition or for private gain.

Part of these financial means were spent on efforts to be elected, merely because since the 1950s election campaigns required increasing amounts of money. As far as I know there is no detailed study of the economics of election campaigns in Sri Lanka. I wish to stress two corollaries of the commoditization of politics. In the first place I assume that politicians can never become political brokers and entrepreneurs without the support of the public service. A politician who pockets x per cent of the budget of a development project plainly needs the cooperation of the administration. I suppose that this is one of the main reasons why the public service is no longer free from corruption – their cooperation has a price. The commoditization of politics turned into a commoditization of administrative services.

In the second place, and in the present context this is more important, the transformation of Sri Lankan politics entails that the prime job of MPs is no longer legislation: MPs have acquired executive functions, in their electorate in the first place. In 1972 this executive function was actively boosted by the then SLFP government in its effort to strengthen the relationship between the government and the people via the MP. This, however, made the MP co-responsible for governing the country. This responsibility was further strengthened after 1977 when MPs could become Deputy Ministers, formally responsible for government policy in specific fields. The net result of this redefinition of the responsibilities of the MP was that a large number of parliamentarians were no longer in an independent position to check the government: here the separation between executive government and parliamentary control completely broke down. The grip of the executive on the Parliament during the Jayewardene government is epitomized by the infamous letters of resignation. In October 1982 Jayewardene made all UNP MPs hand over an undated yet signed letter of resignation to the president.[27] This made these MPs pawns in the hand of the executive: the president could rid himself of any MP at any time.

The second issue is the direct intervention in the responsibilities of the Parliament by the executive, namely legislation, the prime privilege of Parliament. This privilege had been undermined by the dependency of

MPs but was undermined even further by legislation under the state of emergency. According to the Public Security Ordinance the President of Sri Lanka can declare a state of emergency on specified grounds. This was done for the first time during the 1971 Insurgency, and remained during the whole reign of the United Front.[28] The state of emergency was briefly lifted when the UNP came to power in 1977 but was quickly declared again in 1979 for several months. After July 1983 the state of emergency became permanent until 1995, when the Chandrika Kumaratunga government terminated it for most of Sri Lanka, the east and north excepted. This means that for most of the second half of the post-independence period the executive could promulgate regulations without the approval of the Parliament. It did so extensively. Under the cover of emergency it promulgated many regulations that had disputable relations to national security.[29] As we have seen in the Udugampola case, emergency regulations were actually used in the struggle the executive was fighting. The extensive use made by the executive of the state of emergency placed the Parliament offside. The judiciary process was also affected by emergency legislation, because lawyers and judges alike were not always sure which legislation actually applied and which legislative novelties had to be taken into account.

Because the regulations suspended fundamental rights guaranteed by the constitution, fundamental rights became severely restricted as well. This became even more obvious in two instances of legislation promulgated in a constitutional manner, namely the Prevention of Terrorism Act of 1979, and the Indemnity (Amendment) Act of 1988, approved by Parliament in December 1988 when the political crisis was reaching its nadir.

To understand both acts I have to dwell for a moment on the nature of the violent struggle itself. The executive in Sri Lanka had to deal with two guerilla movements, the LTTE, which had been proscribed officially in 1978, and the JVP. The ban on the JVP had been lifted for a while (and in 1982 the JVP leader, Rohana Wijeweera, even contested the presidency). In 1983 the JVP again was proscribed. It was the task of the armed forces to deal with both violent movements. I am saying 'armed forces' (and not the police or the military) on purpose, because the distinction in Sri Lanka between police and army is not very clear-cut. Apart from the circumstance that police and army fall under one and the same minister, the activities of police and military are very similar: the keeping of law and order in Sri Lanka itself. In 1948 the Sri Lankan army was very small. It had never dealt with a foreign enemy and its first deployment was to guard the northwestern shoreline against illegal immigration from India and smuggling: a police rather than a military task.

In the course of the post-independence period both the police and the army were confronted with increasing violence, and the number of casualties among the armed forces grew fast. The first major event was of course the April 1971 insurgency (when scores of police stations were attacked), but this was quickly followed by the violent policies of the various Tamil separatist groups. Although the LTTE has occasionally resorted to veritable battles, the main tactic of both JVP and LTTE was the surprise attack (including, from the LTTE side, the suicide attack). For the armed forces this meant that they were confronted with an extremely elusive yet deadly enemy. Established military tactics assuming two regular armies fighting each other simply did not apply. It is in this context that the Prevention of Terrorism Act must be placed. It was enacted in July 1979, about a year after the proscription of Tamil insurgent groups, in order to combat increasing attacks on government officials, by the LTTE in particular. The main thrust of the PTA is to counter, and to punish, violent attacks on the government. But the various provisos of the PTA contained more than that: under the PTA people could, on mere suspicion, be detained up to 18 months without charge or trial. Detainees need not have been informed of the reasons for detention, and access to relatives and lawyers could be denied. Any confession made by a person was admissible as evidence. The PTA thereby made possible detention on the basis of flimsy evidence and without recourse to constitutionally guaranteed judicial procedures. It severely affected the judiciary because it was not allowed access to suspected persons, and offered considerable licence to violence in the form of torture, extra-judicial executions and disappearances: the PTA greatly facilitated the situation in which an estimated 40,000–60,000 persons are believed to have disappeared during the violent crisis of the late 1980s (see Hyndman 1985: 34–43 for some of the consequences of the PTA: she actually saw hundreds of 'suspects' in detention camps, many of them obviously tortured).[30]

The Indemnity (Amendment) Act of December 1988 covered up all acts, legal or illegal, done or purported to have been done in suppression of 'unlawful activity' as specified in the PTA. The Indemnity Act protected the armed forces by providing indemnity from prosecution as long as their actions had been carried out 'in good faith'. Again, it seems likely that this protection of the armed forces contributed to violent behaviour against anyone the armed forces saw as a threat.

Whereas the Emergency Regulations put the legislative off side, acts like the Prevention of Terrorism Act and the Indemnity Act severely limited the power of the judiciary. How was the judiciary affected? I will focus on three judiciary institutions, namely the Attorney General, the Supreme Court and its members, and the lawyer?

The socio-political position of the Attorney General, the members of the Supreme Court and of lawyers differs. The Attorney General and the members of the Supreme Court are appointed by the government, whereas lawyers form an independent profession. With regard to the Attorney General and the Supreme Court the question arises as to how far the appointments are *political* appointments in the sense that the executive tries to protect its interests by incorporating parts of the judicial process. With regard to the lawyers the question arises as to how far lawyers are still free in the pursuit of their profession. They are usually out of reach of the executive, at least in a formal sense. As members of a free profession they are not answerable to the government. As far as their performance is concerned, they are held accountable only by their own organization and its rules. This, however, does not preclude the possibility of political pressure. I am not arguing that lawyers are politically neutral: lawyers, like other citizens, have their political loyalties.

Already in 1977 Samaraweera drew attention to the diminishing autonomy of the judicial administration via a series of legislative and administrative innovations.[31] Some of these were the direct result of internal pressure from the executive. In 1972, for instance, the Criminal Justice Commissions Law was enacted. It was formulated to deal with the prosecution of hundreds of suspects who had been involved in the 1971 insurgency. Normal courts were unable to handle these cases, because many offences had taken place at a time when the regular law-enforcement process had broken down, and because of the sheer number of cases that had to be dealt with. Modifications of normal procedures were therefore deemed necessary. The resulting legislation, however, went far beyond the requirements of the situation that was the cause of it. For example, legislation provided for the establishment of special courts, the so-called Criminal Justice Commissions, appointed by the

Governor General (and later the President). Three subjects could be brought before the commissions: offences arising out of the 1971 insurgency, foreign exchange frauds, and offences arising out of widespread breakdown of law and order. The third subject especially caused considerable unrest because framed this way it could easily be abused. The failure to provide for the right of appeal from the decisions of the commissions only aggravated the suspicion.

The Administration of Justice Law that became operative in 1974 was meant to provide a clean break with the colonial past. The 1972 Constitution had done so in the political realm. The post-colonial structure of the judicial process was rather complex and still basically colonial: at the top of the hierarchy of courts was still the Privy Council, a body of private councillors of the queen of England! The new law simplified this structure and also brought it more under control of the government of Sri Lanka. Two elements are important here: the position of the Attorney General and the appointment of judges. The 1972 Constitution already had vested the authority for the appointment, dismissal and disciplinary control of judges in the cabinet of ministers. Although members of the Supreme Court were to be appointed by the President, he did so on the advice of the Prime Minister. This aroused fear of judicial dependence: judges, the members of the Supreme Court included, would henceforth be subservient to the political party or parties in power, even though judges of the Supreme Court were, once appointed, not answerable to the government.

Another innovation was that the Director of Public Prosecutions came under the direction of the Attorney General, who was also appointed by the President, presumably on the advice of the cabinet, with the same consequences with regard to his independence: appointments could easily, and perhaps unavoidably, become political appointments. As long as the president was the symbolic head of state, and not really part of the executive, there could be a semblance of independence. From 1978 onwards, however, with an executive president, the Attorney General became a political figure over whom there was no democratic, parliamentary control, not even indirectly, via the Minister of Justice. The Udugampole case suggests that this indeed meant that the Attorney General became a weapon in the struggle for power.

As indicated above, the 1972 Constitution, which made Sri Lanka a republic with a president at the top, stipulated that judges of the Supreme

Court henceforth were appointed by the president. The 1978 Constitution formulated another step in the direction of amalgamation of the jural and the political. It was henceforth an executive president who appointed the judges of the Supreme Court (Article 107). Judges could be removed 'by an order of the president made after an address of Parliament supported by a majority of the total number of members of Parliament' (Article 107[2]). More important, and of immediate concern, was one of the Transitional Provisions which stated that 'All Judges of the Supreme Court and the High Courts established by the Administration of Justice Law, No. 44 of 1973, holding office on the day immediately before the commencement of the Constitution shall, on commencement of the Constitution, cease to hold office' (Article 163). Article 163 opened the road for the wholesale appointment of a Supreme Court agreeable to the political top of Sri Lanka. The 1978 constitution was severely criticized, especially by leftist politicians (and not only on the issue of judicial independence).[32]

Neither in the case of the Supreme Court, nor in the case of the Attorney General has there been a systematic investigation into their functioning in a field that increasingly came to be characterized by the life-and-death struggle in which the executive was involved. The executive has tried to engulf both, but seems to have largely failed in the case of the Supreme Court. The Attorney General, however, succumbed. In the absence of systematic research I present a number of cases to illustrate this statement.

The Udugampola case provides one example of an Attorney General serving the needs of the executive rather than the rule of law. Other examples include the notorious case of the Embilipitiya school boys, and the Mailanthanai case. The Embilipitiya case concerns the abduction and disappearance of 32 schoolboys in 1989. Although there was substantial evidence regarding those who were involved, the Attorney General refused to file a case in court, probably because the armed forces were involved. The same holds true for the second case. In July 1992 an army cum police patrol was ambushed near Batticaloa (Eastern Province), in all likelihood by the LTTE. Twenty-six men were killed on the spot, seven succumbed later to their injuries. By way of reprisal soldiers attacked the Tamil village Mailanthanai, killing at least 33 villagers and burning a number of houses. At the inquest a number of survivors claimed that they would be able to recognize their assailants. As

Mailanthanai is close to Batticaloa, the court case should have been held there. The Attorney General, however, without sufficient legal reason, moved the case to Polonnaruva – 'inexplicably transferred to the Polonnaruva's Magistrate's Court', as the Human Rights Task Force put it.[33] Such a move is legally possible. The reason in this case, however, was not legal at all but political: if the case had been heard in Batticaloa, many witnesses would have been able to come because it is a Tamil area and close to their homes. Witnesses from a Tamil area are not likely to be able or willing to go to a Sinhala area, such as Polonnaruva, much further away. Apart from incurring far higher costs, they would run the risk of being attacked:

> Witnesses from Mailainthani [sic] fear to go to Polonnaruwa and testify against the army men there. If overnight stay becomes necessary, as it most probably will owing to transport problems, they would become easy targets. The witnesses are understandably unwilling to attend the courts at Polonnaruwa. On their absenting themselves warrants will be issued for their arrest. They will then have to furnish bail or be remanded. If they furnish bail and fail to attend court, their bonds will be forfeited. If they fail to pay the forfeit they could be jailed. The witnesses have lost their dear ones, their homes have been destroyed and some of them at least will risk losing their liberty. To them the transfer is a subtle move to scuttle the case.[34]

The 'inexplicable transfer' can be explained as a move to protect the army, at the expense of the victims – and of justice in a more abstract sense. Cases like Udugampola, Mailanthanai and Embilipitiya are explicit and well-known examples of protection of the executive by the Attorney General. A systematic investigation of his decisions will in all likelihood show a general inclination of the Attorney General to protect the executive, the armed forces in particular, against the law.

Although especially in 1978 it was feared that the Supreme Court too would be drawn into the orbit of the executive, this fear did not materialize. Let me again cite a few examples. In December 1982, and in the course of a referendum campaign, a group of *bhikkhu* and other clergymen printed a pamphlet of protest, *Pavidi Handi*. The pamphlet was confiscated by the police (the police officer in charge was Udugampola, see above). Its authors filed a fundamental rights case at the Supreme Court, and won. The policeman was fined. The government, however, paid the fine and promoted him, an act that was widely interpreted as contempt for the law – and for the Supreme Court.

The second case concerns the aftermath of a Supreme-Court case rather than the court case itself. On March 8 1983, Vivienne Goonewardene, a former MP and junior minister and at that time president of a women's organization connected to a number of left wing parties, together with representatives of other women's organizations, went to the American Embassy to present a petition. It emphasized the wish to preserve the Indian Ocean as a peace zone and protested against the establishment of a possibly nuclearized military base on the island of Diego Garcia. They staged a small demonstration and displayed banners and placards. On their way home they passed by a Colombo police office. Of what happened there, two very different versions exist. According to Goonewardene she went into the police office to bail out a photographer who had taken pictures of police intervention; instead of freeing him, she herself was molested and threatened with arrest. According to the police she obstructed a police officer in the execution of his duty when she refused to disband the group of women, and was therefore arrested. Molest and arrest were for Goonewardene sufficient to file a human rights petition – at the Supreme Court, where such petitions belong. The Supreme Court, represented by three judges, did not accept the charge of cruel and degrading treatment, but held that the arrest had been unlawful and unconstitutional. The court ordered the state to pay Goonewardene Rs 2,500 compensation, because the action of the policeman was an executive action. The state therefore was liable for the infringement. The following day the policeman who had wrongfully arrested Goonewardene was promoted.

More important in this context is what happened a few days after the verdict. On Saturday 11 June 1983, the houses of the three judges comprising the court were attacked by mobs of 100–200 people, shouting obscenities and criticizing their verdict in the Goonewardene case. Attempts by two of the judges (the third had moved three years previously, unknown to the instigators of the mob) to reach the police failed: emergency telephone lines were engaged or said to be out of order, policemen refused to listen to complaints, etc.

It is highly unlikely that these attacks were spontaneous. For instance, buses of the Ceylon Traffic Board (CTB) had been used to transport the demonstrators to the three residences. This makes government involvement highly likely.

The incidents raised a storm of protest, not in the least from the Bar Association but also by the press. Lawyers of the Mount Lavinia Courts demonstrated outside the courts in protest against the demonstrations in front of the homes of the Supreme Court judges. The Bar Association required the government to appoint an independent commission of inquiry. *The Island* in its editorial of 13 June 1983 stated:

> Under the principle of the separation of powers it is the role and function of the judiciary to interpret the law and apply it to specific circumstances and if the judges in their wisdom have arrived at a verdict based on law, that is final and binding and there can be no protest going beyond it.

In its editorial of 19 June 1983 *The Island* complained about the lack of commitment of the police, and continued by saying:

> Never before has any single incident generated such a public indignation and horror than this attack by thugs on the judiciary. The judiciary is the last bulwark of the people's rights, the last bastion which separates any society from anarchism and if that bastion is breached then society's lurch towards the tyranny of mob rule will be frighteningly swift.

These words proved to be prophetic – just over one month later, on July 23 1983, an anti-Tamil pogrom took place, in which hundreds of Tamils were killed and thousands had to flee (the background of the pogrom has never been thoroughly investigated but many aspects of it strongly suggest active government involvement).

It seems that after these two incidents, showing government contempt for the highest judiciary authority in Sri Lanka, the Supreme Court has been left to work in peace, both in politically volatile cases and in human rights violations in which the police were also involved.

An interesting case concerns an event that took place in Kandy, early in 1993. Again, the event actuating a fundamental right plea in the Supreme Court is rather fatuous: the petitioner had sounded the horn of his car when the car driven by the magistrate of Kandy was halted in the middle of the road while the driver was talking with the driver of a jeep which had stopped next to the magistrate's car, thereby obstructing traffic. In the afternoon the petitioner was ordered to come to the police station where he was arrested and remanded. Next day he was produced before the magistrate who had been obstructing the traffic. The petitioner never learned why he had been arrested and therefore filed a Fundamental Rights case. The Supreme Court agreed that his fundamental rights had been abused.[35]

More serious is what happened to a number of lawyers. The judiciary is by its very nature involved in conflicts of interests. In a situation in which the executive and its legal and illegal agents use violence to reach their ends, officers of law, such as judges, attorneys and lawyers, may become targets, too.

During the past ten years or so many lawyers have been killed in Sri Lanka. The majority, however, met their fate not as lawyers, but as politicians: Amirthalingam (TULF politician killed by the LTTE); Yogeswaran (TULF politician and MP, presumably killed by the LTTE); Atulathmudali (former minister and at the time of his assassination in 1992 member of Parliament for the DUNF); Chandradasa Ranasingha (law student at the Open University and a member of the Nava Samaja Pakshaya, who disappeared in December 1989 during a combined operation of police and army); Sarath Ratnayake (practising lawyer in Matara but also parliamentary candidate for the SLFP, who was tortured and killed in February 1989 by unidentified persons), or human rights activists: Sam Tambimuttu (gunned down in 1990, probably by the LTTE).

Here I focus on lawyers whose killing was connected to their role *as lawyers*. As far as I know there are five examples of lawyers killed ex officio, all in 1988 and 1989. All five were involved in *habeas corpus* cases. The most notorious case concerned Wijedasa Liyanarachchi, an attorney-at-law, who was abducted, tortured and killed (September 1988). Apart from killings there have been numerous death threats and assaults, as well as ransacking of offices.

None of the cases were seriously investigated by the police. In a number of these cases more may have been at stake than merely *habeas corpus* issues: many young people, students of law included, were at that time sympathizers of the JVP. Some of the lawyers were killed because of this, rather than because they were involved in *habeas corpus* cases. Still, until at least 1993 and the death of president Premadasa, the situation was frightening enough for lawyers. An example can make this clear: Lawyers for Human Rights and Development is an independent organization of lawyers dedicated to the promotion and protection of human rights. During the seven years of its existence it filed hundreds of fundamental rights applications on behalf of people who were illegally arrested, detained and tortured or subject to other kinds of violation of fundamental rights, and hundreds of *habeas corpus* applications on behalf of people illegally detained or who had disappeared after arrest. Moreover, it provided free legal advice and legal assistance to people in distress. Even during the worst period of terror in 1988–89 LHRD could function without any problem. However,

> ... since June 1992 LHRD has faced a very serious security problem. At midnight on June 29, 1992 four gunmen wearing black trousers and black T-shirts with their faces partly covered with dark glasses have come up to the doorstep of the LHRD office ... and inquired of Kalyananda Tiranagama, General Secretary and Mohan Seneviratne, legal officer of the LHRD. While making the inquiry they have held the office peon at gun point. On June 30, between midnight and 2.30 a.m. the office bell was heard ringing 3 times and a Pajero Jeep used by the Security Forces was seen parked near the office. On July 1, 1992, a complaint was made to the Inspector General of Police and the Chief Justice and the Attorney General were informed of this threat. On July 1, night at 9.00 p.m. half an hour after the departure of the Superintendent of Police who recorded the statement of the office staff and one hour before the arrival of police guards, a Pajero Jeep without number plates, usually used by death-squads, was seen parked opposite the LHRD office. Immediately the Police were informed and the Pajero had disappeared by the time Police came.
>
> On July 2, night Police guards were provided from 9.00 p.m. Ten minutes prior to their arrival at 8.50, a gunman has climbed up the ladder leading to the roof top, and entered LHRD premises in the top floor. By the time Police came, the gunman had disappeared.
>
> On July 3, morning LHRD office peon was accosted by a man in civilian clothes and was asked to leave the place within a week. The man has asked the peon to inform Mr.Tiranagama and Mr.Seneviratne to stop appearing in Fundamental Rights applications.
>
> LHRD printer has been asked not to print LHRD newsletters ... On July 8 morning, the man who accosted the peon on July 3, has caught hold of the peon on the road to the office, played back some tape-recorded telephone conversations of LHRD lady lawyers and asked the peon to identify their voices. The peon got panicky and left the job.[36]

Between assassination and a threat like the preceding one lies the forced abduction (and release after a few days), and the ransacking of offices.

The examples succinctly sum up the situation and include an indication from where the threat for lawyers came. During the years of terror thousands of people have disappeared and, although actual proof is hard to deliver, there is no reasonable doubt that the armed forces, the police included, should be held responsible for a certain percentage of these disappearances. Among the legal means available to relatives of disappeared persons to discover their whereabouts is either the *habeas corpus* application or the fundamental rights application. In both cases, army and/or police may be proven guilty, hence the efforts of the police to discourage lawyers who are active in this field. These efforts led to a breakdown of the relationship between the police and the legal profession and even to an exceptional reaction among lawyers: they went on strike, refusing to defend a police officer!

Let me sum up what happened: in the years following independence the Sri Lankan government became more and more involved in a double conflict, one between the Sinhala majority and the Tamil minority, the other between the late-colonial establishment and an ambitious, post-Second-World-War generation. The democratic process as a way of handling conflict failed and government rigidity led to violent opposition. The government answered in kind and in the ensuing life-and-death struggle began to manipulate both legislation and the judiciary, presumably to create greater freedom to fight its enemies. By doing so it contributed to further escalation of violence. Although most of the violence occurred in the years of UNP government (1977–1994), the demise of the separation of powers started earlier, especially during the United Front government from 1970 to 1977:

> Operating most of the time as an emergency regime, the UF government left behind an institutional edifice of centralized democracy, which was fairly elaborate but without functional equilibrium between its legislative, executive, and judicial organs.[37]

Democracy in Sri Lanka: Erosion and Resilience

Sri Lanka's political and moral crisis was at its deepest in the period 1987–1989. These were years of large-scale killing of political opponents and of serious erosion of human rights and democratic values. Yet right in the midst of these years, in 1988, presidential elections were held. Candidates from several political parties participated in these elections. Despite the threats of the JVP, which were backed by violent assaults on candidates and voters alike, 55.32 per cent of the latter found their way to the polling booths. Moreover, parliamentary elections were held in 1994, one year after the violent death of President R. Premadasa in the streets of Colombo during the 1993 May Day rallies. The 1994 parliamentary elections were won by the People's Alliance, a coalition of opposition parties under the leadership of Chandrika Bandaranaike, *and the UNP accepted its defeat in the polling booths!*

In the introduction I put forward the question of how the transformation of the political arena in Ceylon from a promising democracy in the 1940s and 1950s, into an almost Hobbesian war of everyone against everyone in the 1980s could be explained. However, one might equally well ask the opposite question: how to explain that Sri Lanka, plunged into an abysmal moral and political crisis which brought the country to the brink of total chaos, still stuck to a number of basic democratic institutions? Neither the presidential nor the parliamentary elections were flawless (how could they have been, given the circumstances?), but the power shifts *were* based on elections, *and the losers accepting their defeat.*

In an elementary sense Sri Lanka is definitely a democratic state. That it falls short of all conceivable democratic ideals is not surprising, for at least two reasons. In the first place, few, if any, democratic political systems measure up to their ideals. In the second place, very few democracies had to cope with the problems that the Sri Lankan government had to face: it had to deal with Tamil separatist movements (and among these an extremely violent and uncompromising one, the LTTE), with an external threat (in the guise of an Indian Peace Keeping Force), and with an insurgency from within the majority (the JVP).

It is not my intention to discuss extensively the nature of democracy, but in the face of the odds that the various governments of 'the democratic socialist republic of Sri Lanka' have been facing since independence, I cannot leave out the issue altogether. Democracy is a multifaceted concept and a simple definition is not of much help. In the present context I distinguish between two conceptions of democracy. The first is institutional. A political system can be called democratic if it is based on a number of principles such as regular, general elections and the checks and balances expressed in the doctrine of the *trias politica*, and if it allows para-political institutions such as free press and voluntary associations and non-governmental organizations to do their work. The second conception is a moral one. A political system can be called democratic if in addition to institutional aspects, it includes attitudes of acceptance to majority rule and of respect for and protection of minority points of view. Both conceptions of democracy refer to ideals, and they are obviously closely related. The instrumental view to some extent presupposes the moral one. The doctrine of the *trias politica*, for instance, is something one cannot introduce without a morality associated with it.

When Montesquieu in the eighteenth century looked at the way the English were trying to lessen the risk of abuse of power, with an eye to introducing the same thing in France, he was looking at something that had grown in England over the course of several centuries in the relationship between the administration and the administrated. In France, where the power of the king still was on the increase, the introduction of the *trias politica* was impossible. The introduction in Sri Lanka centuries later was possible because the political arena was dominated by an anglophone elite that had absorbed many of the political values of the colonial power.

Sri Lanka seen over the past decades shows movement away from these ideals. Although there still are elections, section four of this chapter shows an erosion of the separation of powers. Also, para-democratic institutions such as a free press have suffered severe losses. Furthermore, those in power, the representatives of the Sinhala majority in particular, have demonstrated little sensitivity, let alone respect, for the Tamil minority. On the other hand, one should take note of the circumstance that even during the darkest years a number of human rights activists have been active: their voice was never completely silenced. And although the press was to a large extent muzzled, it never stopped protesting against restricting the right to free expression. Democracy was besieged, but it was not overwhelmed.

The focus in this chapter is on one aspect of democracy only, the principle of the separation of forces as one of the safeguards against abuse of power. My conclusion is that by meddling with the separation of powers the executive, in its efforts to combat violence, brought about the opposite: it created ample room for even more violence – by shielding the armed forces against judicial action in particular.

Sri Lanka is a highly politicized society in the sense that the interest in the actual political process receives much attention. In fact, politics is one of the most common topics of discussion in most sections of society. But this discussion is predominantly on the level of actual political practices. Even among politicians and political scientists the interest in a more abstract political discourse regarding the principles of political behaviour is almost absent. Sri Lankan social scientists, too, have been extremely cautious as far as politically sensitive research topics are concerned.[38] Far-reaching decisions regarding the political process are based on political expediency rather than on fundamental discussions of democratic rule. A telling example is the move away from the Westminster election principle of 'the winner takes all'. The 'winner takes all' principle means that slight shifts in overall votes can result in vast shifts in Parliament. The resulting discrepancy between the number of votes cast on the one hand and the number of seats in Parliament on the other was particularly dramatic in 1977 when the winning United National Party with 50.92 per cent of the votes gained 140 seats in Parliament, whereas the main opposition party, the Sri Lanka Freedom Party, with 29.72 per cent of the votes kept only eight seats. Such landslides have been characteristic of Sri Lankan politics until the 1978 reforms, which introduced proportional representation. The motive of J.R. Jayewardena to change the system, however, was not a principled effort to bring the composition of Parliament more in line with actual preferences and resulting voting percentages, but a move to prevent a landslide in favour of the SLFP at the next elections (personal communication, 1995).

I am not saying that democracy in Sri Lanka is merely an outward appearance, based on token features, like parties and regular elections. The Sinhala political past (and here I am deliberately restricting myself to the majority) is in terms of regulation of power very mixed. Neither the ancient kingdoms that existed in the northern dry zone until after the first millennium, nor the wet zone kingdoms including the Kandyan one, were democracies. Still, there were so many checks and balances in the political structures of these kingdoms that one cannot call them completely absolutist either. On the other hand, especially irrigation-based village life (and until very recently by far the majority of the population was living in cultivation-based villages) was to a large extent based on consensus reached in sub-caste cum village councils in which all landowning cultivators participated (that is to say: the males). One should be aware that the traditional, *purana* (old) village, with its tank, its paddy fields, its settlement and its Buddhist temple and *dagaba*, is still the model of Sinhala society. The ideals of – admittedly rather romanticized – Sinhala village society are still very much alive on a country-wide scale. Generalized, unnamed and unelaborated ideas of democracy too are very much alive. Again, one should not forget how much the Sri Lankan elite was socialized into British culture. In this respect it is also important to keep in mind that independence and democratic institutions did not come to Sri Lanka through mass mobilization and a fight against the colonial power. They were simply handed over by the British.[39]

However, post-independence confronted Sri Lankan society with a conflict of a rare magnitude. I believe Jayatilleka is right when he says that 'No Third World society has ever faced or faces such a combination of types of conflict'.[40] The tragic fact is that in the case of Sri Lanka the democratic form chosen in the wake of British colonial rule, namely the Westminster majoritarian model of democracy, proved to be the one that intensified rather than diminished the chances of differences in interest turning into conflict, and of conflict turning into violent conflict. Given the presence of a large minority, namely the Tamil population, a consensus model of democracy could have had the opposite effect.[41] The introduction of the majoritarian model of democracy rule in Sri Lanka chosen already during the late-colonial period paved the way for political forms that were undemocratic in the moral sense of the term. In the end this led to violent opposition – and to the dismantling of democracy, as Tambiah put it.[42]

Acknowledgements

This chapter forms part of a book-length study on state formation, ethnicity and violence in Sri Lanka. I am indebted to Gananath Obeyesekere, H.L. Seneviratne, Jan Verhoogt, and the editors of this volume for their constructive comments on various drafts.

Notes

1   Thomas Hobbes, *Leviathan*, Harmondsworth: Penguin Books, 1968 [1651].
2   Steven Kemper, *The Presence of the Past. Chronicles, Politics, and Culture in Sinhala Life*, Ithaca: Cornell University Press, 1991.
3   *Report of the Commission on Constitutional Reform*. Colombo: Ceylon Government Press, 1969.
4   Ibid.
5   K.M. De Silva and H. Wriggins, *J.R. Jayewardene of Sri Lanka. A Political Biography. Volume 1: 1906–1956*, London: Anthony Blond, 1988, pp. 196 ff.
6   K.N.O. Dharmadasa, *Language, Religion, and Ethnic Assertiveness. The Growth of Sinhalese Nationalism in Sri Lanka*, Ann Arbor: The University of Michigan Press, 1992, pp. 290 ff.
7   A. Jeyaratnam Wilson, *The Break-up of Sri Lanka. The Sinhalese–Tamil Conflict*, London: C. Hurst & Company, 1988.
8   Wilson, A. Jeyaratnam, *S.J.V. Chelvanayakam and the Crisis of Sri Lankan Tamil Nationalism, 1947–1977*. London: Hurst & Co, 1994.
9   Victor Ivan, *Sri Lanka in Crisis. Road to Conflict*, Ratmalana: Sarvodaya Book Publishing Services, 1989, p. 6.

10 James Manor, *The Expedient Utopian: Bandaranaike and Ceylon*, Cambridge: Cambridge University Press, 1989.

11 See Dharmadasa, *Language, Religion, and Ethnic Assertiveness*.

12 W.A. Wiswa Warnapala, *Civil Service Administration in Ceylon. A Study in Bureaucratic Adaptation*, Colombo: Department of Cultural Affairs, 1974, p. 244.

13 Tarzie Vittachi, *Emergency '58: The Study of the Ceylon Race Riots*, London: Andre Deutsch, 1958.

14 M.R. Narayan Swamy, *Tigers of Lanka. From Boys to Guerillas*, Delhi: Konark Publishers, 1994.

15 Sirimal Abeyratne, *Economic Change and Political Conflicts in Developing Countries with an Investigation into Sri Lanka*, Amsterdam: VU University Press, Sri Lanka Studies No.5, 1998.

16 Paul Alexander, 'Shared Fantasies and Elite Politics: The Sri Lankan "Insurrection" of 1971', *Mankind* 13, Vol. 2, pp. 113–32, 1997; A.C. Alles, *Insurgency 1971*, Colombo: The Apothecaries, 1972; Mick Moore, 'Thoroughly Modern Revolutionaries: The JVP in Sri Lanka'. *Modern Asia Studies* Vol 27, No. 3, pp. 593–42, 1993; Gananath Obeyesekere, 'Some Comments on the Social Backgrounds of the April 1971 Insurgency in Sri Lanka (Ceylon)', *Journal of Asian Studies*, Vol. 33 No. 3, pp. 367–84, 1974.

17 Peter Kloos, 'The Struggle Between the Lion and the Tiger', in Cora Govers and Hans Vermeulen (eds), *The Politics of Ethnic Consciousness*, London: Macmillan, 1997, pp. 223–49.

18 *Sunday Times*, 5 April 1992, and *The Island* and *Divaina* of 6 April 1992.

19 *Aththa*, 8 April 1992.

20 Quoted in *Daily News* of 8 July 1993.

21 Baron de la Brède et de Montesquieu, *De l'esprit des lois*, 2 vols., Paris: Editions Garnier Frèyes, 1969 [1748].

22 Robert A. Dahl, *Democracy and Its Critics*, New Haven: Yale University Press, 1989, p. 27.

23 *Report of the Commission on Constitutional Reform*, see note 3.

24 F.G. Bailey, *Stratagems and Spoils. A Social Anthropology of Politics*, Oxford: B. Blackwell, 1969.

25 Lorna S. Dewaraja, *The Kandyan Kingdom of Sri Lanka 1707–1782*, Colombo: Lake House Investments, 1988, p. 223.

26 Josine Van der Horst, *Who Is He, What Is He Doing? Religious Rhetoric and Performances in Sri Lanka during R.Premadasa's Presidency (1989–1993)*, Amsterdam: VU University Press, Sri Lanka Studies, volume 2, 1995, p. 121; Peter Kloos, 'Changing Resources, Changing Entrepreneurs', in M. van Bakel, R.R. Hagesteijn and P. van de Velde (eds), *Private Politics, A Multi-disciplinary Approach to 'Big-Man' Systems*, Leiden: Brill, 1986, pp. 54–66; idem, '"Past Political Identities, Present Political Interests". An Indigenous Political Model in Sri Lanka', in M. van Bakel, Renée Hagesteijn, Pieter van de Velde (eds), *Pivot*

Politics, Changing Cultural Identities in Early State Formation Processes, Amsterdam: Het Spinhuis, 1994, pp. 223–34.

27 K.M. De Silva and H.Wriggins, *J.R. Jayewardene of Sri Lanka. A Political Biography. Volume 2: From 1956 to his retirement (1989),* London: Leo Cooper & Pen & Sword books, 1994, p. 545.

28 Phadnis, Urmila, 'Sri Lanka: Crises of Legitimacy and Integration'. In: L. Diamond, J.J. Linz and S.M. Lipset (eds.), *Democracy in Developing Countries. Volume 3: Asia.* Boulder, Colorado: Lynne Rienner Publishers, 1989, pp. 160–61.

29 *Review of Emergency Regulations,* Colombo: Centre for the Study of Human Rights, University of Colombo (in association with Nadesan Centre), 1993.

30 Hyndman, Patricia, 'Democracy in Peril. Sri Lanka: A Country in Crisis'. Report of the LAWASIA Human Rights Standing Committee, 1985, pp.34–43.

31 Samaraweera, Vijaya, 'The Administration and the Judicial System', in K.M. de Silva (ed.), *Sri Lanka, A Survey.* London: Hurst & Company, 1977, pp. 353–75.

32 N.M. Perera, *Critical Analysis of the New Constitution of the Sri Lankan Government,* Colombo: N.M.Perera Memorial Trust, 1979; Colin R. De Silva *Sri Lanka's New Capitalism and the Erosion of Democracy. The Political writings of Dr. Colin R.de Silva in the period 1977–1988,* Batty Weerakoon (ed.) Colombo: Ceylon Federation of Labour, 1988.

33 *Annual Report,* Human Rights Task Force, 1993, p. 29.

34 Ibid.

35 Supreme Court Hearing 15 December 1993.

36 *Quarterly Newsletter of the South-Asian Human Rights Action Programme,* 1992–3, p. 2.

37 Phadnis, 'Sri Lanka: Crises of Legitimacy and Integration', p. 161.

38 Peter Kloos, 'Publish and Perish: Nationalism and Social Research in Sri Lanka', *Social Anthropology* Vol. 3, No 2, 1995 pp. 115–128.

39 Mick Moore, 'Retreat from Democracy in Sri Lanka?' *Journal of Commonwealth & Comparative Politics* No. 30, Vol. 1, 1992, pp. 64–84.

40 Dayan Jayatilleka, *Sri Lanka. The Travails of a Democracy, Unfinished War, Protracted Crisis,* New Delhi: Vikas, 1995; Jagath P. Senaratne, *Political Conflict in Sri Lanka, 1977–1990,* Amsterdam: VU University Press, Sri Lanka Studies, no 4, 1997.

41 Arend Lijphart, *Democracies. Patterns of Majoritarian and Consensus Government in Twenty-One Countries,* New Haven: Yale University Press, 1984.

42 Stanley J. Tambiah, *Sri Lanka. Ethnic Fratricide and the Dismantling of Democracy,* London: I.B. Tauris & Co, 1986.

3 DOMINANT PARTY DEMOCRACY AND THE POLITICS OF ELECTORAL REFORM IN JAPAN

Kazuki Iwanaga

Introduction

Half a century after the end of World War II, Japan is still the only stable industrialized democracy in Asia, with a well-established parliament, political parties that vigorously compete in elections, and a solidly legitimate democratic constitution. The political system is supported by the second largest economy in the world. Japan – from 1955 to 1993 – offers a compelling example of what has been called the dominant or predominant party democracy: the same major party is consistently supported by a winning majority of the voters under free and competitive conditions. According to Alagappa, the characteristics of a dominant party democracy are 'free elections, protection of civil liberties, a dominant party that stays in power over a long period, an interventionist state, a strong central bureaucracy, and management of the political affairs of the country by means of conciliation and consensus-building'.[1]

In the past, South Korea and Taiwan as well as semi-democratic Singapore and Malaysia have, with much variation, sought to emulate features of the Japanese model.[2] The 'learn from Japan' movements in

Singapore and Malaysia in the late 1970s and early 1980s were one of the manifestations of this emulation process. Japan has carefully avoided to spread its own political 'paradigm', after the disastrous experience of the Greater East Asia Co-prosperity Sphere. Nonetheless, in light of Japan's economic performance, questions have been raised in Asia about the Western model versus the Japanese model. The attractive aspects of the Japanese model had been the stability and continuity of its one-party dominant regime which seemed to be performing better than the economies of the West. Many East and Southeast Asians saw Japan as the new champion exemplifying an alternative avenue to democracy, radically different from that of Europe and the United States. They could tell themselves that Japan's system is culturally bound to Asia and shares, therefore, similarities of condition with their countries. Lucian Pye maintains that the Western idea of checking and balancing power and authority tend to limit the appeal of Western-style democracy to Asian leaders whose cultures emphasize a large role for state authority.[3] With the end of Japan's dominant party system and the beginning of unstable coalition governments, the initial enthusiasm for the Japanese model in general has waned.

The Japanese formula for a successful, dominant party democracy has had its negative effects – the role of excess money in politics and corruption. The recent transitions from authoritarianism to democracy in South Korea and Taiwan have been accompanied by the ills of money politics in these countries not dissimilar to those experienced by Japan. In the case of South Korea, the close relationship between the giant economic conglomerates and the government resulted in a series of 'money-for-political favours' scandals involving two presidents. In Taiwan, as in South Korea, political parties, especially the Kuomintang, used their connections to obtain money to bolster their activities. In both countries, the considerable amount of publicity over corruption revealed the openness in their systems – a relatively free press was able to monitor the misconduct of public officials and expose corruption to a greater degree than before. Reforms aimed at dealing with the massive influence of money politics have been pledged by the governments.

Although Japan has had Western-style parliamentary institutions since the late nineteenth century, democracy in Japan is to a large extent a post-World War II phenomenon. During the six and a half years of the

Occupation, various reforms were carried out to transform Japan into a democratic state. A new democratic constitution, written by the Americans, was imposed on a country which has a strong tradition of bureaucratic rule. During the last five decades, Japan has become one of the most stable industrialized democracies in the world.

In the many newly-emerging democracies the choice of an electoral system is increasingly being recognized as a vital element in democratic constitutional design. The nature of the electoral system can make a great deal of difference in which various democratic principles are pursued and whether the stability and management of the political apparatus are maintained effectively. Taagepera and Shugart write that 'electoral rules can make or break a party – or even a country'.[4] Electoral rules are also much easier to change than other components of a political system.[5] Though many scholars agree that the form of an electoral system has important democratic consequences, scholars differ in their prescriptions for emerging democratic states. The choice is primarily between pro-portional representation and plurality elections, but sometimes they prefer mixed systems combining these two principles.

Politically, Japan has been at a number of crossroads in the past and the 1990s seems to be one of the great watershed decades in Japan's postwar democratic history with far-reaching implications for the Japanese political system. The year 1993, in particular, was a critical one in Japan's political history. It marked the end of the one-party dominance of the Liberal Democratic Party (LDP) – the culmination of 38 years in power and the final achievement of change in government. The election also marked the beginning of a period of political uncertainty in Japan with the formation of coalition and minority governments. Japanese politics has at last become a sort of non-zero-sum enterprise in which today's winners may, as coalitions shift, wish tomorrow to form an alliance with today's losers. In 1994, the electoral system for the powerful Lower House of the Japanese Parliament was changed from the 70-year-old system based on a single non-transferable vote (SNTV) in multi-member constituencies to the mixed system combining single-member constituencies and proportional representation (PR). This change in the electoral system is the most radical institutional innovation in Japan since the adoption of the present constitution in 1947.

Is democracy in Japan circumvented? Many scholars and others interested in Japan hold the view that politicians reign but bureaucrats rule. How much power do elected leaders have? Compared with European parliamentary systems, Japan's elected politicians probably rely more on non-elective career bureaucrats in the ministries who are immune from public accountability to formulate policy recommendations and draft legislation. In fact, most laws are drafted by bureaucrats. Senior civil servants often appear in the Parliament (*Diet*) in place of their cabinet ministers to answer interpellations. However, it is the elected politicians who give legal sanction to any legislative proposal drawn up by bureaucrats. The power of the bureaucracy is subjected to the wishes of the parliamentary majority. As Pempel writes: '[I]f the bureaucracy in Japan is powerful, as indeed most evidence suggests, its power remains broadly subject to the preferences set by the parliamentary majority.'[6]

Since the electoral system is 'a major determinant of a political regime',[7] the main purpose of this chapter is to assess the democratic consequences of the Japanese electoral systems – both the multimember constituency system for the Lower House used until 1993 and the new electoral system that combines single-member constituencies with proportional representation. The present chapter also seeks to examine some of the factors that help to explain one-party dominance in Japan. Finally, the long-term factors and short-term catalysts behind Japan's electoral reform will be analysed.

The Political Significance of Electoral Arrangements and the Basis of One-Party Rule

There has been relatively little research into the links between Japanese electoral arrangements and democracy. The previous electoral system used for the Japanese Lower House was unique among established democratic countries, in that it combined multimember districts and a single non-transferable vote. The system had features that distinguished it radically from both plurality and proportional systems. Members of the Lower House were chosen from electoral districts with magnitudes ranging from two to six seats, with most districts having between three to five seats, depending on the population of the district. In a four-member district, for example, the top four vote-getters were elected and the candidate who came fifth lost. Each voter was allowed to cast a ballot for only one candidate in a multimember district, making elections an arena of competition between the parties and among the candidates

within the same party. A voter could not transfer his vote in any preferential manner.

I shall evaluate Japan's multimember election district system in terms
of three democratic criteria: political equality, representation of viewpoints,
and accountability. We may say that an ideal democratic electoral system
is one permitting all voters to cast an equally weighted ballot – the one-
person, one-vote, one-value rule. Proportionality of votes to legislative
seats is central to democracy. There are, however, various reasons to deviate
from this ideal.[8] No known electoral system, moreover, guarantees
absolute numerical equality in the value of one vote. Generally, the disproportionality between votes and seats is large in systems with plurality
elections and small in PR systems.[9] According to Lijphart, disproportionality is 'the deviation of seat shares from vote shares'.[10]

How disproportionate is the Japanese system? One frequent criticism
of the medium-sized election district system is its lack of proportionality
between total national votes for a party and its parliamentary seats. The
medium-sized-district system heavily favoured voters in some districts
over others, and indeed, it was not intended to create proportionality. It
was introduced in 1925 to benefit two conservative parties existing at that
time.[11] The Japanese electoral boundaries were originally established in
1947, when the population was heavily agrarian. It has consistently
favoured rural voters. Despite occasional, albeit limited, reapportionment,
cross-district inequalities in Japan have become an increasingly serious
problem. In extreme cases in the general elections of 1972 and 1993, it
took four to five times as many votes to elect a representative in the most
densely populated urban district as in the most overrepresented rural one.

The public expressed outrage at the gross inequalities in the value of
a vote across constituencies almost every time elections were conducted.
The Supreme Court wrestled with this issue on five occasions after urban
voters filed lawsuits contesting the constitutionality of the elections. In
1976 and again in 1985, it ruled that such a discrepancy is unconstitutional
because it violates the constitutional guarantee of equality under the law.
In response to the Supreme Court's decisions, the most discrepant districts
were reapportioned. Such incremental measures, however, did not solve
the fundamental inequalities. It should be noted that the Court does not
require absolute proportional equality; it permits some disparity in the
value of a vote across electoral districts. In one of the most recent cases
(1995) the Supreme Court decreed, in a three-to-two decision, that the

Lower House malapportionment ratio of 2.28 to one in the 1993 general election was constitutional.[12]

It is often stated that the proportionality between a party's total national votes and its parliamentary seats places the Japanese SNTV electoral system generally between plurality systems and PR systems. It is, therefore, sometimes classified as 'semi-proportional' because it produces less proportional outcomes than PR systems, but more proportional outcomes than single-member district systems.[13] The Liberal Democratic Party has been the chief beneficiary of the system. Powell, for example, writes: 'The small, multimember, but quite inequitably districted Japanese districts tend to favour the largest party, rather than proportional representation of all parties.'[14] In the 1993 House of Representatives elections, the Liberal Democrats obtained 36.6 per cent of the total national vote, but 46 per cent of the seats. The growing disparity in the size of constituencies has raised questions of democratic legitimacy. Governments depended on bias in the electoral system to reward the ruling LDP with a bonus of seats. Its popular votes were translated into a larger share of seats in the House of Representatives to create a 'manufactured majority'.

The rural bias of the Japanese electoral system, and thus excessive representation of rural interests in the *Diet*, affected the policies of successive LDP governments, which aided the agricultural sectors at the expense of urban consumers. The Liberal Democratic Party and the Social Democratic Party (SDP) have strongly supported the policy of rice self-sufficiency, and opposed the liberalization of rice import.

It is interesting to note that, as scholars of electoral systems have pointed out, the single non-transferable vote (SNTV) electoral system caused strategic dilemmas for large political parties, especially for the LDP. Since there is no mechanism for transferring votes from one candidate to another, and since the LDP ran multiple candidates in an electoral district, the party faced the strategic problems of putting up the appropriate number of candidates and dividing the vote equally among them. Strategic errors made by large parties, either to nominate fewer candidates than it has votes to elect or to nominate more candidates than it has votes to select, end up giving seats to smaller parties, which would not have received any seats in the district under PR. On the whole, however, the Liberal Democrats fared better than other parties because they were able to estimate vote shares and run the optimal number of candidates and apportion the vote relatively equally among those candidates.[15]

Although underrepresentation of minority groups and women is 'a typical feature of most legislative bodies throughout the world',[16] it is often stated that underrepresentation of smaller parties and groups is a common result of the single-member district system. In a plurality system like Britain's, minor parties and fringe groups tend to be penalized by built-in biases of the Westminster system, and are thus prevented from acquiring representative legitimacy. Lijphart contends that 'the parliamentary-PR systems almost invariably post the best records, particularly with respect to representation, protection of minority interests and voter participation'.[17] There are several variants of proportional representation. Lijphart makes a distinction between what he calls 'extreme PR', which has no formal thresholds or only few barriers to small parties, and 'moderate PR', which poses threshold barriers to minor parties, such as limiting proportional results by distributing legislative seats only to parties securing a minimum percentage of the vote.[18] Similarly, Diamond contends, 'The purer the form of PR, and the lower the minimum percentage of the vote required for a party to enter the parliament, the more significant parties there will tend to be and the more Parliament will tend to mirror in its political composition the balance of social, cultural, and ideological interests in society.'[19] Between these two formulas, there is a mixed electoral system that rewards majority parties in some districts while compensating minor ones in others.

The previous electoral system for the Lower House resulted in a form of proportional system without a legal minimum threshold rule for securing representation. As a result, it was possible for minor parties to obtain parliamentary seats with little electoral support. Many smaller parties in Japan could rarely have hoped to have any seats under the single-member district system. Under the pre-1994 system, the percentage of the vote required for a party to win seats in the Lower House was low. These electoral arrangements led to a proliferation of parties that could compete successfully with as little as, for example, 2.9 per cent of the national population in the general election of 1993. The multimember district system made it possible for an individual candidate to be elected with as little as 10–15 per cent or even fewer of the votes in a five-member district.[20] In fact, such multimember constituencies gave dissident groups within political parties incentive to defect and form new parties. As Richardson and Flanagan put it, 'Japanese political parties...are highly prone to splintering.'[21] Many parties in Japan have resulted from defections from the large parties, with the Democratic Socialist Party (DSP) in 1960 and the Social Democratic League (SDL) in 1978 splitting from the Japan Socialist Party (JSP), and the New Liberal Club (NLC) in 1976 and more recently three parties – Nihon Shinto (Japan New Party), Sakigake (Harbinger) Party, and Shinseito (Renewal) Party – breaking off from the LDP.

One way of assessing how democratic a country is is the degree to which its government is accountable to the people. For a government to be accountable, the people must have effective means with which to reward or sanction its performance. The only effective means of ensuring accountability in a democratic polity are the mechanisms of an electoral system. The LDP's nearly four decades of permanent tenure tended to undermine its accountability to the citizens. Accountability of government requires a sufficient degree of proportionality so that governments can be defeated by national swings of opinion. One of the most significant aspects of Japan's electoral system was the difficulty of throwing governments out at the end of their tenure of office if the electorate so wished. Pempel notes:

> In Japan...since most candidates receive somewhat between 12 percent and 25 percent of the district's vote, even a 10 percent shift in a major party's support usually means only a 3–4 percent shift in the support level of each individual candidate from that party. In some cases, this is sufficient to ensure defeat for one of them, but the potential for the individual elector to vote effectively against the party as a whole is almost nil. Protest votes are frequently cast against an incumbent but for a different member of the same party or for an independent candidate associated with that party.[22]

Thus, the Japanese SNTV multi-seat system has made it difficult to vote systematically against the ruling party and in a sense contributed to the LDP's dominance in politics. In addition, the capability of the governing party to perpetuate in power under such a system was enhanced by the difficulty of uniting multiple opposition parties for the purpose of defeating the party in power, thereby creating credible alternatives.

Political scientists have rarely attempted to assess the relationship of electoral systems other than the plurality and PR systems to the occurrence of particular party systems. Do any specific electoral rules foster long-term rule by a single party in the industrialized democracies? As Pempel points out, 'electoral systems do little to explain one-party dominance ... no specific electoral system can be said to cause one-party dominance.'[23] All the countries that have experienced long-term rule by a single party by full procedural democracies since World War II – Japan, Sweden, Israel, and Italy – have operated under different electoral arrangements. At the same time, they shared the conditions that generate multipartism. Thus, one necessary, but not sufficient, condition for one-party dominance seems to be the use of PR and other electoral systems that encourage a multiparty system, because one party under a multiparty system usually needs much fewer than 50 per cent of the votes or parliamentary seats to be dominant.[24] Among the industrialized democracies exhibiting a one-party dominance, Japan seems to be the only country with a long-term rule by the LDP having the minimum threshold closer to 50 per cent of the seats in the Lower House, most often more than 50 per cent.

In short, the built-in bias of the SNTV multi-member constituency system makes change in government difficult, while a plurality system tends to produce a more or less regular alternation between two major parties. If the ability of citizens to 'throw the rascals out' is taken as an important element of democracy, one can raise a question as to whether long-term rule by a single political party can be characterized as a genuine democracy. Huntington, for example, considers alternation in power through competitive elections as an essential component of a true democracy.[25] The key indicator of democratic accountability, however, is not actual alternation in power, but its institutional possibility – that is, an assurance that when the opposition receives more votes than the government party, alternation in power will occur. This important feature of full democracy is what separates a dominant party democracy from other semidemocratic and authoritarian regimes dominated by one party. In non-competitive conditions, such as the authoritarianism of Indonesia, Vietnam, Burma, and Laos as well as semidemocracies in Singapore and Malaysia, the opposition parties, albeit competing formally for power, have no real possibilities of replacing the incumbent regime as in full procedural democracies.

In the case of Japan, the ruling party always has to be sensitive to the needs of voters; for if party leaders are insensitive to the wishes of the electorate, they might find their electoral base quickly eroding. Moreover, in the absence of alternation in office, institutionalized factionalism within the dominant party itself became an important mechanism for intraparty competition for the position of prime minister and posts within the cabinet, providing the polity a semblance of checks and balances. Crespo stated: 'Political accountability of government leaders has existed basically through the competition of the factions that make up the dominant party.'[26] Nonetheless, the turnover test described by Huntington was clearly met: there have been several alternations of power since the 1993 general election, and the democratic mechanisms of accountability have been strengthened.

We may also examine the relationships between electoral arrangements and state management. The management and stability of a democratic state requires an electoral system that produces a stable party system and through it an effective government capable of dealing with the political, social and economic problems it faces. Dunleavy and Margetts list three sets of criteria as crucial for the management of a democratic state: governability, party system stability, and handling social conflicts.[27] The relationship among various democratic and state management criteria produce tensions. Many of the crises and problems that both established and new democracies have experienced stem from these tensions. How can state management in a democracy be enhanced without jeopardizing such democratic criteria as representativeness and accountability? One of the most common tensions in any democracy is between governability, on the one hand, and representativeness and accountability, on the other. Governability requires sufficient concentration of power in the hands of the elected government to give effective direction to the society in which it governs. But, at the same time, this criterion is in conflict with representation for diverse social interests in the legislative body and the need to hold government accountable to the people.[28]

Another tension in a democracy can be found in the relationship among party system stability, representativeness, and handling social conflict. If we follow the minimalist definition of democracy in the Schumpeterian tradition, democracy is essentially about political competition, that is, contestation for political power. Democracy needs competition and conflict, but not too much.[29] Conflicts of competing interests are an integral part of democracy as long as they are 'orderly', that is, to be kept within the boundaries of representative democracy. Handling social conflicts is an important dimension of the stability and management of a democratic state. Electoral systems and legislatures are a viable device for keeping conflicts within limits acceptable to the political elites and mass public.

State management becomes more difficult if the election outcomes are not decisive enough to enable the polity to deal with the difficult issues it faces effectively. The governability of a democratic state can be enhanced by an electoral system. Most political scientists generally agree that the electoral system to a large extent determines the party system and through it the type of government.[30] The studies in this field have primarily focused on variants of proportional representation and plurality elections. The PR systems often produce indecisive election outcomes in the sense that no party obtains a majority of seats whereas plurality systems tend to enhance governability by building a plurality of votes into a majority of seats for one single party.

Japan's single non-transferable vote in medium-sized constituencies buttressed one of the important features of the Westminster model: namely, its political system has long been dominated by working majority governments, capable of exerting control over the *Diet* through relatively tight party discipline. Of all the 19 general elections held in Japan since the first Lower House election in April 1946 until the LDP lost control of the Lower House in 1993, only two – the 1947 election that returned a Socialist, Katayama Tetsu, at the head of a Socialist-conservative coalition, and the 1993 balloting that brought about a non-LDP coalition government – have failed to give one party an overall majority in the Lower House. For 18 months in 1947–48 two successive coalition cabinets were formed. From 1983 to 1986, the LDP was in a coalition government with its tiny splinter party, the New Liberal Club, in order to increase its majority, making it the first coalition cabinet since the formation of the LDP in 1955.

The management of a state also becomes more difficult if the party system is not stable enough for leaders or voters 'to adjust or to learn how to predict the consequences of their own and others' actions.'[31] One way of making a party system more stable is to adopt a minimum threshold rule for parliamentary representation. As previously noted, the threshold rules are built into most proportional systems against the fragmentation of the party system. With Japan's multimember constituencies, the party lineup has not remained static. From the adoption of the present constitution in 1947 until 1955, Japan had a highly competitive multipartism in which the electoral system produced governments that were neither very effective nor very stable. Several coalition governments and minority governments were formed. Unstable party politics in a multiparty context of the time resembles the 1993–95 period, which saw the formation of four coalition governments. Yet the very same electoral system that produced coalition governments also delivered a stable predominant party system from 1955 to 1993.

In the first general election following the consolidation (1958), the LDP and the JSP won 98 per cent of the Lower House seats (62 per cent for the former and 36 per cent for the latter), while the Japan Communist Party (JCP) won only two per cent of the seats. However, the 1960s witnessed the beginning of a period of dealignment; the dealignment process was intensified in the1970s, as the support for the two major parties declined and new, minor, parties began to gain electoral significance. Two new centrist parties emerged, with the formation of the Democratic Socialist Party which split from the Japan Socialist Party in 1960, and the arrival of the neo-Buddhist Komeito by the mid-1960s. By the early 1970s, the Communists had revived significantly in terms of popular votes, after two decades of marginal importance in Japanese electoral politics. In the general election of 1972, the percentage of seats won by the LDP and JSP had shrunk to 79 per cent, bringing to a close the era of stable two-party politics established in 1955. In 1976, the New Liberal Club (NLC), a splinter group from the LDP, was created in the aftermath of the Lockheed scandal and by the end of the 1970s the Social Democratic Federation had split from the JSP. The Democratic Socialist Party, the Komeito, and later the New Liberal Club have received a minimum of 25 per cent of the vote in the 1970s and 1980s. The proliferation of political parties would not have been possible under a single-member constituency system.

The rise of several new parties in the early 1990s accelerated the dealignment process, resulting in a highly fragmented party system. New splits of the LDP in the aftermath of corruption scandals, first in 1992 and then in 1993, put increasing strain on Japan's multimember election district system and on the ability of the LDP government to rule the country effectively. From these rifts emerged Nihon Shinto, Sakigake and Shinseito. As a result, the LDP lost its power and was replaced by a coalition government in July 1993. It was primarily splintering within the LDP, rather than a revolt at the ballot box, that broke the LDP electoral dominance in 1993.

The party system during the period 1955 to 1993 has been variously described as a dominant party, a predominant, and a multiparty system. It is not a multiparty system in the precise meaning of the term, because a single party consistently controlled the government without having to share the power in a coalition government.[32] Perhaps the most appropriate way to characterize the Japanese party system is to call it, in the terminology of Giovanni Sartori, a 'predominant party system'.[33] A predominant party system is one in which the same party wins elections over time under competitive conditions, but other parties 'not only are permitted to exist, but do exist as legal and legitimate ... competitors of the predominant party...'[34] A predominant party system differs from an authoritarian one-party system or hegemonic-party systems in that, in the former, parties other than the ruling one can attain power, if they receive the majority of the votes, whereas in the latter the transfer of power is institutionally impossible.[35]

The Dynamics of the One-Party Dominant Regime in Japan

Japan lacks European-type cleavage politics. The country is homogeneous with a very low level of racial, ethnic, language, or religious differences with ensuing turbulence associated with political forces as in many European countries. As Hrebenar argues:

> [T]he religious, language, racial, and ethnic forces behind many of the European parties are almost completely absent in largely homogeneous Japan. Consequently, electoral system facilitators may be more important in Japan than in other nations because many of the other facilitating forces such as federalism, race, and language are not significant in Japanese politics. Rather, most of the new Japanese parties seem to be parties of opportunity facilitated by favorable election laws.[36]

In the 1950s and most of the 1960s the paradigm of Japanese politics was confrontational. The political arena was sharply polarized ideologically between the dominant LDP and the leftist opposition without a viable centre. The leftist opposition parties, the Socialists and the Communists, were seen by the establishment as representing 'anti-system' forces. The sharpest political divisions of the time were those of what one Japanese political scientist termed 'cultural politics' or 'value politics' based on culture or values.[37] The Liberal Democrats were looked upon as representing conservative groups with traditional values while the Socialists were the champion of more modern, 'progressive' value orientations in the society. This division was partly reflected in the relative positions of government and opposition with respect to the issues involving the extent to which 'the excesses' of the democratization and demilitarization reforms enforced under the Occupation period were to be 'corrected' or reversed.

The two diametrically opposed values provided a ground for intense conflict on the political scene. Conflicts were centred on such issues as the constitution, state power, foreign policy, the self-defence forces, and law and order. Since the issues were perceived as part of a broader, cultural context of values and principles, political conflicts in Japan were easily escalated and intensified. In some respects, this polarized political system resembled what Sartori has called a 'polarized pluralism' – a polity characterized by two polarized blocs.[38] Compared with other industrialized democracies, the splits caused by economic differences did not come to the forefront as political issues in Japan. Growing affluence, as a result of the country's rapid economic growth, reduced the salience of class divisions.

During the 1950s and 1960s, the dominant party and the bureaucracy as well as the key supporters of the conservative government were united under the policies of high economic growth, anticommunism, and the Japan–US alliance. The leftist opposition and much of organized labour, committed to Marxism, were opposed to the bilateral security treaty with the US, the self-defence forces, and the revision of the constitution. The conservative LDP performed well in elections as a result of the policies being followed. It is worth mentioning that the ideological polarization between the two camps in Japan was much higher and lasted longer than in most other industrialized democracies.[39]

Pempel, after studying the causes of one-party dominance in several industrialized democracies, concludes that if a ruling party is to maintain its dominance over time it must be flexible enough to attract newer, politically more important support. It can transform itself in two directions. One is the switching of support groups: 'the Machiavellian capacity to betray some portion of the party's original support group in order to attract newer, more vital support'. The other possible direction involves 'less overt betrayal, requiring only that the party, while continuing to make appeals from a clear ideological position, and with due respect to well-entrenched political values and norms, in fact govern far more pragmatically from the political center.'[40]

The Liberal Democrats, in order to regain their steadily dwindling support, moved toward the centrist position by co-opting the issues of the opposition. By the late 1970s and the early 1980s, the LDP, despite its close ties with specific segments of Japanese society, broadened considerably its appeal to those voters who were once alienated from the policy-making process, including those social groups that were concerned about the new issues of environment and social welfare largely ignored by the conservatives in the polarized 'culture politics' of the previous high growth period. It was able to transform itself into a pragmatic, catchall party, or in the words of Curtis, 'Japan's preeminent party of the broad political center.'[41] Thus, the move to the catch-all strategy was prompted by the need to articulate the demands of the country's growing affluent and less supportive electorate in the urban areas. Several points need mentioning.

It is interesting to note that the Liberal Democrats were able to bounce back with much success, because the party was able to respond to the rise of new issue interests in time and broaden its support base: '[H]ad the LDP not responded the way it did, or responded even more slowly than it did, this crisis of social change might have resulted in more power for the opposition parties, much as happened in Italy and Israel.'[42] The implications of the Japanese experience for semi-democratic and new democratic states in Asia are that, in times of great social change, the revitalization of dominant parties are possible only under competitive and pluralist conditions. One-party-dominant regimes in Asia such as semi-democratic Malaysia and Singapore in which opposition parties are allowed to take part in regular electoral competition but are prevented from replacing the ruling regime by a variety of mechanisms including prior containment of liberal participation, have less incentive to respond to societal change, to broaden their support base, and to respond to new demands from opposing groups.

What kind of clientele did the dominant party represent? In the 1950s and 1960s, the LDP tended to appeal to a distinctive clientele. Its strongest constituency consisted of farmers, merchants, and employees in medium and small enterprises. In 1960, the ratio of farmers, merchants, and the self-employed among LDP supporters was 68 per cent while the ratio of white- and blue-collar workers was only 28 per cent. Since then, the rapid industrialization and urbanization eroded the traditional electoral base of the Liberal Democrats and a major shift in the basis of party support occurred by the 1970s. In the 1980 election, the sum of these latter two groups among LDP supporters increased to 52 per cent while the number of farmers and merchants decreased to 47 per cent of the party's vote.[43] Thus, one can see that, during these 20 years, the Liberal Democratic party had transformed itself from a party of farmers, big business, self-employed businessmen, and employees in small enterprises into a mass-based party. Muramatsu and Krauss convincingly argued that 'one of the key explanations of the successful continuance of LDP dominance in Japan indeed lies in that party's flexible adaptation to change, and particularly to its ability to broaden its social interest coalition'.[44]

A country's electoral system appears to play an important role in handling social conflicts. An open electoral system like Japan's multi-member constituencies facilitated easy entry through the legitimate democratic, political processes for small and new political parties. The evidence tends to indicate that when barriers to the entry of new political parties are low, working through the existing electoral system is more common than protest demonstrations. 'Once in the national legislative arena, minorities gain a national forum and their leaders become more closely tied to incentives of democratic involvement. Other groups can then bargain with them in a democratic context.'[45] If Japan had a single-member district system, various groups dissatisfied with the established parties had no way to have their frustration taken out. Under the multimember district system, they could put up their own candidates and contest the elections with a reasonable chance of winning some seats in the *Diet*.

It should be pointed out in this context that norms in the Japanese culture tend to moderate the application of the formal principle of majority rule as a means for resolving disputes. The traditional preference for decision by consensus in Japan implies that the majority has to take into account the interests of the minority. When the LDP, especially in the 1950s and 1960s, exercised its clear majority to ram through controversial legislation despite the strong protests of the opposition in the *Diet* on several occasions, the opposition parties sometimes complained against what the Japanese refer to as the 'tyranny of the majority' – that is, majorities have no right to ignore the views of minority in decision-making in Japanese culture. In support of such an interpretation, the opposition resorted to rioting and mass protest. Under the influence of the traditional Japanese preference for decision by consensus, compromises quite often took the place of forceful decisions.

The wills of the ruling party to make compromises with opposition parties in order to pass legislation were dependent upon the electoral performances of the parties: '[C]ompromises were most frequent when the parliamentary majorities of the LDP were slimmest...'[46] The long-term gradual decline in the LDP vote by the early 1970s provided incentives for political accommodation and compromise. As the LDP's margins of victory began to ebb, the party was forced to seek compromise with the smaller centrist parties. As Krauss writes, 'Compared to dominance by one side..., a multiple-party balance not only gives the leaders of predominant parties incentives to accommodate differences with a minority to stay in power but also gives leaders of minority parties incentives to accommodate in order to share power.'[47]

In addition to the nature of the previous electoral system, the openess of the dominant party not only to demands of social groups and interests not directly associated to it but also to the demands of major interest groups closely linked to the leftist opposition allowed the Japanese political system to contain political conflicts within the system. As previously noted, these were also contributing causes for one-party dominance. The long-term rule of the Liberal Democrats and the absence of alternation of power helped to determine the degree to which various interest groups have been able to exercise policy-making influence. The closer the interest groups were to the ruling party, the more points of access to political influence they had. Naturally, those interest groups closest to the LDP had direct access to the party leadership and to its various decision-making organs, but the groups most closely associated with the leftist opposition, especially labour, were not totally excluded from influence in policy-making. Further, their influence was not confined to access to the dominant party.

The powerful bureaucracy was another channel through which groups such as labour could influence policy. The Japanese civil service was not controlled by the dominant party despite the close ties between the two. Although the groups closer to the LDP did have more access to the bureaucracy, opposition groups were not excluded from access and influence. Muramatsu and Krauss observed: 'Although being part of the dominant party coalition does help a group in its relations with the bureaucracy, being in opposition to the ruling party does not exclude it from access.'[48]

Thus by providing points of access to political influence for opposition interest groups, they were integrated into the system. To exclude them from the policy-making process would be to risk turmoil, political alienation and even violence, that could threaten the stability of democracy.

One aspect of the political process in Japan is often criticized as being less than democratic – the excessive place of money in politics. Indeed, money has been looked upon as an aberrant force in the Japanese parliamentary elections, probably more so than in most established democracies. The nature of the Japanese multimember, single non-transferable vote system took most of the blame for this. It gave strong incentives for candidates of the same party to compete for votes with each other in the same constituency, and therefore pushed candidates to campaign on constituency services. This was especially true of the LDP, which was forced to put forward two or more candidates per electoral district in its bid to retain a majority in the Lower House. Since these candidates belonged to the same party, they had to wage election campaigns by ways other than the party's policy line. They had to raise their own money and establish their own individual political machines, personal support organizations known as *kôenkai* which are essentially vote-mobilization organizations. The existence of *kôenkai* has been an important feature of Japan's political landscape and almost every candidate for the Lower House has some kind of personal support organization. It is a device primarily developed for electoral competition among candidates of the same political party under the multi-member district system and provides a reliable bloc of voters to whom it renders particularistic favours in exchange for votes. LDP *Diet* members have also formed close ties with local politicians in their constituencies, called electoral *keiretsu* or electoral coalitions, for mutual assistance in elections.

The high costs of establishing these support organizations are a major cause of 'money politics' and of the increase in the number of *Diet* members, sons or aides of retired or deceased parliamentarians who inherit an existing *kôenkai*. In the 1963 general election, 12 per cent of LDP candidates elected in the Lower House inherited their *kôenkai*.[49] In the early 1990s, approximately 40 per cent of LDP members and a quarter of all politicians in the Lower House were 'second-generation politicians'. Japanese politics at the national level has increasingly become a sort of 'family business'.

A candidate-oriented election campaign in Japan probably costs much more than that of any Western democracy. According to one study, the amount of money spent on politics in Japan is 23 times that of the United Kingdom and more than double that of the United States.[50] In short, in order to keep the wheels of Japan's democracy moving under the previous electoral system, large amounts of money were required for election campaigns and for the maintenance of the well-oiled political apparatus. Since this money flowed in from business, rampant corruption was an inevitable result.

One of the most problematic consequences of Japan's electoral system was that the multimember constituencies tended to encourage the pork-barrel style of politics. Candidates could win a seat by focusing on some narrow segment of the electorate in a district instead of appealing to voters at large as in the single-member districts. A successful politician in Japan will act as an effective 'pipe' between constituents and the grant-giving bureaucrats in Tokyo, and a politician was expected to show his value to his constituency by obtaining government contracts for local development projects such as new roads, bridges, and public buildings. Flanagan claims that 'Japan's political culture ... has institutionalized and protected the politician's role of go-between.'[51]

The Politics of Electoral Reform

What are the conditions necessary to transform the reformistic impulse into new electoral systems? The popular surge toward political reforms in the early 1990s was the consequence of several interrelated factors. One can identify the long-term trends behind electoral reform and the short-term catalytic events that actually helped to change the system.[52] The long-term factors include: the gradual fragmentation of Japan's predominant party system due to partisan dealignment; the subsequent rise of electoral support for smaller parties; the disproportionality of election outcomes; the low level of political accountability; the problems of public disillusionment with LDP governments; and a series of corruption scandals which led to the loss of public confidence in the Japanese political system. Demands for electoral change were also generated by increasing concern about citizen alienation from politics. All these conditions created a serious political situation where Japan suffered from a 'legitimacy deficit', a crisis of legitimacy in its political system and the potential for electoral reform. The short-term catalysts include various events and leaders surrounding political reform. Many Japanese, both politicians and the public, demanded a radical restructuring of the electoral laws for the Lower House including the electoral system. In order for Japan to overcome its 'legitimacy deficit', the government had to carry out political reform.

The debate about electoral reform has partly revolved around the consequences of alternative electoral systems. Many in the LDP preferred the single-member districts, arguing that they would lead to regular alternations in power between two parties, while other LDP *Diet* members opposed changing the electoral system. But underlying these arguments were contested visions about the principles of representative democracy. For advocates of the single-member constituency system, the principle of responsible party government took precedence over the inclusion of all parties in strict proportion to their share of the vote. For them, the primary purpose of elections was to produce an effective, stable government, thereby avoiding a fragmented *Diet*. For critics of the single-seat constituencies, especially for smaller parties which preferred the PR system, the case for reform was based on the unfairness of the electoral system to minor parties.

Data from many surveys in Japan indicate increasing citizen alienation from politics, declining confidence and trust in government, and declining party loyalty. The decline in the role of political parties in Japan can be seen in various ways. Party identification is weak in Japan. In fact, many studies show that a high proportion of the Japanese electorate does not identify with any political party, and even among those who identify themselves with a party, many have weak identification.[53] In recent years, party identification has dropped sharply and the proportion of the public which shows no party preference has correspondingly increased. Moreover, Japan has experienced relatively high electoral volatility in recent elections, that is, voters have made a different choice from the one they made at the previous election. Such electoral destabilization has been damaging to the functioning of Japan's political system.

Between 1973 and 1989 there had not been much serious discussion of reforming the existing multimember constituencies.[54] In the 1989 Upper House election (held in the wake of the 'Recruit corruption scandal', involving the sale to LDP politicians of undervalued shares in the Recruit Cosmos real estate company in exchange for political influence), the ruling LDP lost its majority position for the first time in its history. The party's unprecedented defeat was due in large measure to the Recruit scandal, the introduction of the unpopular consumption tax and the partial liberalization of agricultural imports. In the aftermath of the scandal, the LDP's Political Reform Committee emphasized in a report the need for electoral reform and pointed out the very problem of Japan's single nontransferable vote, multimember-constituency system:

[E]lections tend to be more candidate-oriented than party-oriented. If one party tries to get an absolute majority in the House of Representatives, it cannot avoid running multiple candidates, thus causing intra-party fights in the election... These intra-party fights have accelerated the tendency of politicians to consider interest politics and the organization of supporters more important than policies in their day-to-day political activities... Politicians have spent a large amount of money on particular interests for their constituencies... This tendency has caused political corruption and discredited the quality of politicians as representatives of the people...[55]

Since many leading LDP *Diet* members were involved in the scandal, Toshiki Kaifu, a relatively inexperienced politician, but one untouched by the scandal, was elected leader of the LDP. From the beginning of the Kaifu government, electoral reform was definitely on the political agenda. In April 1990, the Advisory Council on the Electoral System reported in favour of a system combining first-past-the-post single-member constituencies and PR (proportional representation).[56] On the basis of the report, the government submitted the political reform legislation to the *Diet* in July 1991 providing for a 471-seat Lower House, elected through a mixed system of first-past-the-post single-member districts for 300 seats and PR for 171 seats.[57] The legislation was also to prohibit financial contributions to individual candidates and to introduce public financing of parties. The reform legislation did not materialize because there was opposition within the LDP and the opposition parties, fearing for their survival, were also opposed to the introduction of single-seat constituencies.

The momentum for reform disappeared at least temporarily as the reform-oriented Kaifu cabinet was replaced by Kiichi Miyazawa, a more traditional leader of the LDP in November 1991, partly because more than two years had passed since the Recruit scandal. However, a new series of corruptions was uncovered in 1992 and once again created the pressure for electoral change. In the aftermath of the disclosure of the corruption scandals, the ruling LDP was so deeply damaged that several of its influential members defected from the party. The LDP acknowledged that the multimember constituency system was the heart of the problem: intensive competition among candidates of the same party drives up the costs of election campaigns, thereby encouraging politicians to seek financial contributions from various sources. The party claimed that the introduction of single-member constituencies would put an end to corruption and factional politics. There were several other arguments advanced by proponents of the single-member-district system.

One was that election campaigns will be fought on the policy platforms that each party has built rather than on the qualities of individual candidates. Next, because the party that wins is likely to secure a majority in the lower house, the government will be well poised to exercise strong leadership during its term of office. This will enable it to formulate clear-cut policies and respond swiftly to domestic and foreign issues. Moreover, the single-member-constituency system does not give the majority party permanent power, and so increases the level of public accountability. Should the government party betray the people's expectations, it will be voted out of office in the next election.

The government headed by Prime Minister Miyazawa was under strong pressure from a reformist group within the LDP and the public to pursue political reform. Miyazawa's cabinet then introduced legislation to the *Diet* proposing the introduction of 500 single-member, winner-take-all constituencies. Miyazawa's proposals would have resulted in an overwhelming victory for the LDP in an election for the Lower House.[58] Prime Minister Miyazawa lost a non-confidence motion when a group of reformists within the LDP voted with the opposition and against their party.

In 1993 there was an increasing loss of public confidence in government, which manifested itself in two important ways. First, it led to what Huntington calls an 'anti-incumbent reaction':[59] the Japanese electorate finally voted the LDP out of office in 1993. It also led to a decline in the average Japanese citizen's sense of political efficacy, and to withdrawal from politics and a marked decline in voter turnout. As Huntington puts it, 'A sense of decreasing political efficacy leads to decreased political participation.'[60] The proportion of citizen participation in elections is seen as a key indicator of the health of democracy in a country. Public disillusionment with politics was clearly reflected in the 1992 Upper House election – only about 50 per cent of the Japanese electorate bothered to vote, a record low voting turnout since the end of World War II.[61] A new postwar low voter turnout of 59.65 per cent in the 1996 general election, far below the previous record of 67.26 per cent marked at the 1993 general election, was registered. Decreased political participation was regarded as an indication of the voters' dissatisfaction with the established political parties and the political system.

By the early 1990s, many Japanese had come to identify the multimember-constituency system with clientelism, political corruption and political fragmentation. Indeed, it was, as the reformers of the electoral system for the Lower House put it, the basic cause of corruption, the 'root of all evil'. Electoral reform was seen as a remedy to these problems. With the end of one-party dominance, the political reform movement gathered steam. The 1993 election was a watershed for the cause of electoral reform. The coalition government of all the parties except the LDP and the Communists headed by Prime Minister Morihiro Hosokawa dealt with this problem head-on and introduced the electoral-reform package including substantial public financing for political parties that have five or more seats in the *Diet* and more than three per cent of the vote in national elections. The long and intensive debate as well as the general mood in the country, especially among the *Diet* members, made it impossible to introduce any election system based on a single allocation rule. As a result, the new electoral system came to contain a combination of different principles. The original proposal of the coalition government was to elect 250 representatives by the plurality system and 250 seats by a nationwide vote using PR. However, the allocation of seats was soon changed to 274 single-member constituencies and 226 for PR. The political reform legislation passed the Lower House, but was rejected in the Upper House, as LDP politicians voted against it.[62]

After last-minute agreements between Prime Minister Hosokawa and Yôhei Kôno, leader of the LDP, the final version of the reform package was approved by both houses of the Japanese *Diet* to replace the medium-sized electoral district system in 1994. By this time, most LDP politicians backed the reform package despite the fact that it was aimed at destroying their patronage bases. The electoral reform also included various direct measures to put an end to corruption and money politics in Japan. They included public funding of political parties, prohibition of financial contributions to individual candidates, and limits on the number of fund-raising organizations and strict limitations on the amount a business organization can contribute annually to each fund-raising group.

The 500 seats of the lower house are distributed into two categories: 300 are to be elected in single-member constituencies, and 200 from party lists in 11 large-bloc constituencies. A voter casts two separate ballots, one for individual candidates in single-member districts and the other for a political party in a proportional representation system. Unlike the German system, there is no linkage between the plurality and PR seat allocations. The new electoral arrangements permit 'dual candidacy' – a candidate can run simultaneously in a single-member constituency and under the PR system.

What changes can we expect from the reform of the electoral system? The political landscape of Japan has already begun to change significantly from what it was before the 1993 election. The experience of the next few elections will provide a test of the relationships between the new electoral system and various criteria of democratic theory and state management. The first general election under the new system was held in October 1996. It provided an excellent opportunity to study the impact of the two types of electoral systems within the same political system at the same time.[63] Nevertheless, the fuller meaning of the effects may not become clear until the succeeding elections have given a prospective within which it may be judged.

The adoption of the mixed system combining single member constituencies and proportional representation has already begun a political realignment process in Japan through a coalescence into two major political parties. In fact, many observers in Japan foresee a two-party system in place of the previous LDP dominant party system. A number of parties have already disappeared and coalesced into larger organizations to seek to ensure their survival. Two centrist parties, the Democratic Socialist Party and the Clean Government Party (Komeito), as well as two relatively new splinters of the LDP, the Renewal Party (Shinseito) and the Japan New Party (Nihon Shinto), were dissolved and merged with five other smaller parties to form Shinshinto (New Frontier Party). The formation of Shinshinto, with 178 seats in the Lower House, was the largest party merger since the unification of the Liberals and the Democrats into the LDP in 1955.

With the new electoral rules, the old style one-party rule might never be restored. Many of the factors that are said to have caused long-term rule by a single party in Japan have either disappeared or weakened. As previously mentioned, certain features of the previous electoral system facilitated the perpetual existence of the LDP in power by militating against the unifications of political parties opposed to the dominant party, thereby preventing the Japanese electorate from voting systematically against the ruling party. The 300 single-member constituencies may very well work against long-term dominance by a single party. Although the electoral rules in themselves by no means guarantee anything specific about the outcomes of elections, the available evidence tends to suggest that an electoral system that facilitates multipartism is a necessary condition for the emergence of one-party dominance.[64]

In the era of the LDP dominant party system, the ruling party and the bureaucracy had developed close ties and coexisted in a situation of mutually beneficial relationships. But, with the collapse of one-party dominance in Japan, the foundation of the so-called iron triangle of LDP politicians, bureaucrats and big business that was seen as the essence of the power structure in Japan was considerably undermined.

With the introduction of a new mixed electoral system, the reformers hoped to encourage voters to look more at the parties and their policies than individual politicians and what they can do for their constituencies. Compared with previous elections, where personality and faction-based politicking prevailed, the parties and the issues played a more important role this time around. Opinion surveys taken during the 1996 election campaign support such a conclusion. For example, a survey taken by *Asahi shimbun* asked a sample of the people in Shizuoka, a city often considered a typical example of the average Japanese electorate, a miniature of Japan, questioned as to what extent the two crucial issues – consumption tax and administrative reform – served as a basis for their vote for individual parties. More than half of respondents said these issues more or less formed a basis for their vote.[65]

The new electoral rules, with the accompanying political reform laws, are also intended to reduce the role of factional politics. The factions were often regarded as an outgrowth of the single non-transferable, multi-member district system, under which the LDP put up multiple candidates for each district. These candidates were supported by different factions of the party. The reformers hoped that the introduction of the plurality elections in single-member constituencies would obviate the need for factional backing. The new electoral system did not fully eliminate the existence of LDP factions. In forming his new LDP minority government after the election, Prime Minister Ryûtaro Hashimoto observed the traditional LDP rule of maintaining balance among the different factions through ministerial posts.

The new electoral rules will considerably weaken intra-party competition in elections and reduce the massive influence of 'money politics' and corruption that were often described as being associated with the previous electoral system. The reformers hoped that, with only one candidate from each party running in each single-member district, there would be no need for LDP candidates to differentiate themselves from other candidates of their own party and therefore they would not have to preoccupy themselves as much with money politics as they had in the past. Despite the electoral system change, the 1996 Lower House election demonstrated once again the importance of *kôenkai* in electoral politics. Since the new district boundaries of the single-member constituencies, about half the size of the earlier multi-member districts in most cases, split *kôenkai* into uneven parts, many candidates in the election tried to obtain support from the personal support organization of their previous rivals within the same party or from other parties.[66] Although candidates spent a considerable sum of money in reorganizing their *kôenkai* to fit the new electoral district boundaries, many candidates carried out election campaigning with their support organizations still organized around the old districts. In the long run, however, one can foresee the strengthening of party organizations at the expense of *kôenkai*.

The basic characteristics of political finance have been changed under the new system. Starting in January 1996, the government launched funding for party activities. The public funding of much of the parliamentary election costs can reduce the effect of excess money in the electoral process. The generosity of that public finance, the highest per capita government payment for politics among the established democracies that have a public funding scheme, reflects the willingness of the Japanese government to tackle the sources of political corruption. It is, however, doubtful whether the role of money in the electoral process will be significantly reduced with the availability of public finance. Large sums will still be raised for individual politicians at election time. Nonetheless, there will be some levelling of the advantages of incumbency for the parliamentary elections because candidates for office can now count on the public purse to share the cost for election campaigns.

Although using the new electoral system's combination of a single-member district system with proportional representation will forestall extreme disproportionality of election outcomes, there is some question as to whether it will improve representation. The evidence from the Japanese upper house PR system has shown that a separate PR ballot facilitates the entry of new parties. The legal threshold of three per cent had some constraining effect on representation. My recent study shows that the threshold barrier prevented only the most marginal parties from gaining seats in the Lower House.[67]

In democracies, equality for women and minorities must be respected. Since the 1970s, as the Japanese society shifted toward the post-industrial phase, Japanese have been increasingly concerned with, to borrow Inglehart's term, 'post-material' values such as the rights of women and environment.[68] Women in Japan have not made substantial strides through the political process. A recent study of women's representation in parliaments for 27 long-established democracies during the period 1989–1993 has shown that Japan, with its multimember district for the Lower House, had the lowest figure, a mere 2.3 per cent.[69]

What will happen to women's representation when Japan changes from multimember to the mixed system? The evidence we have suggests that it will lead to higher levels of women's representation. Under the proportional side of Germany's mixed system, for example, more than twice as many women are elected than in the single-member constituencies.[70] The Japanese experience suggests that different electoral systems in the same cultural settings lead to a different proportion of women in parliament. Electoral arrangements can make substantial differences in societies with unfavourable societal conditions for women's recruitment to parliament. For example, women's parliamentary representation increases greatly when one moves from multimember district system of the Lower House to the proportional representation side of the electoral system for the Upper House. The latter averaged 24 per cent women legislators while the former averaged two per cent in the period 1987–1993.[71] In the Upper House election in 1995, women candidates were elected to 26 per cent of the seats from the national constituency operating under PR. Thus, a change to a proportional representation for 200 of 500 seats in the Lower House could provide more equitable legislative representation of women and smaller parties. However, the research evidence from Malta's experience may serve as a caution against optimistic expectations that the adoption of proportional representation will automatically result in greater parliamentary representation for women.[72]

Despite more women presenting themselves as candidates than ever in the general election of 1996, 153 in total (127 in single-member districts and 26 in the proportional representation poll), only 23 of them were elected, constituting a mere 4.6 per cent of Lower House members. Still, this is a substantial improvement over the 1993 general election (2.7 per cent). A majority of women candidates, 16 in all, were elected through proportional representation. This illustrates an advantage that proportional representation has over a plurality system. Some scholars claim that the competitiveness of legislative seats adversely affects female representation, that is, women are often disproportionately chosen as candidates in uncompetitive contests for their party. This so-called 'sacrificial lamb hypothesis' seems to be verified to some extent in the 1996 general election.[73]

What will happen to political accountability under the new electoral arrangements? A series of scandals in Japan in recent years has been damaging to democracy. Corruption was exposed to public scrutiny by the media, and the fact that those responsible were punished has shown the viability of democracy in Japan. Accountability requires a free press that can check and scrutinize governmental power and is willing to expose corruption, and an independent legal system ready to prosecute and punish official abuses. Moreover, public accountability requires the electoral means of making changes in power possible, so that those in power are periodically subjected to the voters for approval or disapproval in a competitive, free and open election. The high level of accountability has long been considered a major advantage of the plurality system. The introduction of the plurality rule for 300 single-member districts will, therefore, increase political accountability.

Considering the political fragmentation, splinter parties and unstable coalition governments since the 1993 general election, the adoption of the mixed system may produce a more stable party system comprising two dominant parties plus two or three minor ones. Each large party will have to rely on support from all segments of the electorate, and to appeal to most social groups and interests. As most advocates of plurality elections suggest, single-member constituencies may encourage the competing parties to adopt a majority-forming posture, since they would have to avoid being too specific in their appeals.

By giving voters not one but two different voting methods, the new electoral system combines the strengths of plurality rule in single-member districts – accountability and governability – with such democratic values as representation of minority views and proportionality associated with proportional representation.

Conclusion

Several lessons emerge from the experience of Japan and the literature about the democratic consequences of electoral systems. The first is that electoral systems matter. No electoral system is perfect. By their very nature, all electoral systems have biases. This study tends to suggest that the system of a single non-transferable vote in multimember districts produced outcomes that were less than optimal in terms of proportionality and accountability. A serious problem arose under this system. It has often been noted that the repeated scandals that plagued the LDP were due to the fact that the system encouraged individual candidates within the same party to compete with each other for votes, through personal favours and constituency services. This should not be taken as meaning that the multimember constituency system is always a bad choice, for it can preserve other democratic and state management criteria, such as the representation of viewpoints and governability. As we have seen, Japan's electoral system has proved superior to PR systems as far as governability is concerned. Throughout most of the post-war period, Japan had single-party, majority governments, and a strong executive in relation to the parliament. I have shown that, in conjunction with the LDP's ability to respond to the rise of new issue interests in time and broaden its support base, the pre-1994 electoral system made a major contribution to long-term one-party dominance. Further, the relationship that was established between the LDP and the powerful bureaucracy during its 38 years in office enabled the government to establish the political, economic, and social conditions that transformed Japan into one of the most stable dominant party democracies in the world.

The second lesson is that, as the Japanese experience of electoral reforms shows, radical change in the institutional and constitutional foundations of the political system in an Asian country with a Confucian culture is possible. As we have seen, Japan experienced a 'legitimacy deficit' in its political system – a sense of dismay at political scandals and declining political responsiveness. The Japanese finally responded to the destabilizing consequences of partisan dealignment, the low level of government accountability, increasing disproportionality of election results, and a series of corruption scandals. Electoral reform was seen by both politicians and the Japanese public as completing a democratic process that would put an end to failures in the political system. However, to argue that all the failings of Japanese democracy would simply vanish if only the correct institutional 'recipe' could be found, was a sort of chimera.

Japan's decision to shift from a single, non-transferable vote in multi-member constituencies to a mixed system of single-member plurality elections and proportional representation forms an interesting case study of why an established democracy changes its electoral system. Together with Italy and New Zealand, Japan will eventually show us something about what happens when a country changes its electoral system. It is much too early to assess the democratic consequences of the new electoral arrangements. The 1996 Lower House election was the first election fought according to the new rules, and caution should be exercised when attempting to derive evidence of change in the Japanese political arena. The next few elections may provide some empirical leverage on the question of how the electoral system affects various characteristics of a democratic political system. The lack of change in the electoral systems of established democracies has hitherto made it difficult to do a comparative study.

What are the implications of this study for the emerging democracies in Asia? Asia's new democratic states, facing varying socio-political circumstances, need the best electoral systems they can get. As we have seen, different systems produce different outcomes according to democratic and state management criteria. Economically and technologically, Japan has been a model for other countries of Asia and of the world. If the past is to be any guide for the future, the Japanese experience of a mixed electoral system, if successful, may set an example for both established and aspiring democracies.

Which electoral systems are best for Asian countries will depend upon the specific needs of each nation. I am inclined to agree with Gladdish: 'Each national case is highly circumstantial and reflects both history in all its manifestations and, more specifically, the consequences of particular patterns of political mobilization.'[74]

Notes

1 Muthiah Alagappa, 'The Asian Spectrum', *Journal of Democracy*, Vol. 6, No. 1, January 1995, p. 35.
2 Robert A. Scalapino, 'Democratizing Dragons: South Korea and Taiwan', *Journal of Democracy*, Vol. 4, No. 3, July 1993. See also Alagappa, 'The Asian Spectrum', p. 35.
3 Lucian W. Pye, *Asian Power and Politics: The Cultural Dimensions of Authority*, Cambridge, Mass.: Harvard University Press, 1985, p. 339.
4 Rein Taagepera and Matthew Soberg Shugart, *Seats and Votes: The Effects and Determinants of Electoral Systems*, New York: Yale University Press, 1989, p. 2.
5 Ibid.

6 T. J. Pempel, 'Democracy in Japan,' in Craig C. Garby and Mary Brown Bullock (eds), *Japan: A New Kind of Superpower*, Washington, D.C.: The Woodrow Wilson Press, 1994, p. 31.

7 Guy Lardeyret, 'The Problem with PR', *Journal of Democracy*, Vol. 2, No. 3, Summer 1991, p. 34.

8 Lijphart, for example, states that district magnitude, electoral thresholds, electoral formulas, and the size of the assembly explain nearly two-thirds of the variance in disproportionality. See Arend Lijphart, *Electoral Systems and Party Systems: A Study of Twenty-Seven Democracies*, 1945–1990, Oxford: Oxford University Press, 1994, pp. 78–117.

9 For an excellent illustration of the disproportionality between seats and votes under the Westminster model, see Bo Särlvik, 'Valsystemet i Storbritannien' [The electoral system in Great Britain], *Statsvetenskaplig Tidskrift* 1994, årg. 97, nr 3, pp. 225–39.

10 Lijphart, *Electoral Systems*, p. 58.

11 Gerald Curtis, 'Japan', in David Butler and Austin Ranney (eds), *Electioneering: A Comparative Study of Continuity and Change*, Oxford: Clarendon Press, 1992, pp. 222–43.

12 *Mainichi shimbun*, 8 June 1995.

13 Pippa Norris, 'Introduction: The Politics of Electoral Reform', *International Political Science Review*, Vol. 16, No. 1, 1995, p. 6.

14 G. Bingham Powell, *Contemporary Democracies: Participation, Stability, and Violence*, Cambridge: Harvard University Press, 1982, p. 59.

15 Steven. R. Reed, 'The 1990 General Election: Explaining the Historic Socialist Victory', *Electoral Studies*, Vol. 10, 1991, pp. 244–55.

16 Wilma Rule, 'Women's Underrepresentation and Electoral Systems', *PS: Political Science & Politics*, Vol. 37, No. 4, 1994, p. 689.

17 Joseph F. Zimmerman, 'Electoral Systems and Representative Democracy', *PS: Political Science & Politics*, Vol. 37, No. 4, 1994, p. 676.

18 Arend Lijphart, 'Constitutional Choices for New Democracies', *Journal of Democracy*, Vol. 2, No. 1, Winter 1991, p. 73.

19 Larry Diamond, 'Three Paradoxes of Democracy', *Journal of Democracy*, Vol. 1, No. 3, 1990, p. 55.

20 In the 1993 general election, the fifth-place winner in a five-member district in Shiga prefecture captured less than seven per cent of the vote.

21 Bradley M. Richardson and Scott C. Flanagan, *Politics in Japan*, Boston: Little, Brown & Company, 1984, p. 82.

22 T.J. Pempel, *Policy and Politics in Japan: Creative Conservatism*, Philadelphia: Temple University Press, 1982, p. 39.

23 T.J. Pempel, 'Conclusion. One-Party Dominance and the Creation of Regimes', in T. J. Pempel (ed.), *Uncommon Democracies: The One-Party Dominant Regimes*, Ithaca: Cornell University Press, 1990, p. 336.

24 Ibid., p. 338.

25 Samuel P. Huntington, *The Third Wave: Democratization in the Late Twentieth Century*, Norman and London: University of Oklahoma Press, 1991, pp. 265–70.

26 José Antonio Crespo, 'The Liberal Democratic Party in Japan: Conservative Domination', *International Political Science Review*, Vol. 16, No. 2, 1995, p. 206.

27 Patrick Dunleavy and Helen Margetts, 'Understanding the Dynamics of Electoral Reform', *International Political Science Review*, Vol. 16, No. 1, 1995, pp. 15–17.

28 Diamond, 'Three Paradoxes', p. 53.

29 Ibid., p. 49.

30 Lardeyret, 'The Problem', p. 31. See also Lijphart, 'Constitutional Choices', p. 72.

31 Dunleavy and Margetts 'Understanding the Dynamics', p. 16.

32 The only exception was the formation of a LDP-New Liberal Club coalition government in 1983.

33 For the characterization of the Japanese party system, see, for example, Ronald J. Hrebenar, 'The Changing Postwar Party System', in R.J. Hrebenar (ed.), *The Japanese Party System: From One-Party Rule to Coalition Government*, Boulder: Westview Press, 1986, pp. 6–7; Hitoshi Abe, Muneyuki Shindo and Sadafumi Kawato, *The Government and Politics of Japan*, Tokyo: University of Tokyo Press, 1994, pp. 28–31; and Pempel, *Uncommon Democracies*, 'Introduction' pp. 2–5.

34 Giovanni Sartori, *Parties and Political Systems*, Cambridge: Cambridge University Press, 1976, pp. 195ff.

35 Crespo, 'The Liberal Democratic Party', p. 199.

36 Ronald J. Hrebenar, 'Political Party Proliferation, the New Liberal Club and the Mini-Parties', in R.J. Hrebenar (ed.), *The Japanese Party System: From One-Party Rule to Coalition Government*, Boulder: Westview Press, 1986, p. 210.

37 Joji Watanuki, 'Patterns of Politics in Present-Day Japan', in Seymour M. Lipset and Stein Rokkan (eds), *Party Systems and Voter Alignments: Cross-National Perspectives*, New York: The Free Press, 1967, pp. 456–60.

38 Sartori, *Parties and Political Systems*.

39 Scott C. Flanagan, 'Electoral Change in Japan: A Study of Secular Realignment', in Russell J. Dalton, Scott C. Flanagan and Paul Allen Beck (eds), *Electoral Change in Advanced Industrial Democracies: Realignment or Dealignment?*, Princeton, N.J.: Princeton University Press, 1984.

40 Pempel, *Uncommon Democracies*, 'Conclusion,' pp. 349, 351.

41 Gerald Curtis, *The Japanese Way of Politics*, New York: Columbia University Press, 1992, p. 71.

42 Michio Muramatsu and Ellis S. Krauss, 'The Dominant Party and Social Coalitions in Japan', in T. J. Pempel (ed.), *Uncommon Democracies: The One-Party Dominant Regimes*, Ithaca: Cornell University Press, 1990, p. 302.

43 T.J. Pempel, 'The Unbounding of Japan 'Japan, Inc.': The Changing Dynamics of Japanese Policy Formulation', *Journal of Japanese Studies*, Vol. 13, No. 2, Summer 1987, p. 292.

44 Muramatsu and Krauss, 'The Dominant Party', p. 283.

45 Powell, *Contemporary Democracies*, p. 223.

46 Pempel, 'Democracy in Japan,' p. 32.

47 Ellis S. Krauss, 'Conflict in the Diet: Toward Conflict Management in Parliamentary Politics', in Ellis S. Krauss, Thomas P. Rohlen and Patricia G. Steinhoff (eds), *Conflict in Japan*, Honolulu: University of Hawaii Press, 1984, p. 234.

48 Muramatsu and Krauss, 'The Dominant Party', p. 296.

49 Yoshikado, Nishio, *Nihon seiji no kiki*[Japanese politics in crisis], Tokyo: Tokyo shimbun shuppankyoku, 1994, p. 24.

50 *Asahi shimbun*, 16 January 1995.

51 Scott C. Flanagan, 'Mechanisms of Social Network Influence in Japanese Voting Behavior,' in Scott C. Flanagan *et al.*, *The Japanese Voter*, New Haven: Yale University Press, 1991, p. 160.

52 Norris draws a distinction between long-term conditions and short-run catalysts contributing toward electoral change. Norris 1995, pp. 3–8.

53 Richardson and Flanagan 1984, p. 83. See also Ichiro Miyake, 'Type of Partisanship, Partisan Attitude, and Voting Choices', in Flanagan *et al.* 1991, p. 226.

54 The first attempt to change the electoral system of the Lower House was made in 1955, when the LDP government proposed the introduction of single-member constituencies.

55 Cited in Rei Shiratori, 'The Politics of Electoral Reform in Japan,' *International Political Science Review*, Vol. 16, No. 1, 1995, p. 84.

56 *Yomiuri shimbun*, 27 April 1990.

57 *Tokyo shimbun*, 10 July 1991.

58 According to Shiratori, the LDP could capture between 70 and 80 per cent of the Lower House seats with fewer than 50 per cent of the votes under the single-member constituency system. See Shiratori 1995, pp. 81–82.

59 Huntington, *The Third Wave*, p. 265.

60 Samuel P. Huntington, 'The United States', in Michel Crozier, Samuel P. Huntington and Joji Watanuki, *Crisis in Democracy*, New York: Columbia University Press, 1975, p. 84.

61 The 1995 Upper House election also showed a record low voting turnout, a mere 45 per cent.

62 Seventeen socialists defected from the party and joined the LDP *Diet* members in the Upper House to vote on the reform bills. See Abe, Shindo and Kawato1994, pp. 151–53.

63 For the consequences of the 1996 general election, see Kazuki Iwanaga, 'Transition in Japanese Electoral Politics: Democratic Consequences of the 1996 Lower House Election,' *The Stockholm Journal of East Asian Studies*, Vol. 8, 1997.

64 See, for example, Pempel, *Uncommon Democracies*.

65 *Asahi shimbun*, 26 October 1996.

66 Steven R. Reed, 'The 1996 Japanese General Election', *Electoral Studies*, Vol. 16, No. 1, 1997, p. 123.

67 The total share of the vote for the four parties denied representation in the proportional side of the Lower House election because the three per cent threshold was a mere 3.6 per cent of the total vote. For the relationship between Japan's new electoral rules and the number of effective parties, see Kazuki Iwanaga 1997.

68 The term, 'post-material values' is taken from Ronald Inglehart, *The Silent Revolution*, Princeton, N.J.: Princeton University Press, 1977.

69 Rule, 'Women's Underrepresentation', p. 689.

70 Ibid., p. 691.

71 Ibid.

72 John C. Lane, 'The Election of Women under Proportional Representation: The Case of Malta', *Democratization*, Vol. 2, No. 2, Summer 1995, pp. 140–57.

73 For an account of women's legislative representation in Japan, see Kazuki Iwanaga, 'Women in Japanese Politics: A Comparative Politics', Occasional Paper 37. Stockholm: Center for Pacific Asia Studies, Stockholm University, June 1998.

74 Ken Gladdish, 'The Primacy of the Particulars', *Journal of Democracy*, Vol. 4, No. 1, January 1993, p. 54.

4 DEVELOPMENT AND DEMOCRACY IN MALAYSIA

A COMMENT ON ITS SOCIO-HISTORICAL ROOTS

Shamsul A.B.

For decades, since the 1960s, there was a belief, especially held by scholars in the United States, that with increased modernization in Asian countries there would be a parallel increase in its secularization, hence the diminished role of religion in the political sphere.[1] However, this has been proven wrong by the religious fundamentalists (Hindus, Muslims and others) who, since the 1970s, have been active and successful not only in voicing dissent against the 'Westernized' form of modernization but also in offering alternatives conceptualized and based upon non-Western notions and practices. In the 1990s, a not dissimilar situation has occurred. This time it involves a more 'worldy religion' called 'democracy' and its relationship to 'development'. There has been a general expectation held by Westerners that economic growth in the Third World, particularly in Asia, would eventually lead to political democratization. It seems yet again that they are proven wrong. The old and new NICs in East and Southeast Asia have grown economically while their governments remained bureaucratic, authoritarian, and militaristic.[2]

However, in the last decade, interesting developments have taken place within Asia that demonstrate that we cannot reject totally the 'increase development, increase democracy' thesis. There have been two opposing trends regarding this: the first rejects the thesis and the second supports it. Cases for the former are as many as for the latter. Singapore, Malaysia and Indonesia (until recently) represent the former and South Korea, Taiwan and Thailand represent the latter.

The South Korean case confirms the dictum that development does bring about democracy.[3] During the 1980s, when it was modernizing using the heavy industry strategy, a sequence of political challenges was directed at the bureaucratic authoritarian industrial regime. This took place owing to a global economic change and the resultant restructuring of economic opportunity that altered South Korea's social structure, which in turn changed the balance of social and political forces within. Indeed, the national economy was experiencing stress as rising labour costs were affecting the competitiveness of South Korean export manufacturing globally. Powerful industrialists, who have grown too strong for the state to dominate, a burgeoning middle class dominating presence in the society making continuous demand for the creation of a truly civil society, and workers and students who have become more daring and militant in their protests, all put pressure on the state to adjust the economic system to improve their respective conditions. The climax was in 1987 when labour unrest and broad demonstrations directly challenged the authoritarian South Korean regime thus starting a movement for greater democracy in the electoral system. Today's democratic South Korea is as developmentalist as it was during the authoritarian days.

Singapore's case is just the opposite. It could be seen as offering a brand of paternalistic authoritarianism that has been justified by Lee Kuan Yew, Singapore's former prime minister, as follows: 'I do not believe that democracy necessarily leads to development. I believe that what a country needs to develop is discipline more than democracy. The exuberance of democracy leads to indiscipline and disorderly conduct which are inimical to development'.[4] It is implied in this statement that a docile labour would attract foreign investment or foreign investors, which is perceived as good for the economic growth of the country. (Ironically, the investors themselves come from countries that hold the principles of democracy dearly). Also implied is that the bureaucratic elite would have more flexibility in making and implementing policies for economic growth, theoretically on behalf of 'the people', if the conflicting interests and demands of the various classes – workers for higher wages, educated middle class for more freedom, industrialists for more room to make money – could be controlled and homogenized for the sake of political expediency with greater economic rewards.[5]

However, recent economic problems and crises, especially relating to the sudden depreciation of the currencies in Southeast Asia, are beginning to give signals that 'the rule of the strong ruler' is going to end sooner than expected and perhaps democracy is finally coming after all, albeit delayed, with development. The source of the eventual democratization of the strong states is not the middle class nor the working class. The latter two need the catalyst provided by the corporate players to launch a successful democratization movement. Thus, I would like to suggest that it is going to be the group of 'local corporate players' or the 'national bourgeoisie', who are going to be the prime movers of democratization in these 'strong states'. After all, they themselves have emerged from the successful policies of the strong states; they became credible corporate players in the international market as a result of receiving the state's support in all their international endeavours and became big players in the domestic economy through the state's interventionist policies that sponsored their successful participation in the domestic economy. When these corporate players and their businesses become too strong for the state to dominate, the latter will find it difficult to dismiss the demands of the former when they are facing financial or 'survival' difficulties. Together with the middle class, the corporate players could create political initiatives advantageous to pro-democracy movement in the country. The South Korean and Taiwan cases are useful examples to consider in this context.

However, in a country like Malaysia, there are other considerations one has to bear in mind when talking about development and democracy. Analysts on the state of democracy in Malaysia are usually pessimistic regarding the possibility of 'democracy being restored' (though they never really discussed when it began or ended) or 'democracy being truly implemented' (an expression of an 'American dream' kind). Some, however, are happy to adopt the easy way out by labelling democracy in Malaysia as a 'half-breed' type (though we are never really told what the original, true breed is), calling it 'semi-democracy' or 'quasi-democracy'.[6] The discussion is obviously influenced by an institution-oriented analytical construct most favoured by a majority of political scientists studying Malaysia whose appetite and dependence on election results is well-known.

The single most glaring analytical inadequacy that has beleaguered attempts to come to grips with the theme 'development and democracy' in Malaysia is its ahistorical nature.[7] Although, admittedly, discussions on Malaysian development experience, as a theme by itself, are strongly grounded in history, they are, however, not so when discussed in combination with democracy. In the latter, the tendency is to emphasize the democracy aspect and less development, hence the overly 'contemporary' nature of discussions on development and democracy in Malaysia. For instance, any such discussion will inevitably address issues related to the well-known New Economic Policy (1971–1990), popularly called the *bumiputera* policy, the general elections,[8] human rights, minority groups, the infamous ISA (Internal Security Act) and detention without trial, and the impotence of the trade unions. Important as these issues are, we could say that this is the first time, in the context of Malaysian studies, that they have been framed and examined within the sphere of the current global interest called 'development and democracy', hence their 'contemporariness'.

What is missing in the recent general discourse on development and democracy in Malaysia is a historical dimension of the concept and practice of 'development' under discussion, particularly as it should be understood, internationally, in the context of the Bretton Woods system and the post-war world order,[9] and locally in the context of the local economy devastated by war and the emergency.[10] Especially crucial is the first decade of post-war Malaysia (or Malaya then) during which institutions, presently perceived as central in the discussion of democracy in Malaysia, were established, such as the constitution and modern electoral politics. It was during this period too that the social roots of the so-called 'non-democratic rules' of today are grounded.

It is therefore the aim of this brief chapter to trace and outline the origin and circumstances surrounding the emergence of what could be viewed as the installation of democracy-related institutions in Malaysia which took place when Malaysia's 'development project and path' was crafted and launched by the colonial government soon after the Second World War and eventually became the grid within which Malaysia's modernization programmes came to be organized affecting the social life, some positively and others negatively, of millions at the grassroots. I shall begin with a historical sketch of the period 1945 and 1955, considered by many as a period of social and political instability, and examine the challenges that the British colonial government had to contend with then. This will be followed by a discussion of the efforts made by the British to establish peace and stability in the political and economic sphere (read 'development and democracy') through the following three critical strategies: (i) the introduction of tight security and legal rules; (ii) initiating activities that fostered ethnic bargaining; and (iii) establishing an institutional framework for central planning, popularly known as the five-year development plans.

Post-war Malaysia: Challenges to the Shaping of a Future

The decade immediately after the Second World War, that is, from August 1945 to July 1955, was indeed a critical period in Malaysia's modern history. This period was characterized by two opposing trends. On the one hand, there was a near-anarchic situation as a result of the war-torn conditions and the negative consequences which developed in turn. On the other, the colonial state was feverishly trying to rebuild the economy and society through various means, some of which were coercive. Finding a middle path between anarchy and harmony was indeed a most difficult task during this period. Finally, some form of harmony emerged from this rather eventful period. The social, economic and political basis of this harmony later became the building block of Malaysia's subsequent development and its attempt to create, for whatever it is worth, a democratic atmosphere.

This period saw the setting up of many of Malaysia's present-day administrative structures, political arrangements and public policy making institutions, which could also be viewed as the bare elements or structures of democratic rule. Admittedly, many of the pre-war colonial bureaucratic structures and organizations, too, were either retained or reconstituted to serve the post-war colonial government. Therefore, it is imperative for us to narrate in some detail what happened during this critical period. I shall proceed by examining the challenges that the British colonial government had to face for more than a decade after the war because it was, arguably, the most tensed and troubled period in Malaysian political history. Then, we shall examine the efforts undertaken by the government to bring back and maintain peace and order within the country.

There were at least four major challenges that the British colonial government had to deal with in the first decade after the war: racial strife, labour unrest, communist insurgency, and widespread opposition to a new system of government which the British planned to introduce. They were all interconnected in the sense that each was ethnically related, involving either a particular ethnic group against the government or two ethnic groups on opposite ends.

The racial strife was bloody and tragic, as one could imagine. It went on almost during the whole of the first decade after the war, occurring sporadically in different parts of the country. The most severe of the racial clashes took place just after the war ended, in August 1945, hardly a week after the Japanese had officially surrendered and the senseless killing went on non-stop for about two weeks in many parts of the country. Initially, it was between the Malays, who sided with the Japanese, and the Chinese, who fought against the Japanese. Later, the racial clash spread to involve Malays and Chinese who neither supported nor opposed the Japanese. However, subsequent clashes were not as severe and widespread but enough to create similar destabilizing effects within the country.[11]

Labour protest, in the form of strikes and rallies, became a common event, too, after the war, particularly in the first half of 1946. The height of the protest was in early 1947, when there was a countrywide strike and demonstration demanding better wages. It was conducted mainly by rubber plantation and tin-mine workers belonging to the General Labour Union. Increasing violence, especially against European planters, was worrying the colonial government to the extent that it had to impose rules that curbed substantially trade union activities in the country. The protesters were mainly Chinese and Indian workers because they formed the majority of the working class in Malaysia then, with the Malays mostly in the peasant sector.[12]

Behind the labour protest were the guiding hands of the Malayan Communist Party (MCP), largely a Chinese-dominated organization. It had strong influence within the trade union and changed its political strategy when the unions were reduced almost to welfare associations by the colonial government. The MCP then encouraged the unions to lead the workers 'to the road of violent action'. Murders and attacks on European estate managers and pro-management workers increased alarmingly to an extent that the colonial government was forced to proclaim a state of emergency throughout Malaya on 18 June 1948.[13]

For the next 12 years, that is until 31 July 1960, the emergency continued, during which the government fought a war against the communist insurgents. In that period more violent clashes between government forces and the MCP guerrillas occurred, including assassinations of high-ranking military and police officials. Needless to say, the economy was badly affected during the initial period of the emergency, especially the modern rural agricultural sector, i.e. the large rubber plantations and numerous tin mines all over the country. It is necessary to note that the local component of the government forces which fought the Chinese-dominated MCP was Malay.

To make matters worse, before and during the emergency period, there were a number of communist-inspired countrywide economic boycotts which occurred from time to time. They involved mainly Chinese wholesalers and shopkeepers but mostly for short periods, causing havoc in the already unstable economic and political situation.

In January 1946, the colonial government introduced the Malayan Union, a constitutional plan for the Malay Peninsula, excluding Singapore, that proposed to confer a common citizenship on her peoples, irrespective of race and origin.[14] It was perceived by the indigenous peoples as a programme which would mainly benefit the immigrant population. The scheme provoked an immediate and impassioned constitutional controversy which threatened to undermine the very basis of British rule in Malaya.

There were widespread political protests by the Malays opposing the introduction of this new system of government. This totally took the British by surprise and was definitely not the kind of problem that they would have liked to have. So, barely three months later, the decision was taken to abort the Malayan Union scheme, and in February 1948 the Union was replaced by the Federation of Malaya.

The introduction of this new system made the immigrant population rather unhappy because, despite being given citizenship almost immediately, they had to accept the special rights and privileges awarded to the indigenous peoples. From then on, the issue of special rights and privileges became one of the central contentious issues in inter-ethnic relations in Malaysia.

In short, British Malaya had its share of racial strife, near-anarchic situations, and socio-political instability just after the war. This was not dissimilar to the situation experienced, in recent times, by Sri Lanka or Bosnia-Herzegovina, perhaps in a lesser magnitude but no less bloody and merciless.

The Search for Development and Democracy

While there was conflict and fighting, the British were working tirelessly to rebuild the economy and society to bring about development and democracy. There were very good reasons for this. Malaya was its richest colony, with a large section of its economy belonging to British interests.[15] It was still contributing substantially, in financial terms, to the coffers of the British government, even in the war-torn situation. Therefore, there was never a lack of motivation on the part of the British to persevere with the difficult situation in the country.

Their efforts at reconstructing the economy and restoring stability could be categorized into the following: (i) to restore peace and security, (ii) to create an environment suitable for ethnic bargaining, and (iii) to introduce planned change through five-year plan programmes. These initiatives necessitated the establishment of new administrative organizations. To operationalize most of these efforts, the British felt that it was necessary to introduce legislation not only as bureaucratic guidelines but also to regulate society and defuse any opposition that could destabilize the country. Let us examine each of these efforts in turn, beginning with those carried out to create peace and security in the country.

Security

From the day the Japanese surrendered, in August 1945, to the day the British surrendered their precious colony to its rightful owner, in August 1957, Malaya, to all intents and purposes, was under military rule of one kind or another. As mentioned previously, this period was characterized by near anarchy in the political and social spheres and great difficulty in the economic sphere. Consequently, the British saw fit that military rule was most suitable to deal with the situation in its effort to restore peace and harmony, thus allowing the rebuilding of the economy and society.

When it took over from where the Japanese left, in early September 1945, the British Military Administration (BMA) was established to suppress the anarchy as well as to allow the British to re-establish their rule. The BMA rule lasted until March 1946. It was then replaced by a civilian colonial government, which lasted until June 1948, after which the emergency was imposed that lasted until July 1960. During the emergency period, the running of the country was conducted within the context of a military administrative framework but with the civilian face maintained prominently.

This was possible because the role of restoring and maintaining peace and order was largely carried out by the police force though the central command was in the hands of the army generals.[16] There was definitely a larger number of police personnel in the field than of the army. The latter was in fact a fragmented group, made up of troops from other British colonies – Nepalese, Fijians, Indians, New Zealanders, Australians.

Except for a number of British officers, the police force was local in content. It was divided into uniformed (such as the jungle fighting units) and non-uniformed (such as the undercover Special Branch). Although most of the members of the police force were serving full time, there were also those who served on a temporary and part-time basis. The part-time ones were sub-divided into conscripts and volunteers. They were in fact the 'front line' fighters as well as the 'eyes and ears' of the government with the difficult task of winning the 'hearts and minds' of the public.

For strategic, military and security reasons the government instituted and implemented a number of measures to control and discipline the society. Three such measures were (i) the introduction of the identity card for every citizen thus separating the 'accountables' and the 'undesirables' as it were; (ii) a massive resettlement programme, shifting thousands away from the fringe jungle areas often frequented by communist insurgents thus alienating the latter; and (iii) the introduction of laws that allowed the government to detain without trial, for an extended period, anybody it considered a danger to 'national security' (read 'British interests in Malaya').

However, there were two different facets of British military rule in Malaysia (then Malaya): before and after 1950. One was quite different from the other in its features. Compared to the earlier British Military Administration (BMA) facet, the post-1950 emergency one was relatively less troublesome to the British, for various reasons, thus resulting in different security measures being applied.

During the BMA phase, the situation was more traumatic and difficult in view of the fact that the whole economy and society were in almost total disarray as a result of the war, thus allowing the near-anarchic situation to develop. For instance, the black market was a massive economic activity during that period and the BMA became popularly known as the 'Black Market Age'. Racial strife was so intense and bloody that the much-talked-about 13 May 1969 racial riot in Malaysia's capital city of Kuala Lumpur paled into insignificance. Therefore, most of the security measures taken by the British during the BMA were directed mainly towards restoring basic order and public confidence in the government.

The initial part of the emergency period, from 1948 to 1950, was indeed a difficult one, too, but not as anarchic. The main challenge for the government was to maintain order and rule of law in the face of violent militaristic opposition from the communist insurgents. Since the war-torn economy was still being rebuilt, this encounter became more difficult to the government in view of the limited economic capacity and resources.

Things began to change after the introduction of what was called the Briggs Plan (named after the British army general who introduced it) in May 1950, in conjunction with the emergency military rule. The plan had two key aspects: one administrative in nature and the other logistic. Through the former, Briggs consolidated a coordinating structure which gave civil administration, the police, and the army the chance to meet regularly and to cooperate effectively. This structure bypassed the un-responsive state administrations and gave the federal government more flexibility in putting its policies into effect. Briggs established a chain of committees from federal to district level called the War Council/ Executive Committees. It operated both ways; top-down as well as bottom-up.

The second key aspect, involving logistics, emerged as the means by which civil administration could reassert its authority in times of crises, such as the state of emergency. A massive resettlement programme to move the entire rural Chinese population into fortified and defended compounds, called the 'new villages', was created and implemented. By the end of 1951, half a million Chinese were resettled in these new villages.

In both cases, the Briggs Plan received strong opposition. In the first key aspect there was opposition from administrators at the state/ provincial government level, who felt left out and not consulted. So there was a certain amount of foot dragging involved. But the new chain of committees proved to be so successful that the dissenters from within were immediately recognized and they shied away. The resettlement programme was resisted by some Chinese but adhered to in silence by others. There was much suffering when this programme was implemented, especially for those who felt up-rooted from the economy and social organization that they had been used to for generations. But they also realized the grave security implications if they were to resist.

The implementation of the Briggs Plan was indeed expensive but the government knew that it was the only hope to really bring back lasting peace and order in Malaysia (then Malaya). Therefore, when the Korean War broke out in 1950, which brought an unexpected phenomenal increase in the demand and price for natural rubber and tin hence much money for the government coffers, the Briggs Plan received a tremendous boost and was implemented with great success.

The Briggs Plan also provided the brilliant administrative structure that the British needed to ensure an all-round development in the country, economically and politically. Thus the progress of the 'ethnic bargain' and, especially, the success of the five-year development plans, or planned change effort, then was intricately linked with the security measures and organization provided by the Briggs Plan.

One could even argue that the British were so confident of the state of security in Malaysia then, owing to the successful implementation of the Briggs Plan, that they were willing to relinquish their colonial master position and thus gave Malaysia its independence already in 1957, three years before the emergency rule ended on 31 July 1960. In other words, Malaysia achieved its independence during a period of military rule, a fact which often escapes the minds of many analysts on Malaysian affairs, past and present, and has wider political, economic implications in understanding Malaysia today.

We shall now turn to the 'ethnic bargain' efforts encouraged by the British semi-military rule to foster goodwill and stable inter-ethnic relationships within the country. In short, the British realized that the future of Malaya had to depend upon its ability to ensure some form of consensus, however fragile, between the ethnic groups, in what had come to be known as the 'ethnic bargain'.

Ethnic Bargain

Through the British-initiated policy of importing workers from China, India and Indonesia to exploit the richly endowed Malaya, a classic Furnivall's plural society was created in due process in British Malaya. A significant feature of this society was its demographic composition, in which the immigrant population was almost equal in number to the indigenous one.

In fact, there was also ethnic identification to economic activities and geographical areas, namely rural and urban, and other forms of social divisions which are normally found in a society (e.g. gender, class and sector). Malays were mainly rice growers in the rural area, Chinese were dominating the commercial sector based in the urban areas, and most of the Indians, largely Tamils, were rubber plantation labourers.

In a sense, the potential for a multitude of problems to develop from this plural society was enormous. This was witnessed quite frequently before the Japanese came to occupy Malaya. When they came, the state of ethnic relations in Malaya was quite fragile. It worsened and finally disintegrated under Japanese rule because the Japanese clearly favoured the indigenous population over the immigrant population, especially Chinese. Fresh from a victory in the Sino-Japanese war, the Japanese were very brutal against the Chinese in Malaya. Therefore, during the Japanese occupation period, the Malays and the Chinese were in a confrontational position, fighting each other as proxies, Chinese for the British and the Malays for the Japanese, thus heightening the already tense Sino–Malay relationship and transforming it into open animosity. It came to the boil the moment the Japanese left, thus leading to a prolonged racial strife for at least a decade after that.

The security problems and the subsequent imposition of some form of British military rule in the post-war period, as mentioned before, was related to racial strife. In fact, the ethnic configuration of security-related problems in British Malaya was dominant indeed.

Therefore, besides trying to restore law and order, the other main task of the British was to restore the inter-ethnic relation which deteriorated during the war and disintegrated immediately after the war. The 'healing' efforts took various forms but the whole exercise was not an easy one.

The attempt by the British to establish a civilian government through the formation of the much-troubled Malayan Union scheme was the first of such efforts. The British thought that by giving everybody equal status as citizens of the new union everything would be solved. But the British received a rude shock when the Malays rallied all over the country protesting against such a union and the British caved in.

The immigrant population would have been the main beneficiaries if the Union had been implemented. But it was not to be. Nonetheless, for a period of about three months the immigrant population did experience the kind of nation (the Malayan Union) that they found most suitable to them and would have preferred to continue. This did not happen, as it was soon replaced by the Federation of Malaya in 1948. The latter restored the primacy of indigenous dominance in the governance of Malaya, which, in the former, was done away with. This became a source of discontentment amongst the immigrant population, who believed that they had made enormous contributions to the economic development of the country. While appreciating the contributions of the immigrant population, the indigenous groups were quick to point out that the immigrants' contribution was not made out of any nationalistic or philanthropic motives but rather incidental because they came to Malaya to earn a living and were paid by the British or Chinese masters for whom they were working.

The implementation of the Malayan Union rule, though very brief, has had many socio-political consequences which generated a host of activities that eventually allowed the 'ethnic bargain' to be conducted in a peaceful manner.[17]

It brought about the establishment of a number of political parties in a short period of time, that is between 1946 and 1952, which signalled the beginning of electoral politics in Malaysia.[18] Most of these political parties were ethnic-based. The UMNO (United Malays National Organization) and the PAS (*Parti Islam SeMalaya* or Pan-Malayan Islamic Party) were Malay-based parties with the latter using Islam as its ideology. There was the MCA (Malayan Chinese Association) for the Chinese and the MIC (Malayan Indian Congress) for the Indians. Though there were other political parties which came later, the UMNO, PAS, MCA and MIC became the four major parties in Malaya until Independence in 1957.[19] Most political parties today are ethnic.

The establishment of the Federation of Malaya, in fact, provided a national and state/provincial political framework, within which these political parties were allowed to operate because the British were intent on establishing self-rule by the locals which they hoped would eventually lead to an independent Malaya. The majority of Malayans who were members of the Federal Council within the colonial government and its executive arm were recruited from these political parties.

Through the Federal Council, various committees and commissions were set up to deal with various aspects of governance, in particular, in nurturing good inter-ethnic relations. Thus the Council provided the umbrella through which the various ethnic groups, each represented by its leaders, could meet and discuss matters related to the improvement of ethnic relations. These meetings were usually mediated by the British, who were keen to see things proceeding properly and quickly because they were at the same time trying to cope with security threats such as the militant opposition from the communist insurgents.

The introduction of modern electoral politics, mainly through local council elections in the urban areas of Malaya, such as Penang and Kuala Lumpur, also provided the opportunity for political parties, particularly the UMNO and the MCA, to form a coalition, called the Alliance, and contested against other parties on a common platform. This meant that the Malay UMNO and the Chinese MCA had to come to some agreement and understanding as to how to deal with their differences and survive together as partners in the political contest against other political parties. The Alliance was indeed the product of an ethnic bargain. Since then 'coalition politics' has remained the main feature of modern Malaysian electoral politics. Even the opposition parties adopted this model, with the creation of, for example, the Socialist Front, in which the Chinese-dominated Malayan Labour Party joined hands with the Malay-dominated Malayan Socialist Party. It is through such coalitions that the process of 'ethnic bargaining' became institutionalized in Malaysian politics.[20]

The British endorsed the coalition politics model and accepted it as the best formula for ethnic harmony in British Malaya, and the prospect of giving Malaya its independence became more realistic from the British point of view. The coalition politics formula seemed to work very well when the Alliance won almost all the seats contested in the 1955 general elections, the first of such elections in Malaysia.

A special feature of the 'ethnic bargain' was that it was a bargain or negotiation conducted by the elite of each ethnic group on behalf of the rest. Often the elite, who were all English educated and people of high position or from well-to-do families, were selected by the British themselves. Thus, the elite did not necessarily represent the interests of the non-elite, 80 per cent of whom were illiterate. Besides, the character and interest of the leaders of the Alliance (moderate, administration-minded Malays and well-to-do Chinese and Indian businessmen) seemed to the British to offer future political and economic stability and a reasonable insurance for their own investments.

The ethnic bargain was at its height when the constitution for an independent Malaya was drawn up.[21] The representatives of every ethnic group were jostling for advantages of all sorts to protect the interest of their lot. Subsequently, after much negotiations, with the British as mediator, a constitution was realized.

In a way the Malaysian constitution is not only a legal document, like any other constitution, but also a sort of 'social contract' between the ethnic groups in which the interests of each of the ethnic groups were guaranteed, protected and written into the constitution. It is also important to note that the nature of the contract reached was to underlie not merely the form that the new state would take but also the manner of its politics and much else during the first decade of independence.

In essence, the understanding reached was that in the interests of leadership groups and, it was argued, of society as a whole, Malay entitlement to political and administrative authority should be accepted unchallenged, at least for the time being, in return for non-interference in Chinese control of the economy. With those understandings as a starting point, a process of reconciliation of interests would be embarked upon, aimed explicitly, for the Malays, at measures intended to redress the balance of economic power and implicitly, for the Chinese, at gradual admission to the franchise and to the political power flowing from this.

Subsequent problems have centred upon two issues: first, the extent to which the two leadership groups have continued to remain acceptable to the communities for which they professed to speak, and second, the fact that one side of the bargain (the increment of political power for the Chinese) operated largely by passage of time, while the other (the increment of economic power of the Malays) did not. Some aspects of these problems have not really been resolved even until the present day, hence the ethnic bargain is still alive and continues to be an important feature of the Malaysian 'democratic' plural society.

There were other opportunities available for the various ethnic communities to express their differences, to trade solutions and to show one another their goodwill. But the best of all the opportunities that was made available by the British was the public policy instrument called 'development planning', which we shall examine briefly next.

Development Planning

In the economic sphere, the post-war reconstruction of colonial Malaya was facing tremendous difficulties as a result of lack of funds. The British nevertheless, following the famous Marshall Plan technique and Bretton Woods system, established an institution called 'development planning' and introduced a five-year plan for the nation. The first was called the Draft Development Plan 1950–1955.[22]

The outbreak of the Korean War in 1950 was a blessing in disguise for British Malaya. There was a sudden demand for natural rubber and tin, mainly for the production of war-related items. Almost overnight, the economic fate of British Malaya changed from that of a struggling poor state to one which was abundant with funds. Hence the funding of the five-year plan, the emergency and the overall effort of economic reconstruction for war-torn Malaya was assured.

The exercise of planning and institutionalizing it, especially in the context of British interests in Malaya, was not new. While World War II was raging, the British government was provided with an opportunity to review their position in the country because they were unhappy with the rather odd patchwork of political authority that they had installed in Malaya. For this purpose they set up a special committee, known as the Malayan Planning Unit, to draw up a plan under which one centrally governed political unit covering Peninsular Malaya was to be created. Hence the birth of the Malayan Union idea.

Against this background, the launching of the Draft Development Plan of the Federation of Malaya, 1950–1955, a five-year development plan document, was not a surprise at all. The influence of the American-initiated Marshall Plan and the Bretton Woods system in the economic reconstruction of war-torn Europe, at least in terms of idea and concept, should not be dismissed here because there is strong evidence to show that this was the case.[23]

It was in essence an exercise of economic planning, if a partial one, initially meant to rebuild the war-torn Malayan economy. The need to plan was essentially forced by the lack of, in fact dwindling amount of, funds in the coffers of the Malayan colonial administration. So, though planning priorities were set up, strategies for implementation were thought out clearly. Whatever they had to spend was carefully decided.

With the unexpected arrival of large sales of rubber and tin during the Korean War, the economic planning changed its direction, not simply at drawing priorities to save funds or use funds purposefully but it also became an attempt at consciously directing the course of Malaya's economic, political, and social future.

There was also an attempt at redistribution, mainly a result of active demand from the Malay community, and hence the establishment of statutory bodies such as RIDA (Rural and Industrial Development Authority). It was quite clear then that state intervention was the name of the game conveniently or necessarily justified by the existence of political situations such as the state of emergency.

The process of deliberating over the five-year plans gave the different representatives of each ethnic community in Malaya a most valuable extra opportunity to put across their complaints, views and hopes, particularly pertaining to economic matters. What this meant was that to a great extent ethnic factors determined the structure and roles of institutions and defined the basic priorities of public policy hence making ethnicity institutionalized and rigid in its manifestations.

To ensure the successful implementation, evaluation, and monitoring of these ethnicized development policies, the whole exercise of 'development planning' in Malaysia, from its beginning, was closely associated with the Briggs Plan of the emergency. The War Council Committee of the Briggs Plan, with its excellent top-bottom-top bureaucratic structure that avoided interventions from state/provincial administration, provided the much-needed administrative framework for the successful implementation of the 'development plans'.

Continuous information, not only about security matters but also on any other matter including 'development' issues, flowed from top to bottom and bottom to top. Therefore, if disputes arose at the district level, they could be sent up the chain for consideration and a binding decision. In this way, planning in Malaysia became very much centralized and to a certain extent operated like a military command structure.

For instance, when the Ministry of National and Rural Development was established in 1959, the Minister-in-Charge, who was the Deputy Prime Minister himself, declared that the government was to adopt the War Council Committee model as its administrative framework to allow smooth top-bottom-top flow of information and evaluation during planning and implementation of development projects. Thus the 'War Model' became the 'Peace Model'. Since then, military idioms have been dominating 'development planning' in Malaysia, such as the term 'operations room', 'war against poverty' and 'economic intelligence'.

Therefore, the institution of 'development planning' was not only closely connected to the 'ethnic bargain' process but also to the 'security measures' introduced by the British colonial government. Without doubt, these three elements became the 'three pillars' of Malaysia's socio-economic development before and after independence. Casting this on a larger social canvass in Malaysia one could easily argue that these very same elements have also been the 'three pillars' of development and democracy in Malaysia.

This does not imply that these are the only elements which are crucial in Malaysian development and democratic experience and in its effort to construct and maintain some semblance of 'national unity'. The fact that Malaysia's economy and society are also shaped by global circumstances, most of which are beyond Malaysia's control, only demonstrates that there are other elements in the making of Malaysia's development story.

Conclusion

It is quite clear, from the above, that contemporary discussion on 'development and democracy' in Malaysia suffers from a serious analytic-cum-historic problem. Analytically, 'nation' and 'state' – two quite separate constructs – formation in Malaysia is not sufficiently problematized in the discourse, hence the concept of 'democracy', too. This is further complicated by the fact that there seemed to be a refusal to accept the idea that 'democracy' is a contested concept.[24] Had the discourse on democracy in Malaysia taken cognizance of the above-mentioned analytical concerns, it would have included, as an integral part of it, a detailed discussion on how the present state of the so-called 'democracy building' in Malaysia has been inextricably intertwined with problems of security, ethnic bargain and planned change, during the post-war British colonial rule era, that became the basis and grid within which state and nation formation in Malaysia have been shaped thus far.

Had the discourse taken into consideration the central role of planned change in Malaysia's development story, especially its militaristic elements, as established then by a politically and economically troubled post-war British colonial regime, one could perhaps see the linkage between the persistence practice of the so-called 'undemocratic' alloca-tion of resources amongst the different social groups in Malaysia, especially the communal-based ones. [25]

In other words, there is an urgent need to historically contextualize many of the 'undemocratic' practices of the present-day Malaysian state in its effort to bring about economic development as well as to create some form of democratic rule. But it should not become an exercise to justify them so as to accept these practices. Instead, it would allow the much-needed analytical space for a truly democratized analysis and discourse to prevail, which for the moment, in the Malaysian studies context, is dominated by a kind of 'epistemological hegemony', practised by Malaysians and foreigners, informed mainly by a rather problematic (or double-standard) notion of democracy, human rights and development propagandized by the powerful United States of America and its allies.

Notes

1   See Robert Bellah (ed.), *Religion and Progress in Modern Asia*, New York: Free Press, 1965. See, also, a recent detailed and critical re-examination of the ideas advanced in Bellah's volume, Charles Keyes, Laurel Kendall and Helen Hardacre (eds), *Asian Visions of Authority: Religion and the Modern States of East and Southeast Asia*, Honolulu: University of Hawaii Press, 1994.

2   See the excellent collection of essays on this theme, with regard to Asia, in Frederic C. Deyo (ed.), *The Political Economy of the Asian New Industrialism*, Ithaca: Cornell University Press, 1987.

3   For a brief but insightful analysis on the transformation that took place in South Korea in the 1980s, see Hagen Koo, 'The Interplay of State, Class and World System in East Asian Development: The Cases of South Korea and Taiwan', in Frederic C. Deyo (ed.), *The Political Economy*.

4   See *The Economist*, August 27 1995, p. 15.

5   See Christopher Tremewan, *The Political Economy of Social Control in Singapore*, London: Macmillan, 1994; Michael Hill and Lim Kwen Fee, *The Politics of Nation Building and Citizenship in Singapore*, London: Routledge, 1995; Geoffrey Murray and Audrey Perera, *Singapore: The Global City*, Folkestone, UK: China Library, 1996.

6   See Harold Crouch, 'Malaysia: Neither Authoritarian nor Democratic?', in Kevin Hewson, Richard Robisan and Gary Rodan (eds), *Southeast Asia in the 1990s: Authoritarianism, Democracy and Capitalism*, Sydney: Allen and Unwin, 1993; William Case, 'Semi-Democracy in Malaysia: Withstanding the Pressures for Regime Change', *Pacific Affairs*, 66(2), 1993; Zakaria Ahmad, 'Malaysia: Quasi-Democracy in a Divided Society', in Larry Diamond, Juan J. Linz and Seymour Martin Lipset (eds), *Democracy in Developing Countries*, Vol. 3, Boulder: Lynne Rienner, 1989; Johan Saravanamuttu, 'The State, Authoritarianism and Industrialization: Reflections on the Malaysian Case', *Kajian Malaysia*, 5(2), 1987; and Beng-Huat Chua, *Communitarian Ideology and Democracy in Singapore*, London: Routledge, 1995.

7   For an enlightening political history of the hegemonic 'Emergency Powers' in Malaysia, see, the excellent but little quoted study by Rais Yatim, *Freedom under Executive Power in Malaysia: A Study of Executive Supremacy*, Kuala Lumpur: Endowment, 1995.

8   There is an unproportionately huge literature on general elections in the study of 'Malaysian politics'. Therefore, it is not surprising that the Malaysian general election as a political phenomenon is also useful in the recent discourse on democracy in Malaysia. See Loh Kok Wah, 'Developmentalism in Malaysia

in the 1990s: Is the shift from the politics of ethnicisms underway?', a working paper for The First Malaysian Studies Conference, 11–13 August 1997, Kuala Lumpur, Malaysia.

9   See, Philip McMichael, *Development and Social Change: A Global Perspective*, Thousand Oaks, California: Pine Forge, 1996, pp. 45–56.

10 There is a recognized corpus of material on the Emergency in Malaysia, both fiction and non-fiction. Some of the latter, mainly academic analyses, are as follows: Anthony Short, *The Communist Insurrection in Malaya 1948–1960*, London: Frederick Muller, 1975; Richard Stubs, *Hearts and Minds in Guerrilla Warfare: The Malayan Emergency 1948–1960*, Singapore: Oxford University Press, 1989; Robert Jackson, *The Malayan Emergency: The Commonwealth's War 1948–1966*, London: Routledge, 1991; John Coates, *Supressing Insurgency: An Analysis of the Malayan Emergency, 1948–1954*, Boulder, Colorado: Westview, 1992; Peter Dennis and Jeffrey Grey, *Emergency and Confrontation: Australian Military Operatins in Malaya and Borneo 1950–1966*, Sydney: Allen and Unwin, 1996.

11 For a useful interpretation of the events during this period, see the contributions of Cheah Boon Keng, *Red Star Over Malaya: Resistance and Social Conflict During and After the Japanese Occupation 1941–1946*, Singapore: Singapore University Press, 1983 and *The Masked Comrades: A Study of the Communist United Front in Malaya, 1945–1948*, Singapore: Times Books International, 1979.

12 On this topic, the best account is found in Michael Stenson, *Industrial Conflict in Malaya: Prelude to the Communist Revolt of 1948*, London: Oxford University Press, 1970.

13 See note 9.

14 See Albert Lau, *The Malayan Union Controversy 1942–1948*, Singapore: Oxford University Press, 1991; Anthony J. Stockwell, *British Policy and Malay Politics during the Malayan Union Experiment, 1942–1948*, Kuala Lumpur: Malaysian Branch of the Royal Asiatic Society, 1979.

15 For further details, see, James Puthucheary, *Ownership and Control in the Malaysian Economy*, Singapore: Eastern Universities Press, 1960.

16 For a useful account on the role of the Police Force in post-war and post-colonial Malaysia, see, Zakaria Ahmad, 'The Police and Political Development in Malaysia: Change, Continuity, and Institution Building of a Coercive Apparatus in a Developing, Ethnically Divided Society', PhD dissertation, Massachussets Institute of Technology, U.S.A. 1977.

17 For a useful guide to the literature view on aspects of the 'ethnic bargain', see, Zakaria Ahmad, 'Introduction: History, Structure and Process in Malaysian Government and Politics', in Zakaria Ahmad (ed.), *Government and Politics of Malaysia*, Singapore: Oxford University Press, 1987.

18 For a useful commentary on the early experience of electoral politics in Malaysia, see T.E. Smith, *Report on the First Election of Members to the Legislative*

Council of the Federation of Malaya, Kuala Lumpur: Government Printer, 1955 and 'The Malayan Elections of 1959', *Pacific Affairs* 33, 1960, pp. 38–47.

19 See John Funston, *Malay Politics in Malaysia: A Study of the United Malays National Organisation and Party Islam*, Kuala Lumpur: Heinemann, 1980; Heng Pek Koon, *Chinese Politics in Malaysia: A History of the Malaysian Chinese Association*. Singapore: Oxford University Press, 1988; Rajesway Ampalavanar, *The Indian Minority and Political Change in Malaysia, 1945–1957*, Kuala Lumpur: Oxford University Press, 1981.

20 The most useful interpretation of coalition politics in Malaysia are found in the two contributions of G.P. Means, namely, *Malaysian Politics*, London: University of London Press, 1970 and *Malaysian Politics: The Second Generation*, Singapore: Oxford University Press, 1991.

21 See the two significant contributions of the following authors, F.A. Trindade and H.P. Lee, namely, *The Constitution of Malaysia: Its Development 1957–1977*, Kuala Lumpur: Oxford University Press, 1978 and *The Constitution of Malaysia, Further Perspectives and Development, Essays in Honour of Tun Mohamed Suffian*, Kuala Lumpur: Oxford University Press, 1986.

22 See Martin Rudner, *Nationalism, Planning and Economic Modernization: The Politics of Beginning Development*, London: Sage, 1975; Shamsul A.B., 'Economic Dimension of Malay Nationalism', *Developing Economies*, 1997 (September), pp. 240–261.

23 Please see a recent work by Yunus Lubega Butanaziba, 'The Making of Administrative and Economic Development plans for Malaysia, 1945–65: the International Hand', MA thesis, Faculty of Arts and Social Sciences, Universiti Malaysia, 1997.

24 For a discussion on this, see W.B Gallie, *Philosophy and the Historical Understanding*, London: Chatto and Windus, 1964, p.158–159; and, also, Z.A. Nizami and Devika Paul (eds.), *Human Rights in the Third World Countries*, Delhi: KIRS Publications, 1994.

25 Perhaps, as in the Malaysian case, if we also go back into the history of the Nordic countries we would now understand better why the Nordic states currently push the issues of democracy and human rights in the Third World so strongly, perhaps as a form of moral repudiation of their immoral past, especially in the light of a recent exposé regarding their pre-Second World War policy of mass sterilization of those considered to be 'less-than-perfect humans'.

5 PRINCIPLED AND UNPRINCIPLED DEMOCRACY

THE CHINESE APPROACH TO EVALUATION AND ELECTION

Børge Bakken

In China there is much talk of the relative importance of morality (*de*) and law (*fa*). The Chinese traditional belief is that power can be restrained and that the good society will develop through morality and strict standards based on objective norms. Moral education (*deyu jiaoyu*) becomes highly important in this model of thinking, and discussions about good emperors, righteous men and just cadres rather than feasible democratic organizational set-ups dominate. The moral elitism of traditional China maintains that the sage or virtuous man (*junzi*) of Confucian thought rules over the small man (*xiaoren*) of low moral standing. This moral elitism constantly strives towards perfectability and describes an 'exemplary' society. A perfect social order depends on perfect human beings.

Debates concerning the Chinese 'moral order' and even democracy have focused very strongly on the 'improvement' and 'quality' of the human material. The focus has been on human engineering by socialization and evaluation. Everyone could be a sage and achieve this highest ideal state of morality. Self-sacrifice and moral self-evaluation constituted the core of the Confucian *junzi* as well as the Maoist 'new man' (*xinren*). In a modernized reform version there is much talk of 'science', and official China maintain that there is a scientific way to judge morality based on the 'objectivity' of norms. During the past decade of reforms we have experienced a 'social engineering' (*shehuyi gongcheng*) approach directed towards the improvement of 'human quality' (*ren de suzhi*). This debate is strongly linked to psychological theories and biological assumptions from the eugenics debate. Despite modernization and reform, justice is still mainly a discourse about the good (now sometimes interpreted as the efficient) ruler rather than one about the checks and balances of democratic institutions, law and a legal system. The discussions on 'modern person-ality' (*xiandai ren*) claim that an objective basis of morality can be found with technocratic accuracy.[1] Models of 'objective norms' and 'righteous persons' define the Chinese approach to education, and countless models (*bangyang* or *mofan*) are set up to be evaluated. Correct behaviour is always linked and evaluated with close reference to such models.[2] Chinese modernity undoubtedly has and will continue to have indigenous cultural traits which differ from its Western equivalent. Consequently, the approach to democracy will be different in various ways to the dominant Western approach. It is a long way, however, from such an understanding to the acceptance of a specific Eastern or Asian 'moral approach' to democ-racy. This 'moral approach', however, puts much stress on surveillance and control, and in particular statements of 'cultural objectivity' has obvious undemocratic traits built into it. I shall try to shed some light on this problem by using examples from recent Chinese debates on democracy.

China is a rapidly changing society, and norms and standards are not at all 'objective'. While norms used to be strongly rooted in the tradi-tional culture and gained almost general consent, such consent has now been uprooted by modernity. Norms become increasingly diversified in the anomic process of modernization. The government can still define what is 'objective', however, but norms more and more lose their social and cultural moorings. 'Objective norms' take the form of 'super-social norms', and perfectionist norms of 'exemplarity' are firmly based on the definition of the power-holder.

Democracy and the Dangers of Perfectionism

The ideal of complete perfection of political systems and human beings is thought by Chinese democracy theorists like Jin Guantao, Yan Jiaqi, Hu Ping and Su Wei to be impossible and undesirable. Instead they suggest democracy as the best, although *im*perfect (and this is an important distinction) solution. The Chinese aversion towards everything imperfect explains some of the scepticism that these theorists have met in China. There can, however, be no repose for humanity in a 'good society' defined once and for all in an exemplary norm. Perfectionism presupposes that its proposal is unique and the best in the world. Thus, to maintain its superiority it denies the existence of other doctrines and the rights of others. The stress on perfection and exemplarity thus leads to autocracy.[3] Jin Guantao has attacked the notion of 'perfect values'. A democratic institutional design is not the final and perfect solution of the problem of evil in society, but it is better than the autocratic or authoritarian solution we see today. Hu Ping further argues that a democratic system of elections cannot assure that the best person is elected, but at least it can ensure that people can call back their representatives by voting against them.[4] In Hu Ping's terms China should adopt this 'possible, good system' rather than what he regards as the impossible 'best possibility'.[5] In other words he follows the rationality of Thomas' theorem which holds that 'good enough is best', while the principle of 'only the best is good enough' might have too costly consequences to be successfully implemented in practice. The Great Leap Forward of the late 1950s and the Cultural Revolution of the 1960s and 1970s were both 'best' projects of perfection. While the first led to disaster and widespread famine, the second ended in chaos. The search for perfectability led to disaster. In the same way the search for perfect 'human quality' will have counter-productive effects, these democracy theorists claim. Instead of perfection it will lead to moral elitism and utopian perfectionism. Platonic as well as Confucian efforts to seek perfection in politics have obvious limitations. Such theories do not see evil and imperfection as part of reality, according to Ding Chu. Commenting on the debate about Chinese democracy, he has claimed that he would rather have two evil people who check each other than an angel without check.[6]

In Jin Guantao's view the Cultural Revolution was the decisive blow against the beliefs in utopian perfectionism. Jin's assumption is partly correct since faith is crumbling rapidly in today's China, but still the 'campaign' (*yundong*) defines the Chinese approach to political participation. In contrast to the ballot box approach, the campaign is based on an assumption of moral and political improvement and final perfection. The ongoing campaigns of 'spiritual civilization' (*jingshen wenming*) are still linked to the notions of 'perfection' and 'exemplarity' and stand in sharp contrast to the real existing pragmatic attitudes of the reform era. The logic of exemplarity and perfectability is still dominating China, and in the following I shall look at some of the literature and practices of this approach.

Ping versus *Xuan*. On Moral and Evaluative Democracy

Shifting the focus from the works of Chinese democracy activists and theoreticians, let us first look at some of the system-loyal writings of moral order and 'moral evaluative democracy'. This debate is linked to 'perfectionism' and 'exemplarity', and the imperfect alternative made by Chinese democracy activists is not at all appealing to this line of thought. The literature on 'moral evaluation' is vast in China today. Often the type of democracy being discussed in this literature indicates a very important distinction between Chinese and Western conceptions of 'democracy'. In China, evaluation is said to represent an 'objective' democracy where the exact knowledge of objective norms and standards forms the basis of the process. Moral and political evaluation is defined as insight in necessity. The Chinese 'democracy of evaluation' is contrasted to a Western 'democracy of election'. An interesting article by Jin Rong discusses the importance of *ping* – evaluation – and the uselessness of *xuan* – election. Jin critiques the fact that certain work-units have recently neglected the systematic evaluation of their employees. Instead of evaluation (*ping*), the units have used election (*xuan*) procedures in finding right persons for right tasks, etc. Elections are used instead of evaluation, ballot instead of judgement. The educational aspects inherent in evaluation disappear from the process in such cases. Some people simply vote according to their own likes or dislikes, whether they are related to people, whether they have connections or *guanxi* with them, etc. If we use elections instead of evaluation, the unity and stability of the work-units will disappear, Jin claims. Some want the new procedures of election because it is so much faster, and because it avoids the quarrels associated with the evaluation procedure. Some people might have had bad experiences with the evaluation process, Jin admits, but their reactions are exaggerated and 'like someone who is one day bitten by a snake, they get afraid of the rope to the well for three years'.[7] Jin's suggestion is that the ballot box is not based on a principle of goodness or perfection; it becomes unprincipled and without any moorings in the correct and principled social norm.

It is interesting to note that the argument of rampant nepotism is cited against elections, and that factional infighting is blamed on elections, since much of the arguments *for* elections go in the same direction. The explanation for Jin's outburst is easy to spot. The lack of a standard against which to judge people is evident in an election; elections are thus unprincipled and chaotic. Furthermore, elections are not objective because they are not linked to an exemplary standard; in fact they are not linked to any standard at all, and there is no element of improvement or education in elections. Surely, it is wrong to be able to choose whoever you like for this or that post or purpose. The educative aspect as well as the building order lies in *ping*, in evaluation. Jin's argument indicates some of the traditional Chinese scepticism towards elections and representative democracy in general, and explains some of the immense importance of evaluation in all walks of Chinese everyday life.

Many authors have touched the theme of evaluative democracy. Instead of emphasizing the ballot box and the ballot paper, the official political 'small group' or *xiaozu* network is presented as the stage on which democracy is intended to develop. The small group is an important basis for moral evaluation and defines quite another institutional set-up than we normally think of as democratic institutions. Within such groups, social norms are 'held' and individuals 'improved' under conditions of maximal visibility through constant evaluation. The groups are supervised by teachers or cadres. A textbook on evaluation techniques suggests that one should 'carry out evaluation in a group with no less than five members'.[8] Large parts of society are organized into such small, informal groups. Classrooms, factories, neighbourhoods, prisons, military camps – all are formed and supervised by higher authorities through small groups. Within these groups each person is expected to analyse his or her attitudes, to reconsider values in the light of an exemplary collectivity. The small group is the core of evaluation, but since evaluation is an ever-present and all-round process it does not stop at the confines of the small circle. There is a control aspect of the *xiaozu* network, and it is closely linked to authority. The idea is that the *xiaozu* network can prevent the emergence of autonomous primary groups, and thereby prevent un-authorized standards from establishing themselves, and cliques and factions from developing. Groups should evaluate each member in order to set the standards in each individual, solve problems, and restore the collective unity.[9]

The small-scale group network thus opens up to a society outside classrooms and work-units. It is often heard that school, family, and society should all form a mutual network of evaluation touching on all walks of life. A typical comment in the journal *Shanghai Education* formulates the idea explicitly: 'Small group evaluation develops a democratic consciousness'.[10] In other words, we see the framework of a Chinese evaluative democracy, based on 'objective' or 'exemplary' norms following an idea of 'moral science'. We do not have to accept that this defines a type of democracy, but at least Chinese educators and theories of evaluation use that term to describe the process of evaluation. Of course it also describes a definition of perfectionism that Hu Ping thinks is alien to the concept of democracy.

The editor of the journal *Research in Higher Education* shares the concern over elections in selecting candidates for titles of honour. Appraisals are often carelessly done through secret ballot, the article claims. Behind the concern lies the fear that the strictly regulated standards for the 'three-good student' – good study results, good moral conduct and good health – could be tampered with. Critical to elections, the article signals its adherence to reform in another way, by suggesting a much wider use of material incentives as an end-product of the evaluation process. Material rewards should be allowed, and both cash awards and bonuses are suggested. Awards for excellent studies (*xuexi youxiu jiang*) should be graded, and awards for making progress in study (*xuexi jinbu jiang*) should also be introduced.[11] Reform-minded articles are often much more likely to support reforms concerning material incentives than to support notions of elective democracy on any level. Democracy is seen in the terms of moral elitism and as a way to award the morally excellent. Various 'morality diplomas' have become widely used. Titles of honour, too, have begun to appear in ranked order, forming a hierarchy of rewards for good and heroic deeds.[12] Titles exist all the way from the national level of model workers or students, down to the local county or even work-unit or classroom levels.

Evaluation, Democracy and Social Disorder

Evaluation is the main way in which exemplary society links people's behaviour, or rather their display of attitudes – their *biaoxian* – closer to the exemplary norm. The Chinese ancients said 'promote the good, suppress the evil' (*yang shan yi e*) and 'only by comparison can one distinguish' (*bi ze ming qi li*). The principle is institutionalized in the process of *pingbi* – 'comparing and assessing' individuals – used within the small groups. Appraisal through discussion is the most common method used in small-group evaluation, and in the larger sessions following up small-group discussions. For many years this method was discredited.[13] However, in schools it was reintroduced in the early 1980s, to 'strengthen moral education' as it was formulated.[14] The educative aspect is evident. While binding individuals to norms, evaluation at the same time improves 'human quality'. Even if this approach is participatory, improvement and surveillance define the process. According to the theory individual evaluation represents a 'restraining or binding force (*yueshu li*)'.[15] The fear of chaos or *luan* has deep roots in Chinese society, and the more recent memories of chaos during the Cultural Revolution and the breakdown of the Soviet Union have strengthened the fear of modern disorder. Contrary to official fears that democratic institutions will cause disorder, Wang Huning, a Fudan University political scientist, has claimed that the lack of division of power and of democratic institutions caused the chaos of the Cultural Revolution.[16] There was no official or institutionalized outlet for frustration and fundamentalist Red Guards were instead influenced by the repeated Chinese mistake of emphasizing the perfectionist doctrine of moral elitism.

Today the regime upholds legitimacy not by economic growth only, but by a combination of growth and order. This is reflected in the slogan of creating 'material and spiritual civilization' where 'material' stands for growth and 'spiritual' for order. Social order is an argument on both sides of the debate, and an important part of the 'reform-faction' consists of neo-authoritarians such as Zhang Binjiu. He believes that democratic institutions may provide an open channel for social upheaval and civil fighting. The alternative that they advocate is a model of semi-centralized power to maintain social order in the transition towards democracy.[17] Other advocates of Chinese democracy claim that such neo-authoritarian institutional arrangements would instead create social and political disorder due to the lack of institutions and proper procedures to deal with corrupt leaders. Neo-authoritarianism might also lead to a permanent succession crisis that continually threatens chaos or even civil war when the ultimate ruler is dead. Neo-authoritarianism is also based on the moral elitism of the old system and there is no guarantee that it will develop in the direction of democracy. On the contrary, Hu Ping argues, the project of neo-authoritarian government has the weakness of an authoritarian institutional arrangement that invests individual power in one or a few persons presupposed to be morally superior.[18]

Educative Evaluation and the Objectivity of Norms

Evaluation based on strict moral standards and exemplary norms is seen as a way of linking individuals to the greater society. Through evaluation the individual 'small self' (*xiaowo*) is lifted up to the level of the collective 'great self' (*dawo*) that is society. In the words of one moral educator: 'Evaluation will prevent the bad influences coming in the wake of opening up and reform'.[19] The chaotic change of values must be held together through so-called objective evaluations manifested through the detailed measurement of behaviour or *biaoxian*, subsuming individual behaviour under the logic of a strict exemplary standard. During the reforms moral and political correctness is supported by modern notions of 'objectivity' and 'efficiency'.

Evaluation is claimed to be based on 'the objective character of objective values (*keti de jiazhi de duixiang xing*)' and an evaluative democracy must be based on education. In the Chinese debate on evaluation there is much talk of 'fostering' (*peiyang*) worthy successors, and keywords like 'direction' or 'guidance' (*zhixiang xing*) are frequently used to lead the populace on the right path leading to exemplary, objective order.[20] It has been claimed that the guiding function of evaluation will raise moral efficiency (*deyu de xiaolü*),[21] and the campaigns and movements of spiritual civilization are often expressed in the language of such 'moral economy'. The concept of 'value objectivity (*jiazhi duixiang xing*)' is used to characterize the evaluation process. There are both internal and external yardsticks for evaluation: the internal yardstick lies in conscience, while the external yardstick is social intelligence, social opinion and the objective standards of society.[22] Such 'objective' evaluation lies at the core of the disciplinary concept of human quality.

There is a range of evaluation techniques, there are oral and written types of evaluation, open and hidden ways of judging individuals. Evaluation concerns education and improvement, discipline, rewards and punishment. The corrective and improving effect of evaluation is its most important characteristic, which the ballot box lacks, or at best only has in minimal quantities. Moral selection is often described through the picture of a universalistic ideal of equitable allocation for jobs, education and other scarce resources. The particularistic reality of China, however, makes evaluation into a very subjective way of controlling such resources. 'Fixed norms' (*kebi zhibiao*) should be established, and one should 'make objective evaluations through seeking truths from facts'.[23]

Also the evaluator is evaluated. In schools it is part of the daily routine for teachers as well as students to write self-assessment reports. The teacher evaluation form (*jiaoshi kaohe biao*) is also to include comments from all responsible persons at every office in the school administration.[24] Cadres are also thoroughly evaluated; and their evaluation, like that of teachers, is important background material for their further selection for jobs – or for purges or rehabilitation in political campaigns, for that matter. Evaluation concerns everything from one's moral and political world outlook, down to matters of whether primary school children keep their schoolbags tidy, or wash their hands properly.[25] As there is a small-group network at the basic levels, there is also an evaluation network outside the smaller unit. Individuals should be evaluated constantly. Daily evaluation is recommended in schools, and an overall appraisal is made in the end. China might not be a society of 'perpetual penalty' as in the Foucault expression, but it certainly is close to one of perpetual evaluation.

Evaluation is regularized, bureaucratized and frozen into files. The personnel file (*renshi dang'an*) starts in school and follows you from work-unit to work-unit. Even if the file has lost some of its controlling functions during the reforms, it is still a very important control factor deciding and restricting your life and career.[26] When ideological orientation or attitude towards the exemplary norm is used as a starting point for the distribution of social mobility, we can speak of virtuocratic evaluation and virtuocratic mobility.[27] In contrast to meritocratic processes such evaluation is characterized by a low level of measurability, it follows subjective criteria for evaluation, and draws diffuse and flexible lines for the definitions of who can be regarded as worthy. Such moral judgement is a nice breeding ground for connection networks and stategic, overt obedience.

The Measurement of Morality

Bureaucracies are interested in measuring and quantifying their success. The ballot box offers accurate measurement, but the count of votes is hardly an easily controllable entity. 'Objective' methods of controlling virtue are instead introduced, and Zhang Yutian uses the concept 'vague mathematics' (*mohu shuxue*) as a description of the quantified moral evaluation system.[28] His moral mathematics is based on an aggregate (v) which is made up of ideological (x) and moral (y) 'systems' to form a quantified expression of correct moral and political conduct.

There are historical roots to this measurement of morality. The late Ming/early Qing period saw the use of a type of moral account books, or ledgers of merit and demerit attempting to seek moral assurities in numbers.[29] The ledger of merit and demerit was used for the improvement of individuals, and to encourage good and exemplary deeds while discouraging bad behaviour. It was assumed that the gods rewarded and punished human behaviour according to certain established moral standards. These books list good and bad deeds, using merit and demerit points to enable the user to measure his or her moral standing in a precise way. Belief in the system of merit and demerit can be traced back to pre-Han times. For a period parallel to the belief in number-mysticism, through to the late twelfth century when the first ledger of merit and demerit was produced, the system primarily served a religious purpose. In Taoist texts, it was seen as a means of earning immortality, in Buddhist texts, rebirth in a higher level of existence.[30] Later, the ledgers served a more secular purpose, as a means of attaining social and career goals like success in the examinations, official positions, etc. The ledger system was later adopted by the educated elite as an instrument for strict moral and social discipline. By the eighteenth century the ledgers were commonly incorporated into the collections of moral instructions frequently published by gentry officials. The belief in the salutory effect of good deeds found in the ledgers is still very much a part of Chinese moral education. One of the most famous of these books was the Song dynasty work *Gong guo ge* or 'Ledger of Merits and Demerits', and the book was intended as a guide to exemplary morality.[31] The practitioner of this system is urged to keep an account of everyday behaviour. By keeping a daily tally of merits and demerits based on a system of points, and by taking monthly and yearly inventories, one was always able to determine the standing of one's moral account.[32] This type of 'objectivity' is also being followed in modern evaluation. The alleged justice resulting from such measurement still of course is moralistic rather than democratic.

Evaluation: Democracy or Surveillance?

Chinese textbooks on evaluation, however, see the process as something 'natural' and all-embracing, and evaluation is directly linked to the issue of democracy. Some enthusiastically claim that 'evaluation develops a democratic consciousness' among people.[33]

In a description of reforms of moral evaluation techniques, a microcosm of the evaluating and controlling techniques in a system based on a moral responsibility principle is presented.[34] Such articles on evaluation reform are interesting because they stress the connections between control and participation, and indirectly tell us a great deal about a view of democracy alien to a Western eye. Democracy in this connection is linked to the objectivity of norms, and is focused on the principle of self-management or self-supervision (*ziwo guanli*). One should foster abilities in self-supervision 'to fit the needs of society'. The method should also contribute to human improvement and 'create a new self' among the participants. Such suggestions of moral reform build on quite traditional ideas about regulation through written records. 'Democracy through participatory self-surveillance' rests with the file – the written registration of behaviour. Not only individuals, but the family should be involved in the recording process. The first method is to establish a 'contact transmission record' (*lianxi chuandi bu*) in schools regulating the contact between school and home. The record should ambulate between school and home every week. It should carry notes on the students' moral behaviour, the rules of study, attendance record, test record, level of hygiene, delivering of homework, and carefully describe the students' conduct at home for later inspection. Freedom and democracy lie in a moral science based on reliable knowledge of the moral order: and this is precisely the knowledge offered through the evaluation process.

The message seems to be that democracy lies in correct information, but also in finding a correct way to utilize the surveillance potential of the evaluated individuals themselves. In school participation should be learned through the selection of 'class cadres' from among the students. A system of rotation of class cadres is suggested to utilize the resources of control and surveillance from the whole class collective, and to try out more democratic methods of participation. This system has received due support in educational journals, and has found its way into schools and textbooks of pedagogy and evaluation techniques. 'Small class teachers' and 'hygiene supervisors' should be tested on a rotation basis. The student class teacher can set up an own 'cabinet'. The system allows the students on a rotation basis to read other students' diaries, to make home visits, give notes to the parents, correct homework and write remarks in the students' records (*jilu*). After the term is finished the 'small class teacher' is evaluated by fellow students who give marks for performance. These remarks come into the school file later. The 'hygiene supervisor' should check hygiene in general, including hairstyle, fingernails, clothes and oral hygiene, whether fellow students use a civilized vocabulary or whether they swear and use dirty words. Bad behaviour should be criticized in the small group. If serious mistakes are reported, negative marks should be given. The idea is that the class is easier to control if the resources of the students themselves are used to keep control. At the same time it develops each student, it provides a better understanding of the work of the class teacher and underlines the necessity of authority. In university each department posts up a notice of commendation (*tongbao biaoyang*) or criticism.[35]

The democratic character of evaluation is often emphasized in education journals. The small group evaluation should be discussed. Students can dissent if they wish; they can reconsider decisions, and re-examine a case through these discussions in a democratic way. Self-understanding and democracy are thus promoted, and students can better regulate their behaviour and bring it in line with the objective norms.[36] The stress is here on mutual evaluation, not on the democratic discussion as such. Evaluation through comparison should not be performed in order to show off one's wealth and self, but to compare oneself against the standard.[37] Order lies in principled evaluation compared against a moral standard, chaos in the unprincipled election.

The 'building' character of evaluation should not only be understood in terms of individual improvement. It concerns the building of the entire civilization, and is seen as a means to enhance both science and democracy. Evaluation procedures not only reflect the narrative of order, but also touch upon the narrative of progress as does the 'spiritual civilization' movement itself. In the standards of evaluation the themes of work ethic, thrift and professional knowledge also appear. It is explicitly said that the evaluation process is closely connected to the four modernizations and economic development.[38] 'Only communist morality fits the needs of the development of the socialist mode of production', says Wang Xingzhou. Such morality is an important factor in promoting the development of society and 'the basic and objective standard for the moral evaluation of people's behaviour.'[39]

Such general statements, however, are not accurate enough for the systematic and 'scientific' approach to the construction of standards that has emerged during reform. Long lists of measurable standards have been set up to form a 'moral quality index'. There is now an attempt to include values of modernity in those long lists. One such index operationalizes morality into 47 items.[40] The index emphasizes productive values, but the authors nevertheless underline the importance of morality. Moral quality is an even more important measure than age and social status, it is claimed.[41] Both traditional and modern values are used in this index, but the aim is here to introduce modern standards within the same frame of ledgers used for the same type of evaluation as we have now discussed. One part of the index concerns the qualification of the work force and includes such attributes as study habits, self-strength, creativity and effectiveness. Other items are also related to a high work ethic.[42] Modern change is again controlled through the construction of fixed but orderly and gradually adapting standards, approached through an orderly process of objective evaluation. Attitudes towards the norms are again ordered or frozen into written files.

Perfectionism and Simulation

Morality has been a dominating approach to the Chinese conception of democracy and we have seen that moral elitism defines the Chinese approach to the 'good society'. This moral elitism has a tendency to develop into structural obstacles to democracy, and some of the Chinese democracy theorists have claimed that perfectionism leads to social breakdown and catastrophy. Let us look at some internal contradictions of moral elitism.

Moral elitism and the establishment of 'objective', exemplary norms are the foundations for transforming and improving the populace. However, this system also bears a price tag – that of 'hypocrisy'. Here I am not thinking primarily of a moral hypocrisy, but rather the structural 'ways of lying' inherent in an exemplary society that forces people to behave in prescribed ways, and to follow exemplary 'objective' standards. This 'lying' – or I should rather use the concept 'simulation' – is a counter-productive consequence of the disciplinary techniques of moral elitism; among them the reward systems of the exemplary society, its evaluation procedures and its regulation through files. When talking about the 'Chinese ways of lying', I do not mean to promote any sort of Western chauvinism and ethnocentric criticism of another type of culture. Instead I shall show that moral elitism is full of structural contradictions, and no passable road for democratic development. Let us look at the experiences from other cultures, mainly our own European pre-democratic tradition to underline the argument. Perez Zagorin has discussed the phenomenon of simulation in more general terms in his *Ways of Lying*,[43] suggesting an approach that may lead us to a conception of the 'structural lie' – a situation where one is forced to 'lie' to survive or cope with society.

Dissimulation describes the subject matter of Zagorin's book; his main question is to ask how people in the early modern states armed themselves morally and ideologically to resist oppressive regimes, divinely appointed kings and the Catholic Church. Religious dissimulation was found among the Reformation Protestants who, far from openly committing themselves to the new faith, dissembled their beliefs by a feigned conformity to Catholicism. 'The phenomenon of dissimulation is as widespread as the world and as old as nature itself', Zagorin explains.[44] There is a difference between the terms dissimulation and simulation, but the two constitute different sides of the same coin. The two words each denote deception, with the further possible connotation of lying. For the sake of precision it is said that 'dissimulation is pretending not to be what one actually is, whereas simulation is pretending to be what one actually is not'.[45] If we follow this definition in the example of present-day China, we see that simulation more than dissimulation describes the practices of evaluating *biaoxian*, as individuals are rewarded for pretending to be some exemplary person they are actually not by following perfect, 'objective' norms they do not share.

Simulation and dissimulation can serve as means to hide from view – a refuge from oppressive powers. Dissimulation has been central in all kinds of religious dissidence in the early modern era. Historians have accordingly come to designate as 'Nicodemism' the dissimulation used in self-protection by various sorts of Protestants and sectarians during the Reformation and Counter-Reformation. The Chinese practice of simulation is different from the dissimulation of Christian Nicodemism, but the aspect of self-protection from the visibility to rulers is common for both.[46]

The practice of dissimulation is found not only in the Christian tradition. In Shi'ite teaching there is *taqiyah*, which has been defined as 'a doctrine of legitimate dissimulation'; and in the European secular tradition Machiavelli's book *The Prince* is of course the work on dissimulation *par excellence*.[47] The Spanish Jesuit Balthazar Gracian's *Manual of the Art of Discretion* from 1653 is another work describing the assets of dissimulation. He was the originator of the maxim *'Nescit vivere qui nescit dissimulare'* – He who does not know how to dissimulate does not know how to live.'[48]

That China is currently a society out of touch with the ideals and standards prescribed for perfect behaviour strengthens the tendencies towards simulation. The phenomenon of *feng pai* – the 'wind style' – is illustrative of simulative social protection. After the purge of the Cultural Revolution 'Gang of Four' in 1976, it had already become a rule that if the political wind happened to be blowing eastward, then a person should lean eastward; if the wind happened to be blowing westward, then a person should follow the same direction. The best strategy of behaviour was to follow the mainstream. The 'opportunist' strategy is for many the only active and 'natural' way to cope with the system.[49] The stronger the moral elitism prescribed, and the more inflexible the rules and standards of the exemplary society tend to be, the more simulation does the system produce.

Since the Chinese exemplary structure breeds simulation rather than dissimulation, social performance and theatre are not so much about hiding away as they are about presenting the expected exemplary surface – pretending to be what one is not. Theatre is part of the parading of norms, and is seen as part of the educative process of fostering and improving people. The play is well-rehearsed, and the script is well-known to all. Even if the acts are theatre performances, and even if everybody knows it is play-acting, the show goes on: not because people feel morally obliged to play the act, but because the acting is an important tool both for self-promotion and to 'get things done' even in the affairs of daily life. Theatre and simulation represent flexibility within a system of inflexibility. The act of performing super-social norms is an integrated and crucial part of a career ladder for positions and prestige in society. The acts in themselves are often instrumental acts, justifying our description of them as social theatre or simulation. Rather than terming the phenomenon a 'culture of hypocrisy' we should talk of a 'culture of simulation' or even a 'structure of simulation' since the social theatre is a reaction to structures that force people to act in certain ways. The rampant corruption and connection building (*guanxi*) in Chinese society must also be judged by this reality.

There is also another problem brought about by the exemplary structure that is highly counterproductive for upholding the system. This relates to the possibilities for planning. The 'ways of lying' are thus not only or not even primarily a question of morality. Alvin Toffler has grasped some of this problem in his description of the dilemma of the central planner. This dilemma neatly describes the problems of a bureaucracy built on an order of exemplarity:

> You can't make good decisions unless you can continually monitor their effects. For this you need people who are located on the periphery to tell you what's happening. You need information and you need it on time. You most especially need information about your errors. It is called negative feedback. But that's the last thing you, as a central planner, want to hear. You're always afraid your boss will punish you. Whole careers are built on denying error. So the people down below, not being stupid, sugar coat the information or just plain lie, or send in the truth too late, or play any number of other games with the information.[50]

If people cannot participate in making decisions and have no responsibility for them, it is the best strategy to tell the leaders what they want to hear, give useless information, tell as little as possible or simply lie. Toffler argues that every planner needs internal devil's advocates, critics and 'nay-sayers' who have nothing to lose by talking back and opposing the planner. Since the alleged participatory system of evaluation is not actually a participatory system as much as it is a control system, the planner ends up in isolation, in a world of lies, illusions and anachronisms. Whole economies can be destroyed as a result of this false information. This probably happened during the Great Leap Forward in 1958, when over-optimistic plans were built on local reports that were highly exaggerated because they were part of a career system built on saying yes, denial of error and the feigned 'overfulfilling' of production quotas. The overall irrationality of the bureaucratic system linked to large-scale campaigns built on enthusiasm more than on rational calculation of possibilities merged together, ending in the famine years of the early 1960s. Democratic institutions would undoubtedly have been counter-forces to crazes like the Great Leap Forward.

The well-organized and well-rehearsed 'campaign' or 'movement', the *yundong*, is occupying a very central place in the Chinese social fabric. Political and moral campaigns, or *yundong* are still the very foundations for political and public activity in China. If there was still considerable 'freshness' in the mass campaigns of the late 1950s, the situation is worse now that the formal skeleton of a mass movement is often all there is left of 'spiritual civilization'. Mass campaigns in China have become increasingly formalistic, and their stifling character no longer has the power to transform people. 'Objective' standards are still overtly paraded, but covertly the same standards are more and more neglected. Sun Longji holds that the only effect of the moral campaigns is now that they are restrictive forces upholding order in a smaller group over a short interval of time.[51]

Moral elitism has been described as a form of Chinese democracy. Democracy does not function without participation. The procedures of evaluation and the involvement in political campaigns are undoubtedly participatory. At the same time this set-up of moral elitism is more about power and control than about democracy or morality for that sake. Since democracy is meant to control the abuse of power, I can see no hope for a democratic development along this line of moral elitism.

'Village Democracy', 'Democracy Movement' and the Rule of Law. Voices of Chinese Democracy?

China has been experimenting with direct elections and a system of 'village democracy' since the early 1980s, and in 1987 the Village Committees Organic Law of the People's Republic of China (Experimental) was formed. Grassroots elections were delayed by the events following the Tiananmen crackdown in 1989, and were not implemented in earnest until after 1990. The dissident movement is critical of the reform and Xiao Qiang, leader of the New-York-based 'Human Rights in China' dismisses the reform as a mere show having no value whatsoever in forming democratic institutions in China.[52] I think that it is correct to emphasize that the reforms are more about practical local village governance and the quest for stability in the rural areas than about democracy as such. It is definitely not meant to challenge the ruling elites' monopoly of power. In fact, the law was pushed through in the National People's Congress by hardline Long March veteran Peng Zhen.

'Village democracy' is strictly village based, and there are no signs that this form of local governance will move into the cities where the situation is very different. Urban residence or neighbourhood committees and work units take care of local affairs there, and preclude people's engagement in local politics rather than enhance it. Nor do the new village reforms represent a radical departure from Chinese history, as village self-sufficiency and decentralization have been used to rule the vast countryside for centuries. The new aspect about the most recent system of village self-governance is that villages are now raising their own revenues. When the commune system was broken down, it meant that villagers could lease land, grow crops and make money. It also meant that collective funds for public goods and services were no longer available. Allen Choate has noted an 'instrumentalist' attitude towards village democracy among Chinese officials.[53] They stress the usefulness of village democracy because it holds promise for economic development. The ability to lead the village to get rich is the main platform for candidates who run for office.

Even if 'village democracy' does not represent a rights-based approach to democracy, the reform is more than a mere show. Allen Choate concludes that it is about a civil society and democracy, although it is not a matter of liberal democracy. People who are not party members are now elected to village committees, in some cases even on secret ballot in competitive elections where each adult has a vote. By 1997 voters had cast their votes in secret ballot in six out of the twenty-two provinces which had implemented the reforms. During the village elections in Liaoning province in 1995 around 60 per cent of the former village leaders lost their posts.[54] Available figures indicate that in some provinces as many as 25–50 per cent of the successful candidates are non-party members.[55] Some of them become party members after they are elected, but the majority continues to be outside the party. In other cases, however, the village assembly – dominated by older men and party members – *selects* the candidates according to their own standards. Often the township (*xiang*) party committee retains the right of veto,[56] and village officials have no power to alter the directives given by the central government. When the Western media discovered 'village democracy' and reported extensively about the new reforms, the Chinese Ministry of Civil Affairs decided to downplay the politically explosive term 'village democracy', and started referring to 'local governance reform' in the villages. I think Linda Jakobson sums up the development well when she claims that the Chinese leadership 'is pursuing a means of implementing good governance, not democracy'.[57]

There is no immediate reason for optimism when we look at the Chinese scene of democratic discourse. The voices of institutional democracy are few and scattered, and instead of powerful democratic institutions, neo-authoritarianism and evaluative approaches of moral elitism dominate the scene. Even if the protest movement of 1989 used the name 'democracy movement' the process of democracy was little understood. Even here the tendency towards moral elitism and lack of compromising strategies was evident.

The importance of morality or *de* is not only a rudiment from traditional Chinese thinking. It reproduces itself in modern society, and is still utilized by the regime for controlling purposes. At the same time the argument of moral purity has firm moorings all the way down to the grass-roots of society. The importance of law or *fa* in democratic development has not been thoroughly understood, not even among the Chinese opposition. One of those who have stressed the importance of law is the human rights activist Guo Luoji, formerly professor at Nanjing University. Guo has been an active spokesman for democracy and law ever since the Great Leap Forward in 1958.[58] In a speech held in Boston in June 1995, six years after the Tiananmen massacres, Guo makes a very interesting comment on the protest movement and its leaders.[59] The tragedy of the massacre in Beijing in 1989 was not only that people were brutally killed by the regime. Another tragedy lies in the fact that the protest movement itself had not developed a democratic consciousness, and that some of its leaders propagated the traditional and emotional moral issues of patriotism and blood-sacrifice rather than democracy and human rights. Some of its leaders even propagated that students should sacrifice themselves, and claimed that 'blood should run like a river' (*xue liu cheng he*) in order to 'open up the eyes of the Chinese people'.[60] Guo sums up that the movement in the end turned out to be an 'non-democratic movement (*bu minzhu yundong*)', and represented a step back from the more democratically oriented movement at Tiananmen in 1976. Other student leaders, however, are about to rethink the failed strategy from 1989.

Guo points out another important factor, the lack of understanding of the role of law in democratic society. He uses a thought-provoking metaphor in his speech to illustrate this point. The Chinese goddess of democracy, erected at the Gate of Heavenly Peace during the days of demonstration, held a torch in her hand. The Statue of Liberty, however, which is the original after which she was modelled, also clutches a book to her chest – a law book. Her Chinese equivalent lacks any trace of such a book. Just the burning torch, but no law-book to direct the march forward into democracy. Even the student movement resorted to heroism and moral elitism, the *de* of traditional China, without focusing on law, the *fa* of a democratic China.

In an article in the *Harvard Human Rights Journal*, Guo is developing his arguments about law.[61] He quotes Wang Hanbin, deputy director of the Law Committee of the Standing Committee of the NPC who said: '[I]n accordance with the stipulations of the Criminal Procedure Law, our nation's criminal procedure does not operate on a principle of guilt or innocence. Rather, we take facts as the base, and use law as our standard'.[62] The meaning of 'taking facts as the base' fully articulated would state: 'taking facts as grounds to prove the guilt of those who otherwise are innocent', Guo emphasizes. Again, there is a standard which stands over the individual. Taking 'facts as the base' and 'using law as our standard' are both aimed at finding guilt. The basic flaw of the Chinese legal system is that there is no presumption of innocence in that system. Some people are presumed 'guilty' by others for not following the prescribed standards, and consequently lose their dignity. Those who presume others to be guilty and who are representing the prescribed moral and legal standards enjoy privileges in their return for their accusations. As I see it in light of my own discussion, the standard in itself is the important factor here, not the presumption of innocence, which is an unprincipled presumption.

I do think the traditions of moral elitism with their stress on moral standards and perfectionism – even fundamentalism – and power and control are serious obstacles to a democratic development. Democratization cannot build on traditions of moral and evaluative elitism. However, the official image of 'good society' that we find in China is not a fixed and 'objective' cultural image. Even if democracy is not a necessary product of modernization and economic growth, weak voices of the 'imperfect' are heard.

Notes

1 See for instance Mu Guanzhong, 'Renkou suzhi xinlun' [New discussion on human quality], *Renkou yanjiu*, No. 3, 1989, p. 56. I discuss the technocratic approach to 'human quality' in my book: Børge Bakken, *The Exemplary Society, Human Improvement, Social Control and the Dangers of Modernity in China*, Oxford: Oxford University Press, 1999.

2 Bakken, *The Exemplary Society*.

3 On this debate see *Democratic China*, No. 2, 1990 quoted from He Baogang, 'Designing Democratic Institutions and the Problem of Evil: A Liberal Chinese Perspective', manuscript given to me by the author, Canberra 1995, p. 8.

4 Hu Ping in *Zhongguo zhi zhun* [China Spring], July 1988, p. 50, quoted in He Baogang 1995, p. 6.

5 Hu Ping, *Gei wo yige zhidian* [Give me a fulcrum], Taibei: Lianjing chuban gongshi, 1988, p. 178.

6 Ding Chu, in *Zhongguo zhi chun* [China Spring], No. 79, December 1989, p. 37, quoted in He Baogang 1995, p. 17.

7 'In the original Chinese: *Yi ri bei sheyao, san nian pa jingsheng.*' See Jin Rong, 'Yi 'xuan' dai 'ping' bu kequ' [Substituting 'evaluations' with 'elections' is not to be recommended], *Renshi yu rencai*, No.3, 1989, p. 25.

8 Zhang Yutian *et al.* (eds), *Xuexiao jiaoyu pingjia* [Evaluation in school education], Beijing: Zhongying minzu xueyuan chubanshe, 1987, p. 237.

9 Ibid., p. 15.

10 Hu Wei, Tang Yuan and Ouyang Hongsen, 'Guanyu pinde pingding zhibiao tixi de yanjiu [On the study of moral quality index systems], Part 4, *Shanghai jiaoyu*, No. 12, 1986, pp. 11–12.

11 Editorial article, 'Gaoxiao "san hao" xuesheng pingding gongzuo you dai wanshan' [The evaluation work of 'three-good students' in universities must be handled well], *Gaodeng jiaoyu yanjiu*, No. 3, 1986, pp. 98–99.

12 *Zhongguo jiaoyu bao*, 1 April 1986, p. 2.

13 Ibid., p. l20.

14 *Zhongguo baike nianjian 1982* [China encyclopaedic yearbook 1982] Beijing: Zhongguo dabaike quanshu chubanshe, 1982, p. 577.

15 Xie Hongmao and Chen Weifeng, 'Daxuesheng suzhi zonghe ceping tansuo' [Exploring the comprehensive appraisal of university students], *Fujian gaojiao yanjiu*, No. 1, 1991, p. 64.

16 Wang Huning, '"Wenge" fansi yu zhengzhi tizhi gaige' ['Cultural Revolution' and the reform of the political system], *Shijie jingji daobao*, 29 September 1986.

17 On Zhang Binjiu's theory and other neo-authoritarian approaches, see Liu Jun and Li Lin (eds.), *Xinquanwei zhuyi* [Neo-authoritarianism], Beijing jingji xueyuan chubanshe, Beijing 1989.

18 See Hu Ping, *Zai lixiang yu xianshi zhijian* [Between ideal and reality], Hong Kong: Tianyuan shuwu, 1990, pp. 151–63.

19 Hu Wei, 'Xiandai deyu pingjia de tedian ji gongneng' [The characteristics and functions of modern moral evaluation], *Shanghai jiaoyu*, No. 7–8, 1987, pp. 16–17.

20 Ibid., p. 18.

21 Ibid., p. 17.

22 Wang Keqian, 'Shilun jiazhi he pingjia' [On values and evaluations], *Shehui kexue jikan*, no.1, 1990, pp. 19–21.

23 Zhang *et al.* (eds), *Xuexiao jiaoyu pingjia*, pp. 236–37.

24 *Ha'erbin shi shangye xuexiao guanli zhidu* [The administrative system of Harbin business school], Harbin (Internal school document), 1987, p. 90.

25 Xia Daoxing, 'Gaige sixiang pinde ke kaocha de changshi' [An attempt to examine the reform of ideology and morality classes], *Jiaoxue yanjiu (xiaoxue ban)*, No. 4, 1987, p. 38. For a detailed description of evaluation of 'labour requirements' for primary school children, see Li Yuqi and Xie Yupu, 'Sheji laodong kepian shanghao laodong ke' [Planning a good labour class by using a labour card], *Hebei jiaoyu*, No. 10, 1989, p. 14.

26 Bakken, *The Exemplary Society.*

27 See Susan Shirk, *Competitive Comrades: Career Incentives and Student Strategies in China*, Los Angeles, Berkeley: University of California Press, 1982.

28 Zhang *et al.* (eds), *Xuexiao jiaoyu pingjia*, p. 240.

29 Colin A. Ronan and Joseph Needham, *The Shorter Science and Civilization in China*, Cambridge: Cambridge University Press, vol. 1, pp. 157ff.

30 Cynthia Brokaw, 'Guidebooks to Social and Moral Success: the Morality Books in 16th and 17th Century China', *Transactions of the International Conference of Orientalists in Japan*, No. 27, 1982, pp. 137–41; Cynthia Brokaw, *The Ledgers of Merit and Demerit. Social Change and Moral Order in Late Imperial China*, Princeton, NJ: Princeton University Press, 1991.

31 Ibid., p. 121.

32 Yü Chün-fang has noted that in theory and practice this system of merits and demerits bears a strong resemblance to the ritual complex of merit-making in contemporary societies where Theravada Buddhism is practised. One accumulates merit or demerit and, once acquired, it entails automatic consequences. This ideology of merit-making is clearly shared by the compilers of morality books. Merit is similar to money. For instance Burmese do careful merit bookkeeping in order to 'calculate the current state of their merit bank'. A quantified prayer practice is shown by the masters of the Buddha-beans who count beans for mentioning the name of the Buddha in prayers. See Yü Chün-fang, *The Revival of Buddhism in China. Chu-hung and the Late Ming Synthesis*, New York: Columbia University Press, 1981, pp. 121–22, 128.

33 Hu Shoufen, *Deyu yuanli* [Principles of moral education], revised edition, Beijing: Beijing shifan daxue chubanshe, 1989, p. 184.

34 Ren Xiao'ai, 'Jianli tuanjie, minzhu, pingheng, hexie de shisheng guanxi. Xin shiqi banzhuren gongzuo chuyi zhi yi' [Build a united, democratic, balanced, and harmonious relation between teachers and students. My humble opinion on class teacher work in a new era]. (Part one), *Beijing jiaoyu*, No. 9, 1988, pp. 37–38, and (Part four), *Beijing jiaoyu*, No. 12, 1988, pp. 16–17.

35 Xie Hongmao and Chen Weifeng, 'Daxuesheng suzhi zonghe ceping tansuo' [Exploring the comprehensive appraisal of University students], *Fujian gaojiao yanjiu*, No. 1, 1991, p. 65.

36 Ibid., pp. 63–66.

37 Shi Jun, 'Mangmu 'panbi' bu keqi' [Blind 'climbing' is not desirable], *Renshi yu rencai*, No. 8, 1990, p. 38.

38 Zhou Lu, Yang Ruohe and Hu Ruyong, *Qingshaonian fanzui zonghe zhili duice xue* [Studies in how to deal with comprehensive control of juvenile crime], Beijing: Qunzhong chubanshe, 1986, p. 211.

39 Wang Xingzhou, 'Guanyu daode pingjia de jiu ge wenti' [On some problems of moral evaluation], *Dongbei shida xuebao (zhexue shehui kexue ban)*, No. 3, 1987, pp. 3–4.

40 The 47 items are: (1) hygiene habits, (2) individual habits, (3) public welfare work, (4) house work, (5) study habits, (6) habits of collective life, (7) civilized

language habits, (8) approach to public affairs, (9) thrift, (10) self-respect, (11) self-love, (12) self-dignified conduct, (13) self-confidence, (14) self-criticism, (15) independency, (16) self-support, (17) self-strength, (18) self-control, (19) sense of pride and dignity, (20) respect for parents, (21) respect for teachers, (22) friendliness towards fellow-students, (23) respect for working people, (24) reliability, (25) to decline modestly (*qianrang*), (26) modesty, (27) honesty, (28) feelings of sympathy, (29) understanding, (30) making a clear distinction between right and wrong, (31) loving the collective, (32) cooperation and unity, (33) democratic feeling, (34) respect for discipline and law, (35) duty and responsibility feeling, (36) concrete (no empty words) in matters relating to work, (37) thirst for knowledge, (38) will-power, (39) decisive character, (40) creativeness, (41) effectiveness, (42) abilities of forming social relations, (43) consciousness of participation, (44) uniting strength, (45) power of leadership, (46) ability to adjust to change, (47) aesthetic judgement. See Hu Wei, Tang Yuan and Ouyang Hongsen, 'Guanyu pinde pingding zhibiao tixi de yanjiu' [On the study of moral quality index systems], (Part 1), *Shanghai jiaoyu*, No. 9, 1986, pp. 13–14.

41 Hu Wei, Tang Yuan and Ouyang Hongsen, 'Guanyu pinde pingding zhibiao tixi de yanjiu' [On the study of moral quality index systems], (Part 2), *Shanghai jiaoyu*, No. 10, 1986, p. 8.

42 Hu Wei, Tang Yuan and Ouyang Hongsen, 'Guanyu pinde pingding zhibiao tixi de yanjiu' [On the study of moral quality index systems], (Part 3), *Shanghai jiaoyu*, No. 11, 1986, p. 14.

43 Perez Zagorin, *Ways of Lying*, Cambridge, Mass: Harvard University Press, 1990.

44 Ibid., p. 1.

45 Ibid., p. 3.

46 The phenomenon is known as Nicodemism, and the term derives from 'Nicodemites', the name the reformer John Calvin gave the members of underground churches among Catholics who betrayed their faith by conforming outwardly to Catholic rites but in reality supported Protestantism. Its origin lay in the Gospel of John, which depicts the Pharisee Nicodemus as a believer in Christ who concealed his faith for fear of the Jews and came to hear Jesus secretly by night. See John 3, 1–2: 'There was a man of the Pharisees, named Nicodemus, a ruler of the Jews: The same came to Jesus by night, and said unto him, Rabbi, we know that thou art a teacher come from God: for no man can do these miracles that thou doest, except God be with him'.

47 See Niccoló Machiavelli, *The Prince*, Toronto, Bantam Books, 1981 (The original was published in 1513).

48 Here quoted from Zagorin, *Ways of Lying*, p. 6.

49 See Godwin C. Chu, 'The Emergence of the New Chinese Culture', in Wen-Shing Tseng and David Y.H. Wu (eds), *Chinese Culture and Mental Health*, London: Academic Press, 1985, pp. 20–21.

50 Alvin Toffler, *Previews and Premises*, London: Pan Books, 1984, p. 97.

51 Sun Longji, *Zhongguo wenhua de shenceng jiegou* [The deep-structure of Chinese society], Hong Kong: Jixian she, 1983, pp. 90–91.

52 Xiao Qiang in an interview in the Danish daily *Information*, February 1997.

53 Allen Choate, 'Local Governance in China', paper presented at the seminar Asian Perspectives: Focus on China, held in Washington, D.C. March 20, 1997, pp. 12–13.

54 Linda Jakobson, *A Million Truths: Ten Years in China*, New York: M.Evans, 1998, Chapter 6, 'The battle against despotism'.

55 Rod Mickleburgh, 'Rare freedom thrives in Chinese villages', *Globe Post*, Toronto, 30 January 1995.

56 Anne F.Thurston, 'Village Elections in Lishu County: An Eye Witness Account', *China Focus*, 1 May 1995, p. 3.

57 Jakobson, *A Million Truths*.

58 Guo Luoji criticized the Cultural Revolution, but it was only after his criticism of the Deng regime in 1982 that he was not allowed to write or publish. After 1989 he also lost his professorship at Nanjing University and his Party membership. Neither was he allowed to teach any longer. He was finally allowed to leave China, and in exile in 1992 he sued the Party Committee at Nanjing University and the Education Commission for violating his human rights.

59 Guo Luoji, speech manuscript. Speech held 4 June 1995 in Boston.

60 Guo here uses a hotly debated quotation from Chai Ling, the student leader and 'commander of Tiananmen square' during the protest of 1989. Her remarks were made in an interview with Philip Cunningham on 28 May that year and recorded on video. Whether the meaning of Chai Ling's words are interpreted as 'should run like a river' or 'will run like a river' as the debate goes, the theme of sacrifice still remains. According to Guo, she and some others among the leaders of the student-movement totally lacked the will to compromise and the tolerance needed in a democratic organization.

61 Guo Luoji, 'A Human Rights Critique of the Chinese Legal System', *Harvard Human Rights Journal*, Vol. 9, Spring 1996, pp. 1–14.

62 See *Renmin Ribao* [People's Daily], 12 December 1980, p. 4. (Guo 'A Human Rights Critique', p. 13.)

6 SOCIAL VALUES AND CONSENSUAL POLITICS IN COLONIAL HONG KONG

Tak-Wing Ngo

If democracy can take different forms, then so too can authoritarianism. The case of Hong Kong under British rule is perhaps a rare type of authoritarianism. Hong Kong had one of the most liberal and pluralist societies in Asia, yet was until recently still governed by an authoritarian political system. It does not match what O'Donnell and Schmitter called the 'liberalized authoritarianism' since there was no liberalization process.[1] A high degree of civil liberties had already existed for decades. It may be more properly called a 'liberal authoritarianism' or a 'pluralistic authoritarianism'. The use of the prefixes 'liberal' and 'pluralistic' is not to give credit to a regime under colonial rule. Rather it is to highlight the paradoxical nature of the regime: on the one hand, there was no election and no universal suffrage until 1982, no political party until the 1990s and still, on the eve of handover, no fully elected assembly; on the other hand, there had been no shortage of interest-group activities, social movements, and lobbying. In this apparent mismatch, the process of policy deliberation had been painstaking and decisions were not taken by a single power centre. Such a system existed for quite a long time before political reform began in 1985 in preparation for the transfer of sovereignty in 1997. This period of post-war colonial rule prior to the introduction of political reform in 1985 is the focus of this paper.

The paradoxical system of colonial Hong Kong during the period makes a good case for taking up the quest, in this volume, of relations between culture and politics in Asia. This is so because the key to unlock this paradox has been commonly seen as lying in the political culture of the Hong Kong Chinese. We are often told that political acquiescence came from a combination of Confucian values and refugee mentality, allowing a pluralist society to co-exist with an authoritarian political system. This view is re-examined in this chapter: instead of seeing political acquiescence as resulting from some kind of long-existing, cultural values by default, this paper argues that social values are indeed part of the political process, created by and yet constraining the body politic. Using Hong Kong as a case, the following discussion thus aims at highlighting the mutual constitution of social norms and politics in shaping the form of rule.

The Authoritarian Political System

Before we re-examine the cultural explanations, let us first look at the features of this pluralist authoritarianism and the circumstances that gave rise to its paradoxical nature. One outstanding feature is the remarkable institutional longevity of the political set-up.[2] It is remarkable because the basic system of the government was formally the same until the 1980s as that of a hundred years earlier. This system was, as one sceptical observer describes, 'about as democratic as the Soviet Union'.[3] It is commonly seen as a kind of bureaucratic polity.[4] The colonial government bureaucracy is viewed as the only significant political institution in the polity, with almost complete monopoly of political power. Other political actors were co-opted into the political process primarily upon the initiative of the bureaucracy, and were therefore believed to be subordinated to bureaucratic control.[5]

This unchanging political structure was, to a large extent, the result of the China factor. After the Second World War, decolonization occurred in many British colonies. The China factor prevented a similar process to take place in Hong Kong. The new government of China insisted that the Treaties signed by the Ching court to cede Hong Kong to Britain were unequal treaties. The People's Republic of China did not recognize them as binding. Hong Kong was still regarded as a part of the Chinese territory, and the Chinese government would resume its sovereignty at an appropriate moment. The normal decolonization process, and the development of a representative government, had no place in Hong Kong.[6]

The British government legitimized the absence of political reform in Hong Kong with the view that an elected government run by the Hong Kong Chinese would be totally unacceptable to Beijing. It was believed that China's tolerance towards the British colonial rule over Hong Kong would end if the colony made any move towards internal self-government. A government produced by popular election would have unpredictable consequences for both the British and the Chinese governments. On the one hand, sensitive political issues could be raised by candidates during elections. On the other hand, there was no control over the background of the candidates. One well-informed writer has emphasized that the British government would not choose to remain nominally responsible for Hong Kong if decisions were subject to the veto of locally elected communists. Nor would the Chinese government tolerate the governance of the colony to be shaped by elected pro-Taipei councillors. If this happened, the 'delicate equilibrium of British, Chinese and local interests would be upset and the inevitable result would be the reincorporation of Hong Kong into the People's Republic'.[7]

Such a constitutional constraint virtually 'froze' the political structure of Hong Kong until 1985, before the signing of the Sino–British Joint Declaration to hand over Hong Kong to China in 1997. In the 40 years between 1945 and 1985, Hong Kong was governed under a peculiar political regime. It was peculiar since some common political institutions that could be found even in authoritarian regimes were absent. Not only was there no popular form of political representation, but there was also no political party, no election,[8] and no elected assembly. The absence of these normal mechanisms of interest arbitration and political legitimation poses a paradox because such an anachronistic political structure governed one of the most sophisticated economies and societies in Asia with apparent success.

A Modern Dynamic Pluralist Society

The kind of society Hong Kong developed out of the above anachronistic political system is often associated with a democratic form of governments. Dahl calls this a 'modern dynamic pluralist society'.[9] It is characterized by a high level of income per capita, long-run growth in per capita income, a high level of urbanization, a small agricultural population, great occupational diversity, extensive literacy, popularized higher education, a free market economy, and high levels of community well-being in terms of life expectancy, infant mortality, etc.

Hong Kong had more or less attained these levels of modernity by the late seventies. But more important than these was its pluralist character. Following the common law tradition, everything was permitted in Hong Kong except what was forbidden. The people enjoyed a high level of freedoms of expression, association, and assembly.[10] There were a great number of social, economic and political groups and organizations autonomous from government control. This multitude of civic organizations helped to disperse power, influence and resources away from any single centre towards a variety of independent individuals and groups. Such a plurality of groups and resources, as Dahl puts it, allowed the actors to resist unilateral domination, compete with one another for advantages, engage in conflict and bargaining, and pursue independent goals and actions on their own.[11]

Although a modern dynamic pluralist society tends to support the development of democratic government, Dahl is quick to point out that it is neither necessary nor sufficient for democratic governments.[12] He gives the examples of South Korea and Taiwan in the eighties. One of the most important reasons preventing their development into democratic governments was the control over the means of violence by the government. Again, Hong Kong raises an interesting puzzle in this regard. Unlike other authoritarian regimes, the government of Hong Kong did not rule just by fiat or coercion. This was not only due to the fear of provoking anti-colonial feelings if excessive coercive measures were taken. It was also due to the fact that any popular resentment that might result in social unrest would frighten away investment and, at the same time, invite unwelcome ministerial and parliamentary attention from London. Because of these considerations, quite opposite to any rule by fiat, the colonial government was in practice 'painfully sensitive' to public opinion and rarely took steps that might arouse widespread opposition.[13]

The mismatch between an anachronistic authoritarian political system and a modern dynamic pluralist society in Hong Kong was partly sustained by the peculiar geo-political constraint that Hong Kong faced. One writer argues that since the only alternative to colonial rule is rule by socialist China, China unintentionally becomes the bulwark for continued colonial rule. Hong Kong people's realization of the situation, and hence their political quiescence, relieved the colonial government from the need to resort to coercive measures in order to maintain an authoritarian regime.[14] This is reflected in the answer given to an opinion survey conducted in the mid-eighties. Over 70 per cent of the respondents answered that although the political system of Hong Kong was not perfect, it was the best Hong Kong could have under existing circumstances.[15]

This argument falls well in line with the theory of regime transition put forward by Przeworski. He maintains that what matters for the stability of any regime is not the legitimacy of that particular system but the presence or absence of preferable alternatives. A regime will not collapse unless and until some alternative is organized in such a way as to present a real choice for individuals.[16] While accepting the basic premises of Przeworski's argument, I nevertheless contend that his thesis cannot fully explain how Hong Kong's paradoxical political system was maintained under colonial rule. Although this argument can explain the lack of impetus for regime change in Hong Kong, it does not mean that the existing system would automatically function effectively, in response to the demand of a pluralist society. The inadequacy of Przeworski's argument is obvious once we recognize that such a nineteenth-century political system was charged with the responsibilities of running a modern economy, resolving interest conflicts within a pluralist society, enlisting political support without the use of widespread coercion, and upholding a non-elected government without jeopardizing the freedom of expression, the rule of law and the independence of the judiciary. The fact that the regime not only survived, but remained stable and effective thus requires further explanations.

Culture and Politics

Given that Hong Kong is predominantly a Chinese society, the effectiveness of authoritarian rule in the colony has often been attributed to the presence of a Confucian culture. Such a culture is, as argued in the chapter of Geir Helgesen and Li Xing in this volume, one that prefers order, consensus, and strong political authority to individual rights. Huntington puts this cultural factor in persuasive terms which are, interestingly, well-received by both supporters and critics of the Asian regimes:

> Classic Chinese Confucianism and its derivatives in Korea, Vietnam, Singapore, Taiwan, and (in diluted fashion) Japan emphasized the group

over the individual, authority over liberty, and responsibilities over rights. Confucian societies lacked a tradition of rights against the state; to the extent that individual rights did exist, they were created by the state. Harmony and cooperation were preferred over disagreement and competition. The maintenance of order and respect for hierarchy were central values. The conflict of ideas, groups, and parties was viewed as dangerous and illegitimate.[17]

This theme has long been the mainstream explanation in accounting for the effective functioning of the regime in Hong Kong. Lau Siu-kai, for example, suggests that the Hong Kong Chinese, who constituted the majority of the population, were family-centred and politically apathetic. They showed a passive adaption to the political system and resolved their problems through their own familial resources and networks. Social demands were accommodated through private networks and hence were atomized and depoliticized.[18] This was accompanied by a strong sense of political powerlessness, and an ethos of upholding harmony and authority.[19] As a result, there was little demand for political participation and democratic reform.

In such a way, the co-existence of an authoritarian political system with a dynamic economy and stable society is seen as a workable combination rather than a mismatch. It apparently adds another exemplary case of the so-called 'paternalistic Asian authoritarianism', viewed by Fukuyama as a serious contender to Western liberal democracy.[20] In fact, the Hong Kong case has received such wide applause that even the Chinese government has promised to keep its existing system unchanged for 50 years after China resumed its sovereignty in 1997.

This type of cultural explanation suffers from a number of problems stemming from a gross over-simplification of state–society and culture–politics relations. In the first place, we can immediately detect a circularity in the above argument when the absence of social conflicts is taken as evidence of the political aloofness of the Chinese society and this aloofness is in turn used to explain the absence of social conflicts.[21] Furthermore, there is an implicit tendency in cultural explanations to equate political stability with the absence of conflicts. Conflicts abound in Confucian societies. In the case of Hong Kong, the romanticized view of a homogeneous and atomized society with a total absence of social conflicts and political demands is certainly a misrepresentation. Observers have increasingly realized that interest group activities and collective actions – from student activism to labour protests and environmental movements – emerged in the 1970s to become part of the political life in Hong Kong.[22] Stability and effective rule thus depended not on the absence of conflicts, but on how conflicts were managed, accommodated, or resolved. One of the reasons why the democratic form of government is closely associated with a modern dynamic pluralist society is that a democratic government offers an effective means of processing and resolving inter-group conflicts.[23] The question for Hong Kong is thus how interest arbitration was undertaken and how decisions were justified in the absence of both democratic mechanisms and coercive measures.

Using cultural explanations, it may again be hypothesized that social values can facilitate the achievement of compromise and consensus in resolving interest conflicts. This is a possible explanation. But the problem is that cultural explanations tend to assume that paternalistic consensus/compromise can be achieved automatically by cultural default. Such an assumption overlooks two important aspects central to our understanding of political life. First, it ignores the fact that social values (either Three Principles of the People, *Pancasila*, or laissez-fairism) can be manipulated in such a way as to facilitate the achievement of a certain political consensus. Second, it fails to recognize the key role played by political institutions and strategies in linking up the politically constructed social values and consensus. This means that even if we accept a cultural explanation, we still have to work out which particular set of cultural norms is mobilized to serve as a governing ideology; what political strategies and institutions exist to create/sustain that governing ideology; and how conflicts are resolved/accommodated by those strategies, institutions, and values in the political process.

The rest of this chapter elaborates on the above-mentioned premises by looking at how a very specific set of economic and social values (commonly falling under the label 'laissez-faire') were maintained alongside a set of policy networks (namely, the advisory bodies) to facilitate interest deliberation and to achieve political consensus in colonial Hong Kong. In doing so, it hopes to highlight the complicated relations between culture and politics.

Alternative Channel of Political Participation: Government by Consultation

Before discussing the role of social values, let us first look at the kind of political institutions created by the colonial government to meet the demand for political participation in a pluralist society. Just as a feudal monarchy can be modified to exist side by side with a representative government, the anachronistic colonial system can also be modified to perform the need for enlisting political input and support for effective governance. This has been done through the development of the so-called 'government by consultation'. An elaborated advisory system was developed by the government to achieve this governing principle of government by consultation. This system provided a channel of interest representation in the absence of popular electoral participation.

Under this system, members of social groups were co-opted into different advisory bodies to reflect 'public opinion' to the government on policy making. By being sensitive to public opinion, the colonial government could claim that although it was not a government by the people, it was a government for the people.[24] This enabled the government to justify the continuation of colonial rule in the international opinion and the continuation of an authoritarian political system for the colony.

The number of advisory bodies grew from a few dozens in the early post-war years to over four hundred in the eighties. Advisory bodies of one kind or another were linked to nearly all government departments and quasi-governmental bodies. They ranged from statutory bodies with executive powers to *ad hoc* committees. They might be charged with the task of examining a narrow issue, such as the allocation of textile export quota, or might be responsible for broad topics, such as trade and industrial matters. In constitutional terms, the highest policy-making and law-making bodies – the Executive Council (ExCo) and the Legislative Council (LegCo) – were also advisory bodies to the colonial Governor. A Governor could, in principle, reject the advice of the two councils. In that case, however, he would have to explain to the Secretary of State in Britain about his reasons for doing so.

The existence of an advisory system is not unique to Hong Kong. Japan, for example, has between two and three hundred advisory councils, committees, or groups attached to government agencies. In assessing the role of the advisory bodies in Japan, Pempel suggests that they not only function as important 'lightning rods for dissent', but also very often help to reconciliate the differences among their members.[25] Similar functions were also performed by Hong Kong's advisory bodies. Nevertheless, the system in Hong Kong also exhibited a number of distinctive features.

First, in the absence of elected institutions, the advisory system became an informal substitute for political representation. Usually, members of the public were appointed by the Governor or head of departments to sit on the advisory committees. They were appointed in their private capacity, not as representatives of any groups, to offer their personal advice to the government. In practice, however, most were office-bearers of peak associations or major interest groups. The government expected them to reflect their associations' views as well as to persuade their associations to accept government decisions.[26] Members knew that they wore two hats, while the associations knew who spoke for them inside these bodies.[27]

The system worked under a delicate understanding. The co-opted associations were given a voice in the policy process through their informal representatives. In return, they gave support to the policies adopted after consultation. By co-opting leaders of peak associations and major interest groups into the advisory committees, the system served to bring these interest associations into a co-responsibility in public policy formation.[28] In principle, the recommendations put forward by an advisory body did not have any formal binding power on the associations involved. However, unless a decision was detrimental to its interests, an association would not refuse to support that decision because if it repeatedly refused to do so it might lose its seat at the next appointment.

Second, the advisory system was also an informal mechanism of government licensing. By appointing the leader of an interest group into an important advisory body, the government recognized, in essence, the group as indispensable negotiators in a particular area of policy concern. Social groups were eager to have their members appointed because they sought to increase their status as the legitimate representative and spokes-man of a social collective. Co-option into the network was a recognition by the government of a group's representation. The official recognition, or government licensing, and the privilege to participate in policy making in turn became a definite asset for the group in attracting members, especially the economically more powerful ones in the constituency. This subsequently served to enhance the group's representation. The relation-ship between becoming a recognized representative and becoming a partici-pant in policy-making was thus mutually reinforcing.

Third, the advisory system was a source of political legitimation for the colonial government. The apex of this advisory system was the LegCo, a parliament-like assembly responsible for law making, policy debate, and budgetary control. Although the LegCo performed some of the common parliamentary functions, it was formally only advisory in status and its members were, until 1985, entirely appointed by the Governor. The total number of LegCo members (including the president, who was the Governor himself) increased gradually after the Second World War, from 16 in 1950 to 25 in 1970 and to 46 in 1980. Normally, about half of the members were government officials and the other half were appointed members of the public, usually called the 'unofficials'. To increase the representativeness of these unofficials, and hence that of the LegCo as a whole, the government also appointed these unofficials to sit on a whole range of advisory bodies. As a result, the LegCo became the focal point of the entire web of the advisory network. Most of the important advisory committees had unofficial LegCo members appointed either as the chairmen or as senior members.

Setting aside the question of 'representativeness' of the entire advisory system, the consultation exercise was a genuine one. In the LegCo, the ExCo and other advisory committees, the opinions of appointed members were highly respected. The Governor rarely opposed the majority views of the ExCo, especially when there was a consensus among the unofficial members.[29] Likewise, the government seldom acted against the consensual views of the unofficial LegCo members. Although an official majority of LegCo seats was maintained until the eighties, it had not been used to overcome the unanimous opposition of the unofficials since 1953.[30]

It was through this advisory system that popular legitimacy of the government was constructed. Through co-opting selective interest groups into the advisory bodies, the government granted monopolized representation status to these groups. In return, the advisory bodies also enjoyed a certain degree of legitimation because they reflected the views of the 'representative' groups. Ultimately, all major advisory bodies were linked to the LegCo through overlapping memberships. The LegCo was in essence a super-advisory body. With the presence of membership in a whole range of advisory committees, it 'represented' the views across social collectives. This 'representation of views' was the main justification of government rule by consultation.

Although members of the public as well as the unofficials recognized the limit of this kind of participation, they also realized the constraints over constitutional reform under the prevailing Sino–Hong Kong relationship. As mentioned earlier, the majority of people thought that the existing system, although imperfect, was the best Hong Kong could have under the circumstances. For the unofficials, they knew the limit of permissibility under the system of consultation. One analyst observes that these unofficials did not wish to play a really vigorous role. The overriding need to preserve the existing form of governance required that the authority of the government would not be weakened by constant attacks on its competence or on its policies. Criticisms could be made but they should not be pressed home.[31] The system thus provided a constant appearance of unity. The unofficials were seen to be acting in concert with the government. In return, the government appeared to be acting in accordance with the wishes of the community. One veteran unofficial of the LegCo and ExCo, Lydia Dunn, who was later knighted as Baroness, proudly declared that: 'This system is our way, our style of Government.'[32] However, it should be realized that this style of government depended not upon any cultural ethos of respect for order and harmony, but upon pragmatic recognition of the political reality.

Oligarchic Politics

Since all the members of the advisory system (including the ExCo and the LegCo) were appointed by the government, the advisory system was conveniently used as a means of political inclusion and exclusion. It was deployed to enlist the support of the powerful. Stinchcombe argues that legitimation depends not so much on an abstract principle or the assent of the governed. 'The person *over whom power is exercised* is not usually as important as *other power-holders*.'[33] Tilly adds that legitimacy 'is the probability that other authorities will act to confirm the decisions of a given authority'.[34] To gauge the political support of other power-holders, the colonial government was obliged to share policy-making power with them by co-opting them into the various advisory bodies, particularly the ExCo and the LegCo. These co-opted groups supported, or even defended, government policies in exchange for privileges in using public goods, inclusion in the policy process, and access to insider information.

In his influential study of government-business relations, Lindblom maintains that 'public affairs in market-oriented systems are in the hands of two groups of leaders, government and business, who must collaborate and that, to make the system work, government leadership must often defer to business leadership'.[35] This is particularly true for Hong Kong. The post-war government faced periodic floods of refugees into the colony which caused enormous financial burden and social problems. The government relied entirely on the business sector to provide jobs for these refugees and to generate revenue for social service provision.[36] Naturally, the economically powerful businessmen and the organized business interests became the other power-holders from whom elite legitimation was acquired. They were thus the main targets of consultation and co-option.

The dominance of a few political groups in the policy network of the government was very obvious. Generations of political scientists in Hong Kong have documented 'an unholy alliance of businessmen and bureaucrats'.[37] Rear described in 1971 those unofficial members of the LegCo and the ExCo as forming a 'fairly tight-knit group' directly representing the interests of big business and banking, the industrialists and the employers.[38] He examines the background of the councillors and finds a high degree of inter-marriage and interlocking directorship. In another extensive survey of major policy-making bodies in the mid seventies, Davies tracks down their overlapping membership and finds that the advisory bodies were controlled by a relatively small elite group.[39] There were some one to two hundred people who could be found in all parts of the advisory networks. Among the 775 places in the various government councils, boards, and committees in 1975, he finds that 21 per cent of the membership controlled 46 per cent of the total committee votes. Of this 21 per cent, 38.9 per cent were directors in 56 large companies and they held 24 per cent of the directorships.[40] These companies, in Davies' words, were 'the richest, the oldest, and the most all-embracing, and they own more property in Hong Kong than any other equivalent group'.[41]

This system of political representation thus constituted an oligarchy. The domination of business and the exclusion of labour in the top policy networks of the system were very obvious. Having said that, it should be noted that political inclusion and exclusion under this oligarchic system was a matter of degree rather than an all-or-nothing matter. First of all, while labour and other lower class groups were conspicuously absent in the top policy networks, they were accommodated in the less important boards and committees. From the early seventies onwards, such a mechanism of political co-option was extended to the grass-roots level through appointing local leaders into district level advisory bodies and committees. Second, the appointment system allowed the government to expand political representation by co-opting newly emerged groups and sectors into the existing system, without changing the basic structure and rules of the game. For instance, the number of unofficial members in the ExCo and the LegCo had gradually increased over the years. This was accompanied by an increase in the membership of professionals and members of the middle class.[42] One author calls this process of political accommodation one of 'administrative absorption of politics'.[43] He argues that in the absence of democratic participation, existing or emerging elites were co-opted to create a consensual community that helped to legitimize policy decisions.

In sum, the system of political co-option developed in Hong Kong helped to cope with the problem of interest representation. This was done especially by co-opting the economically and socially powerful into the policy process. However, although political co-option constituted an alternative channel for political participation under an authoritarian system, it did not resolve the problem of policy deliberation. The oligarchy – composed mainly of dominant business interests – did not constitute a homogeneous group. Longstreth reminds us that capitalists meet as 'hostile brothers' in the political system.[44] Although they are capable of joining forces to meet an external threat to 'bourgeois class relations', they are more characteristically divided among themselves by their market position, policy goals, ideological orientations, etc. While they did not dispute the fundamentals, that is, the creation of wealth, they disputed over an ever-shifting category of secondary issues – such as trade policy, tax rates, and regulation and promotion of business. How intra-oligarchic conflicts were arbitrated is thus an important issue to look at.

The Formation of Consensus

The problem for the government concerning policy deliberation was how to give more say to the powerful and yet keep the subordinate happy. This was important because the conflict over policies ran the danger of turning into a conflict over the political system. If the less-represented groups were persistently upset in policy outcomes because of their subordinate position in the system, they would likely turn their attention from policy goals to the question of who controlled the policy agenda. If so, the entire system of government by consultation would be jeopardized by ongoing struggles about the question of political representation. The erosion of a democratic system into political chaos in Sri Lanka, discussed by Kloos in this volume, is a good case in hand. The Tamils resorted ultimately to armed struggles against an electoral system that consistently deprived ethnic minorities of their voices in governance.

A similar problem was once foreseeable in Hong Kong. The riots of 1966 and 1967, and the proliferation of social movements in Hong Kong during the 1970s are outbursts of popular dissatisfaction towards oligarchic politics. Subordinate interests being excluded or marginalized in the policy networks had to resort to extra-institutional means of social mobilization to press home their demand. Under the colonial setting, social movements could easily be linked to identity politics, which could eventually become an anti-colonial struggle.

This problem was resolved and avoided by forging a compromise and consensus among members of the oligarchy. Consensus is not to be understood here as the absence of disagreement or simply elite collusion. As Kavanagh and Morris put it, it is more useful to think of consensus as 'a set of parameters which bounded the set of policy options regarded by senior politicians and civil servants as administratively practicable, economi- cally affordable and politically acceptable'.[45] By setting a boundary on the policy options, this consensus set a limit on both the bureaucratic and the business elite about their privilege and relative power. This compromise and consensus formed a pact of alliance among the oligarchic interests. It was reached 'on the basis of mutual guarantees for the 'vital interests' of those entering into it'.[46]

The pact involved the inseparable components of upholding the existing oligarchy and pursuing a laissez-faire policy. Hong Kong has been well known for being the only existing modern economy that came closest to the laissez-faire ideal. It was here that an economic policy was appropriated and re-articulated to become a political mechanism for consensus building. Under the pact, besides the privilege of sharing policy-making power, the oligarchic interests were guaranteed that their vital interest of profit making would be protected and facilitated by the government. In this regard, the British government of Hong Kong had never tried to hide its prime objective of promoting capital accumulation – a phenomenon that we ironically recognize from the 'Asian Values' debate. The government emphasized that the creation of wealth should have higher priority than the distribution of wealth. As a result, a range of pro-business policy measures was adopted by the government. These included low profits tax, limited social welfare provisions, minimal labour protection, free enterprise, and free capital inflow and outflow. They were grouped under the label of a 'laissez-faire' policy. All of them worked to facilitate profit maximization. The oligarchic control of policy-making by big business allowed business to veto labour protective measures and other welfare policies that might lower its profit.

Although the oligarchic interests benefited from the pro-business policies in facilitating wealth creation, they sought more than that. All sought to pursue rent-seeking activities – that is, using their political privilege to obtain preferential resources while transferring the cost to others. If the government allowed a specific group of business elite to undertake rent-seeking activities ruthlessly, those excluded from, or marginalized in, the oligarchy would seek political reform to redistribute political power. This would undermine the whole system of government by consultation. The compromise reached in the pact thus included the absence of preferential policies for selected interests. By insisting on such a pact of constrained privileges, the government sought to resolve the dilemma of allowing domination of some privileged few in the policy process while ensuring that policy outcomes were acceptable to the less well represented and the wider population of players. It represented the solution offered by Wildavsky to Lindblom's problem about business capture of the government: reducing the abuse of public power by business through reducing government intervention.[47]

The principle of non-selective intervention was implemented through a policy commonly labelled again as laissez-faire. In contrary to some existing arguments, this policy was undertaken not because of the lack of government capacity to intervene, but because of deliberate government action.[48] In the words of one Governor, Sir David Trench, 'Hong Kong's generally laissez-faire economic policies have always been based on considered decisions, not mere paralysis of mind and will'.[49] In practice, the policy was not only undertaken with considered decisions, but also maintained with what one analyst described as 'an almost religious fervour'.[50] This was because it represented a constituent component of the pact of alliance that was essential for the maintenance of the existing regime. As a matter of fact, upholding this laissez-faire policy was not easy since it was constantly being undermined by calls for intervention.[51]

With a few exceptions, the post-war colonial government adhered strictly to this principle. Demands for preferential allocation of resources to particular business sectors and market protection for specific enterprises were all rejected. For example, there were repeated demands throughout the fifties and sixties from the manufacturers for government assistance in the form of medium- to long-term loans to industries. All were opposed by the government and the ExCo. Several declining industries made loud appeals to the government for assistance, which fell on deaf ears. The government declined to help the steel-rolling industry and suggested instead that the industry should contract substantially.[52] The enamelware and wig industries asked for labour inducement assistance but were turned down flat.[53] The enamelware industry was at that time the fourth biggest industry in Hong Kong. The appeal from the textile industry suffered the same fate.[54] The government also refused to help industrial upgrading for expanding industries such as the electronics industry. There had been strong pressure for government assistance to the electronics industry since the late seventies. The industry faced serious structural problems, such as reduction in the size of firms and the low level of technology. Industrial research and development was lagging far behind that of other East Asian countries. Proposals such as the imposition of a levy on electronics exports to support common research and product development facilities were resisted by the government. It was not until 1990 that the government eventually approved the establishment of a technology centre, which was not to be fully operational until some years later.

Despite these futile demands for preferential treatment, representatives of those organized interests co-opted into the LegCo, the ExCo, and major advisory committees were willing to restrain their conflicts in order not to undermine the whole system. The existing system allowed them privileged access to information, deliberation in policy actions, and prestige in the community. Through upholding the laissez-faire policy, they shared the common interests of having low taxation, free flow of capital, absence of government interference and low labour welfare. Whenever conflicts arose over the deployment of resources, it was settled with reference to the principle of non-selective intervention.

The Role of Social Values

So far we have discussed the political strategies and institutions responsible for conflict resolution and consensus building in post-war Hong Kong. We can see that effective rule in this pluralist society did not come about automatically by cultural default. Rather, it was upheld by painstaking maintenance of the above-mentioned strategies and institutions. However, it does not mean that cultural ethos or social values played no role in this process. Indeed, social norms and values did help increase the acceptance of such a process. The most important values related to this were freedom and opportunities. Both of them were linked to the notion of laissez-faire.

In post-war Hong Kong, laissez-faire stood as an antithesis to the absence of free enterprise, limited personal freedom, domination of the ruling party, extensive state control, absence of mobility and personal opportunity, and economic backwardness in socialist China. Of course, in reality, personal freedom is not necessarily reduced by having a more interventionist state; the market, when left unchecked, may lead to monopoly rather than free competition; and economic success in many other countries exists side by side with government intervention. However, all these considerations were overshadowed by a strong anti-socialist sentiment.[55] This sentiment was shared by the ruling oligarchy and the ordinary workers alike. As Lau and Kuan put it, '[t]heir common desire is to be left alone, to have nothing to do with politics, and to work for themselves and their families. That is what laissez-faire offers'.[56]

Laissez-faire was also associated with free competition. This belief was promoted by the government as well as the private sector. One high-ranking official described the government's policy as the rules of the jungle:

> [I]n our business community the successful prosper. The unsuccessful are not carried by Government subsidy. Business either sink or swim as they adapt to changing competitive conditions. A policy directed towards survival of the fittest may seem harsh and unfeeling, but it has been shown to be appropriate in the particular circumstances of Hong Kong.[57]

Furthermore, free competition under laissez-faire was seen as enhancing social mobility and personal opportunity. In an opinion survey conducted in the mid-eighties, 84.2 per cent of the respondents agreed that in Hong Kong, provided a person had the ability and worked hard, he would have the opportunity to improve his social and economic status.[58] In an earlier survey, 71.8 per cent of the respondents agreed or strongly agreed with the statement that those who succeeded under conditions of intense competition, such as Li Ka-shing, ought to be the model for the youngsters to admire and learn from.[59]

The opportunities afforded by social mobility and personal advancement allowed the system to justify itself in terms of equality of opportunities rather than uniformity of outcomes. In such a system, the government was expected to be an impartial referee who upheld the rules of the game.[60] Here the principle of non-selective intervention, embodied in the doctrine of laissez-faire, enabled the system to appear as free and fair because it avoided giving privileges to sectional interests. By appealing to the socially valued ethos of free competition and fair play, the colonial government thus appeared as an impartial arbiter, thereby legitimating its rule.

It is through linking the strategy of consensual politics to public ethos that the relationship between values and politics manifested itself in colonial Hong Kong. It should be noted here that freedom and opportunity are not values that dominate the so-called Confucian culture. Nor are they directly related to the nineteenth-century European doctrine of laissez-faire about the theory of macroeconomic management. The prevailing social values and the meanings attached to the notion of laissez-faire depended on a congruence between the ideas and the circumstances.[61] In other words, the pervasiveness of laissez-faire rested not so much on the idea itself but on the way it fitted existing perceptions of the people in contemporary circumstances.

Conclusion

The case of Hong Kong provides some reflections over the issue of democracy in the Asian context. O'Donnell and Schmitter suggest that modern democracy relies on a 'contingent consent' among the political elites.[62] These elites agree among themselves to compete in such a way that those who win electoral support can exercise political authority and make binding decisions until the next round of contest. This consensus is built not on substantive grounds, but on the procedural norms of contingency. Echoing this argument, Przeworski maintains that democratic compromise cannot be a substantive compromise, but can only be a contingent institutional compromise. And since it is not a substantive compromise, outcomes of democratic conflicts are uncertain. The process of establishing a democracy is therefore a process of institutionalizing uncertainty, of subjecting all interests to uncertainty.[63]

The contingent consent – upon which Western democracy rests – relies on the political elites' belief about an equality of opportunity in obtaining ruling power. However, in societies divided by ethnic, religious, linguistic, or economic differences, such a contingent institutional compromise may be difficult to achieve when the subaltern groups see themselves as trapped in a permanent minority position. Democratic breakdown may result, as our Sri Lanka case shows. Here cultural/religious elements may be mobilized to serve as the basis for confrontation, not compromise.

In the case of colonial Hong Kong, although the majority of the population was deprived of any chance of obtaining ruling power, the colonial regime remained stable and effective because the pre-1985 system operated exactly in opposite to the principle of contingent institutional compromise. The Hong Kong system relied on a substantive compromise among political elites. It was a compromise that guaranteed a certainty of policy outcomes. It guaranteed the adoption of pro-business policies yet at the same time preventing the use of public resources to subsidize selected interests. This substantive compromise, although running in contrary to O'Donnell and Schmitter's principle of modern democracy, indeed ensures more equality in opportunity in the prevailing political setting. Given the fact that the introduction of any electoral arrangements into the system was prevented by constitutional constraints, political representation could only be achieved through oligarchic politics. In such a context, the substantive compromise actually allowed a higher degree of uncertainty (though still within limits) than otherwise, under the oligarchic control of ruling power. Under the policy of non-selective intervention, the substantive compromise allowed a higher degree of competition in the social and economic spheres. And through social and economic competition, market winners could emerge to become new elites and hence enjoying the chance of being co-opted into the ruling oligarchy.

Regardless of whether we consider it as Asian-value democracy or Asian-value authoritarianism, the Hong Kong case cautions against the gross generalization of seeing either Asian values as totally compatible with modern democratic principles, or Asian values as only supportive of paternalistic kinds of rule. As our case study suggests, how well dominant social values fit the existing political system depends on concrete historical circumstances. In Hong Kong, the stability and effectiveness of colonial rule relied upon neither coercion nor cultural ethos alone. The conventional belief about the absence of conflict in a Chinese society dominated by Confucian values is certainly ungrounded. Equally ungrounded is the view that since Confucian societies value harmony over disagreement, political means (whether democratic or otherwise) of interest arbitration and conflict resolution are unnecessary. In fact, the case of Hong Kong demonstrates that authoritarian rule was painstakingly maintained by means of political co-option, policy consensus, and manipulation of social values.

This raises questions over the relationship between the functioning of a political regime and the cultural/social ethos. It can tentatively be suggested that while politically constructed/maintained values may increase the acceptability of a political regime, reducing the success or failure of that regime to the existence of certain cultural norms alone is a gross simplification. Furthermore, as the case of laissez-faire reveals, dominant social values may not automatically derive from cultural heritage. Thus, different values and political systems are found in mainland China, Taiwan and Hong Kong, even though they share the same cultural heritage. These values can be the contingent outcome of prevailing socio-political circumstances.

Notes

1 Guillermo O'Donnell and Philippe C. Schmitter, *Transition from Authoritarian Rule: Tentative Conclusions about Uncertain Democracies*, Baltimore: Johns Hopkins University Press, 1986, p. 9.

2 Lau Siu-kai, *Society and Politics in Hong Kong*, Hong Kong: Chinese University Press, 1982.

3 A.J. Youngson, *Hong Kong: Economic Growth and Policy*, Hong Kong: Oxford University Press, 1982, p. 56.

4 Peter Harris, in his *Hong Kong: A Study in Bureaucracy and Politics*, Hong Kong: Macmillan, 1988, describes the system as an 'administrative no-party state'.

5 Lau, *Society and Politics*, p. 26.

6 An early attempt to bring about constitutional reform in Hong Kong, under the so-called Young Plan, was abandoned after the communist takeover of China. Details of the plan are well documented in Norman J. Miners, 'Plans for Constitutional Reform in Hong Kong, 1946–52', *The China Quarterly*, No. 107 September 1986, pp. 463–82; and Steve Yui-Sang Tsang, *Democracy Shelved: Great Britain, China and Attempts at Constitutional Reform*, Hong Kong: Oxford University Press, 1988.

7 N.J. Miners, *The Government and Politics of Hong Kong*, 3rd ed., Hong Kong: Oxford University Press, 1981, p. 32.

8 The only election was the partial election to the Urban Council, a body responsible for municipal services.

9 Robert A. Dahl, *Democracy and Its Critics*, New Haven: Yale University Press, 1989, p. 251.

10 For a discussion of the legal protection and restrictions of these civil liberties, see Raymond Wacks (ed.), *Civil Liberties in Hong Kong*, Hong Kong: Oxford University Press, 1988.

11 Dahl, *Democracy and Its Critics*, p. 252.

12 Ibid., p. 253.

13 Miners, *Government and Politics*, p. 267.

14 Lau Siu-kai, 'Basic Law and the New Political Order of Hong Kong'. Centre for Hong Kong Studies Occasional Paper No. 26, Hong Kong: Chinese University of Hong Kong, 1988, p. 1.

15 Lau Siu-kai and Kuan Hsin-chi, *The Ethos of the Hong Kong Chinese*, Hong Kong: Chinese University Press, 1988, p. 74.

16 Adam Przeworski, 'Some Problems in the Study of the Transition to Democracy', in Guillermo O'Donnell, Philippe C. Schmitter, and Laurence Whitehead (eds), *Transition from Authoritarian Rule: Comparative Perspectives*, Baltimore: John Hopkins University Press, 1986, pp. 51–52.

17 Samuel P. Huntington, 'Democracy's Third Wave', *Journal of Democracy 2*, Spring 1991, p. 24.

18 Lau Siu-kai, 'Utilitarianistic Familism: The Basis of Political Stability in Hong Kong', Social Research Centre Occasional Paper No. 74, Hong Kong: Chinese University of Hong Kong, 1978.

19 Lau and Kuan, *Ethos*, Chapter 3.

20 Francis Fukuyama, 'The Primacy of Culture', *Journal of Democracy 6*, No. 1, January 1995, p. 10.

21 A fuller discussion criticizing this circularity of argument can be found in Tak-Wing Ngo, 'Hong Kong under Colonial Rule: An Introduction', *China Information 12*, Nos. 1/2, Summer/Autumn 1997, p. 4.

22 See the study by Anthony Bing-leung Cheung and Kin-sheun Louie, 'Social Conflicts in Hong Kong, 1975–1986: Trends and Implication'. Hong Kong Institute of Asia-Pacific Studies Occasional Paper No. 3, Hong Kong: Chinese University of Hong Kong, 1991.

23 See Przeworski, 'Some Problems', pp. 56–57.

24 Miners, *Government and Politics*, p. 267.

25 T.J. Pempel, *Policy and Politics in Japan: Creative Conservatism*, Philadelphia: Temple University Press, 1982, p. 18.

26 Interview, Hong Kong, 15 March 1993.

27 Interview, Hong Kong, 10 March 1993.

28 Corporatist writers have emphasized the importance of such a mechanism in achieving policy consensus. See Philippe C. Schmitter, 'Reflections on Where the Theory of Neo-Corporatism Has Gone and Where the Praxis of Neo-Corporatism May Be Going', in Gerhard Lehmbruch and Philippe C. Schmitter (eds), *Patterns of Corporatist Policy-Making*, London: Sage Publications, 1982, p. 261.

29 Miners, *Government and Politics*, p. 82.

30 Ibid., p. 129.

31 John Rear, 'One Brand of Politics', in Keith Hopkins (ed.), *Hong Kong: The Industrial Colony*, Hong Kong: Oxford University Press, 1971, p. 81.

32 Hong Kong, Legislative Council, *Hong Kong Hansard 1977/78*, p. 707.

33 Arthur L. Stinchcombe, *Constructing Social Theories*, New York: Harcourt, Brace & World, 1968, p. 150; emphasis in the original.

34 Charles Tilly, 'War Making and State Making as Organized Crime', in Peter B. Evans, Dietrich Rueschemeyer, and Theda Skocpol (eds), *Bringing the State Back In*, Cambridge: Cambridge University Press, 1985, p. 171.

35 Charles E. Lindblom, *Politics and Markets: The World's Political Economic Systems*, New York: Basic Books, 1977, p. 175.

36 Henry J. Lethbridge, 'Hong Kong Under Japanese Occupation: Changes in Social Structure', in I.C. Jarvie (ed.), *Hong Kong: A Society in Transition*, London: Routledge & Kegan Paul, 1969, p. 126.

37 Harris, *Hong Kong*, p. 57.

38 Rear, 'One Brand of Politics', p. 73.

39 Stephen N.G. Davies, 'One Brand of Politics Rekindled', *Hong Kong Law Journal* 7, No. 1, 1977, 44–84.

40 Ibid., pp. 70–71.

41 Ibid., p. 65.

42 See the discussion in Stephen N.G. Davies, 'The Changing Nature of Representation in Hong Kong Politics', in Kathleen Cheek-Milby and Miron Mushkat (eds), *Hong Kong: The Challenge of Transformation*, Hong Kong: Centre of Asian Studies, University of Hong Kong, 1989.

43 Ambrose Y.C. King, 'Administrative Absorption of Politics in Hong Kong: Emphasis on the Grass Roots Level', in Ambrose Y.C. King and Rance P.L. Lee (eds), *Social Life and Development in Hong Kong*, Hong Kong: Chinese University Press, 1981.

44 Frank Longstreth, 'The City, Industry and the State', in Colin Crouch (ed.), *State and Economy in Contemporary Capitalism*, London: Croom Helm, 1979, p. 160.

45 Dennis Kavanagh and Peter Morris, *Consensus Politics from Attlee to Thatcher*, Oxford: Basil Blackwell, 1989, p. 13.

46 O'Donnell and Schmitter, *Transition from Authoritarian Rule*, p. 37.

47 Aaron Wildavsky, 'Changing Forward Versus Changing Back', *Yale Law Journal* 88, 1978, p. 227.

48 Stephen Chiu suggests that a laissez-faire policy was adopted in Hong Kong because of the lack of state capacity to intervene. See his 'The Politics of Laissez-faire: Hong Kong's Strategy of Industrialization in Historical Perspective'. Hong Kong Institute of Asia-Pacific Studies Occasional Paper No. 40, Hong Kong: Chinese University of Hong Kong, 1994.

49 Quoted in Miners, *Government and Politics*, p. 52.

50 Harris, *Hong Kong*, p. 159.

51 Ibid., p. 10.

52 Hong Kong, Legislative Council, *Hong Kong Hansard 1967*, pp. 372–73; and *Hong Kong Hansard 1968*, p. 431.

53 Hong Kong, Legislative Council, *Hong Kong Hansard 1970/71*, pp. 114–15.

54 Ibid., pp. 496–97 and 542–43.

55 Cf. the resistance to Keynesian interventionist policy in post-war Germany and Italy. Interventionist doctrines were discredited through associating them with the Nazi and Fascist regimes. See Christopher S. Allen, 'The Underdevelopment of Keynesianism in the Federal Republic of Germany', in Peter A. Hall (ed.), *The Political Power of Economic Ideas: Keynesianism Across Nations*, Princeton, New Jersey: Princeton University Press, 1989, pp. 263–89; and Marcello de Cecco, 'Keynes and Italian Economics', in Peter A. Hall (ed.), *The Political Power of Economic Ideas: Keynesianism Across Nations*, Princeton, New Jersey: Princeton University Press, 1989, pp. 195–229.

56 Lau Siu-kai and Kuan Hsin-chi, 'Public Attitude Toward Laissez-Faire in Hong Kong', *Asian Survey*, 30, No. 8, August 1990, p. 779.

57 Hong Kong, Legislative Council, *Hong Kong Hansard 1981/82*, p. 424.

58 Lau and Kuan, *Ethos*, p. 64.

59 Ibid.

60 Wong Siu-lun, 'Business and Politics in Hong Kong During the Transition', in Benjamin K.P. Leung and Teresa Y.C. Wong (eds), *25 Years of Social and Economic Development in Hong Kong*, Hong Kong: University of Hong Kong, 1994, p. 227.

61 See the discussion in Peter A. Hall, 'Conclusion: The Politics of Keynesian Ideas', in Peter A. Hall (ed.), *The Political Power of Economic Ideas: Keynesianism Across Nations*, Princeton, New Jersey: Princeton University Press, 1989, pp. 369–70.

62 O'Donnell and Schmitter, *Transition from Authoritarian Rule*, p. 59.

63 Przeworski, 'Some Problems', pp. 57–59.

7 DEMOCRACY IN INDIA – A HISTORICAL PERSPECTIVE

Bettina Robotka

During the years following her independence, India has been widely understood to be the largest functioning democracy in the world, the living example that the concept of parliamentarian democracy as it is common in modern Western civilization is valid also for Asian countries. India has indeed managed to maintain her parliamentary democracy during the 50 years of her independence. Unlike her neighbours, Pakistan and Bangladesh, she has successfully avoided military dictatorships. Contrary to her southern neighbour Sri Lanka she was able to keep under control separatist move-ments and to avoid civil wars which could have endangered the Indian state as a whole and the functioning of its political system. This assessment has largely been underlined by sucessive parliamentary elections in which changing majorities for parties and party coalitions resulted in peaceful transfers of power.

The history of Indian parliamentary democracy during the last 50 years also depicts the troubles and weaknesses of this system: the infringements of Indira Gandhi's emergency rule in the 1970s, the movements for more autonomy or separation in Punjab, the North-Eastern parts of India and last – but not least – the struggle of the Kashmiris. In order to solve these problems a reform of the existing political set-up – primarily the structure of Indian federalism – seems necessary. If not by all governments, this necessity was at least acknowledged by the United Front government headed by the south Indian politician Deve Gowda (1996–97). The revision of centre–state relations in favour of more autonomy for the latter in financial and social development matters, more power of decision-making and fewer possibilities of interference for the centre (for instance, dismissing state governments that are considered hostile to the centre) were among the main tasks of his government.[1] The failure, so far, to achieve this intention maintains this as a most urgent problem in the restructuring of Indian federalism.

India's federal and parliamentarian democratic system is essentially a colonial legacy. It was introduced by the British after they had conquered large parts of the sub-continent in the course of their rule lasting almost 200 years. A highly centralized and unitary type of state and administration routed the 'loosely woven web of suzerainty'[2] of pre-colonial Indian empires and their practice of political compromise and power-sharing. The British succeeded in passing on their concept of a centralized state and administration to the newly created class of English-educated Indian intelligentsia. From the second half of the nineteenth century onwards this intelligentsia developed a concept of an all-Indian nation, the ultimate aim of which would be independence from foreign rule and self-government in a nation-state of sub-continental dimensions. That nation-state as visualized by the representatives of the Indian National Congress, the leading force of the national movement, included almost all the structural characteristics of the colonial example: federalism with a strong centre and weaker federal units, overwhelming influence of the executive institutions as government and administration over the legislative, and concentration of the distributive power over financial resources at the centre. This bias was visible during the years of anti-colonial struggle when all attempts to accommodate the main minority, the Indian Muslims, failed because all proposals of securities for their participation in political power and of autonomy for the Muslim majority areas were rejected. The painful experience of partition did not, however, alter this stand and the first constitution of independent India of 1950 emphasized the political set-up inherited from the colonial period.

This paper will focus on the historical perspective of Indian democracy. It will try to explore what the traditions of pre-colonial political conduct were, how Western orientalist bias and the efforts of colonial empire-builders interacted in the establishment of a special type of 'colonial democracy'. And it tries to bring out the points of criticism that were formulated in the course of time by the British and Indians alike. As a conclusion, emphasis is laid on the necessary revision of this colonial legacy by connecting the modern Western concept of parliamentary democracy with the Indian political traditions of decentralized rule, regional autonomy and power-sharing.

The Indian State in Pre-Colonial Times

Indian sources of state formation and state-society relations reach back as far as to the Mauryan state of the fourth century BC. The inscriptions of the famous ruler Ashoka (273–232 BC) give abundant evidence about the principles and practice of rule and state building at that time. Most of the written sources of ancient Indian history, like the Puranas, the Arthashastra and the epics *Mahabharata* and *Ramayana* contain information about principles of state building and ruling and describe the virtues a good ruler should possess.

Most sources characterize kingship as a divinely ordained institution.[3] The ruler or king is nevertheless responsible not only to the gods, but to the laws of society (dharma) and society itself. Ashoka, for instance, is depicted as a *dharmaraja*, a ruler who rules in accordance with law. His lawful conduct secures, according to the sources, the prosperity of the ruled country. The famous Indian epos Mahabharata tells the story of the first king Manu. Though he was appointed by the god Brahma there is no doubt that his appointment was made at the request of the people in order to secure the welfare of the society.[4] Among the main duties of the king are mentioned the protection of the people and the service of their well-being. Protection of the people was thought to promote the *dharma* of both the king and his subjects. Service to the people, again, was meant to promote the material well-being (*artha*) of the king and his subjects.[5]

Of course, all the duties of the rulers mentioned above were moral duties in the first place which established the right of the ruler to rule. In case a king did not keep to the prescribed modes of conduct, which should have been rather often the case, the people were morally justified to protest against an oppressive ruler. The means at their disposal mentioned in the scriptures reached from various forms of official protest to open revolt. A quite common practice for the people seems to have been leaving the country of the oppressive ruler by leading families and their followers. In some texts the ruler is described – at least in theory – as liable to fines in case of the violation of law. A council of ministers is mentioned as an advisory body to the king and has the task of safeguarding the interests of the people.[6]

Apart from notions about royal moral qualities, a ruler should acknowledge the political structure of the country. One basic idea was that of the ruler as *chakravarti*, that is a universal ruler over a large country or even empire. Ashoka and others were described as ruling over vast territories reaching from sea to sea, from the Himalayas to the shores of the ocean. The borders of such continental empires are mentioned only vaguely, they seem to have been changeable and under steady re-adjustment through the activities of the king. As Basham observes:

> In this ideal there was no conception of a strong and centralised empire like that of China, but rather of producing a federation of kingdoms loosely subordinate to an emperor who was strong enough to be able to demand periodic tribute from them.[7]

This conception of a loose federation of states implicated that socially, racially and culturally diverse regions could retain a large amount of autonomy and even parts of their traditional jurisdiction. The uniting force of this loose conglomerate of smaller and larger kingdoms was the nominal acceptance of the overlord by paying taxes and tributes to his representatives and providing military aid in times of need. This idea of the state in ancient India prevented the development of a doctrine of 'sovereignty' as it did develop in Europe in the eighteenth and nineteenth centuries with a notion of 'clearly carved out territory with the exclusive jurisdiction of the central power'.[8] With the coming of Muslim rule in India this idea was adopted by the rulers of the Delhi sultanate (thirteenth to sixteenth centuries) and the Moghuls (sixteenth to nineteenth centuries). The Muslim imperial tradition as it developed under the West Asian Abbasids (eighth to ninth centuries) and Saffavids (ninth to tenth centuries) had already added some new aspects to the Indian tradition without basically altering it. As a result, four major levels of power could be identified in the North Indian region of Benares in the eighteenth century:[9] the imperial level of the Moghul court; the secondary level of the Moghul provinces that emerged as more or less independent successor states with the ongoing dissolution of Moghul power; the regional level headed by rulers whose status was granted to them by the imperial or secondary authority and who were loosely incorporated by rituals of allegiance and financial obligations; and last the local level represented by lineage, families and local leaders (sometimes tribal) who derived their authority from the regional or secondary authority. During the eighteenth century the declining power of the Moghuls resulted in the first place in a reduction of the influence of the first, the imperial level, in favour of the remaining three. But this did not mean the end of this kind of imperial idea so far. The West Indian Marathas and the Sikhs of North India as indigenous powers and the East India Company as a newcomer from outside[10] struggled for their respective succession to the imperial level of rule. As it is known, the East India Company routed its Indian competitors by 1820 and declared itself the successor of the Moghul emperor in spirit and substance. This status was confirmed by a weakened and only nominally ruling Moghul king. The avowed policy of the early period of the company's rule in India was that of interfering as little as possible with the inherited power structures and of maintaining the levels of power. This policy, however, could not be upheld for very long. It was abounded and replaced by an imperial idea of a very different kind and of European origin. Utilitarian ideas and practices of strong centralization and authoritarian rule that were unacceptable at home and liberal ideas of representative government that differed essentially from the Indian tradition were introduced into the South Asian subcontinent step by step.[11]

Colonial State Building in India

At the time of the conquest of the Indian subcontinent in the eighteenth and nineteenth centuries there existed a distinct picture among the British and in Europe as a whole about Asian political systems in general and the Indian state and society in particular. It was a picture of an archaic and despotic political system headed by an authoritarian ruler with unlimited executive power, and a society that was helplessly at the mercy of this despotic system.

The notion of the despotic character of oriental political systems was not at all a new one. Its sources can be traced back to the writings of the Greek philosophers Plato and Aristotle.[12] Forgotten, or at least neglected, during a rather long period of transition in Europe during the Middle Ages, this theory of oriental despotism was revived by European philosophers like Montesquieu, Hegel and by economists like R. Jones and A. Smith in connection with the acquisition of colonies. The essence of the theory was not altered. Oriental despotism came to depict a state or a political system where the power of an absolute ruler was unchecked over all the subjects in a highly centralized and oppressive state. The power of the state and its ruler was supposed to dominate all spheres of the society. According to this understanding the overall power was grounded in the command of the state and the ruler over all soil and all the income drawn from it. In the eyes of the promoters of 'oriental despotism' it implicated stagnation in state and society over centuries and denied the possibility of any development. As a matter of fact, this theory influenced the understanding of large parts of the English society and beyond and its thinkers. Marx, for example, derived his understanding of India and his model of the 'Asiatic mode of production' under its influence and even in our century a new version of it was developed by Wittfogel.[13]

Therefore, most administrators who came in touch with India through their service in the East India Company (EIC) were influenced by this theory. Charles Grant was one of them. He returned from his service in India to England in 1793. In his treatise *Observations on the State of Society among Asiatic Subjects of Great Britain* (1797) he described the state of affairs in India as follows:

> Upon the whole then, we cannot avoid recognising in the people of Hindostan, a race of men lamentably degenerate and base, retaining but a feeble sense of moral obligation; yet obstinate in their disregard of what they know to be right, governed by malevolent and licentious passions, strongly exemplifying the effects produced on society by a great and general corruption of manners, and sunk in misery by their vices, in a country peculiarly calculated by its natural advantages, to promote the prosperity of its inhabitants.[14]

Despotism, as Grant and many others understood it, did not only prevent any development in economy or society and the participation of the people in it. It was thought to destroy their character and morality and make them impotent subjects in the hands of the ruling despot, unable to help themselves. This state of powerlessness and stagnation was the point from which the English colonisers defined their role and tasks in India – that of breaking up the existing state and society and of modernizing and improving it.

A decisive role in Indian affairs was acquired by the English utilitarian James Mill. In his *History of India* (1817) he analyses the Indian society on the basis of the facts available in Great Britain at that time, and through the glasses of his utilitarian views.[15] In his description the Indian people appear as 'tainted with vices of insincerity, dissembling, treacherous, mendacious to an extent which surpasses even the usual measure of an uncultivated society'.[16] The reason for this social and moral decay he saw – like others before him – in despotic rule. He writes: 'We have already seen, in reviewing the Hindu form of government, that despotism in one of its simplest and least artificial shapes, was established in Hindostan and confirmed by laws of divine authority'.[17] The aim of this characterization of the Indian state and society was 'to dispel what he considered the silly sentimental admiration of oriental despotism'[18] and to prove the necessity and moral duty of interference on behalf of the British.

The importance of Mill's *History of India* lies in the fact that it suited the aims of the East India Company and was promoted to be the standard work on India for many years to come. It was made the main reference book for the training of young servicemen of the East India Company at their training centre in Hailesbury and influenced generations of administrators. The author himself was rewarded with an influential post in the London administration of the East India Company with extremely strong possibilities to shape policies in India.

Along with the statement that oriental despotism was the basic trouble of Indian state and society, subsequent writers contemplated the forms of government and administration which should be introduced into India instead. On which principles, employing what institutions should India be governed and her improvement be attempted? The conclusions reached at by thinkers and writers of that time seem to be rather surprising. After characterizing India as a glaring example of oriental despotism and contrasting her pre-British history with the progressive and outstanding principles of government in Great Britain, A. Dow, one of the earliest authors of an Indian history, arrived at the conclusion that the rule of despots has to be ended, but the desired improvement of state and society in India can be achieved only through a benevolent authoritarian rule of the morally high-standing British. 'Ironically, as the British were the inheritors of India's past, many of the assumptions about India's peoples that shaped their views of that past found a place in their own government'.[19] During the nineteenth century the notion of 'benevolent authoritarianism' as the appropriate mode of government continued to be upheld by administrators like T. Munro, J. Malcolm and C. Metcalf. They created a system of administration the central figure of which was the collector, representing to the ruled the full authoritarian power of the rulers.[20] With growing utilitarian influence in Indian politics and the firm establishment of the Company's rule in India, greater attention was given to the completion and refinement of the administration. India became a field of trial for administrative innovations developed far away in Britain. In his writings as a leading employee of the East India Company, Mill developed a form of government for India where the state was supreme over all other institutions (including the courts) and entrusted with absolute and binding authority.[21] He visualized a central legislative council composed of a few British experts. He resisted to the last the possibility of introducing representative institutions into India because the low castes of society were not able to represent themselves and would never be. Mill thought that the introduction of British law and the transformation of Indian government from an 'anomalous congries of semi-independent authorities into an uniform and centralised state'[22] was the only way to achieve an improved society. This reform programme dominated the Indian administration for the rest of British rule in India.

It should be mentioned here, however, that there existed a liberal political tradition in ruling India. One of its first representatives was the British historian and educationist T. Macaulay. He and his followers did not deny the possibility of introducing the merits of British culture and political system into India. He even regarded this as part of the 'civilizing mission' of the British. By introducing English education into India and making it available to just a small part, namely the upper layers of Indian society, he sought to create a new social group, a modern intelligentsia which – though Indian by blood and colour – would be English in its education, moral and tastes, and thus function as allies of British rule. Step by step the English-educated Indians would disseminate their knowledge to a broader public. After a time, by way of example, the Indian public would emancipate themselves and get fit for self-government and democracy. Emancipation and the ability to govern themselves was regarded as the final but very distant aim of British rule in India as it was understood by Macaulay and other liberals. But for the time being this distant aim was entirely out of reach in the opinion of the liberals and, therefore, the strongly centralized and authoritarian state was the only possible way to rule India. As a consequence, the liberals did not alter the character of the colonial political system in India.

The Indian uprising of 1857, which shook British rule to its fundaments, convinced the British government that they needed a broader base of allies for the continuation of their rule. As a result, from the 1860s onwards, the political structure of British rule designed basically on utilitarian lines was amended by the introduction of elements of the British political system of representation.

The Councils Act of 1861 provided for the creation of councils in the provinces and of municipalities.[23] It provided for the inclusion of non-official members by the way of appointment. For the first time the appointment of Indians was – at least in principle – made possible. No Indian was, however, appointed until the end of the century. The Indian Civil Service (ICS), the most important ruling body in India, was entirely confined to the English in its upper levels, and only a small number of lower posts were available to Indians. A critique of this state of affairs by the English-educated Indian intelligentsia developed during the 1870s and led to the foundation of an all-Indian organization, the Indian National Congress (INC) in 1885. From the platform of the INC, Indian intellectuals started demanding their share of power by the means of appointments to the councils and the ICS. Partly as an answer to these demands and partly under the pressure of broadening the basis of their rule, a new Councils Act was issued in 1892, providing a further extension of the number of appointed members in the councils. Besides, more Indians were gradually given employment in the ICS. Under the impression of the rising tide of nationalist sentiments and a boycott movement of English goods led by the Congress in the years 1905 to 1907, a new reform was introduced in 1909. For the first time election was made the means of choosing representatives for the non-official members of the councils – of course, by a rather limited franchise. After the World War, which Great Britain had fought with considerable support from India and the Indian people, the British – pressed by high expectations for self-government on behalf of the Indians – introduced another act in 1919. The so-called Montford reforms[24] extended the number of elected representatives in the councils at all levels again, and selected spheres of influence, such as those of public health and sanitation in the provincial governments, were placed within the responsibility of Indian ministers. On the basis of the first constitution introduced by the British into India in 1935, a certain provincial autonomy was introduced and, during the years 1937–39, Indian provincial governments functioned. Throughout British rule in India central executive and legislative power remained firmly in British hands. When the British left India in 1947 they 'transferred power' of the political and administrative system to the succeeding Indian and Pakistan governments, handing over an almost complete structure.[25]

Colonial Democracy in India – the Outcome

The political and administrative system that had been established during the 200 years of British rule on the South Asian sub-continent was a basic inheritance that characterized the newly independent state of India.[26] In the course of its development during independence most of the basic factors that characterized the colonial Indian state have been preserved. It is, therefore, necessary to analyse the effect that was produced by the introduction of 'colonial democracy' on India and Indian society.

The representatives of the East India Company had come to India originally with strictly economic aims of trade and commerce. But after some time they found it difficult to avoid political involvement and responsibility in the territories of their commercial activity. Their efforts to secure and strengthen the position of the company and its exclusive commercial rights in the region led to its involvement in political struggles and, as a consequence, to the conferment upon them of *diwani* rights in the province of Bengal in 1765.[27] The political involvement of the company increased during the following years and by 1857 the company ruled about two-thirds of the Indian sub-continent. The rather aggressive policy of expansion demanded from the British administrators decisions about the manner in which they wanted to administer and rule the newly-acquired territories. The decision was made under the impression of the above-described prevailing notions of the despotic ruling traditions in India and under the decisive influence of utilitarian ideas. It resulted in the establishment in the company-ruled territories of a strongly centralized state and neatly organized administration 'frozen in the impersonal rationality of bureaucratic institutions'.[28] Thus the newly created colonial state overruled the political tradition of pre-colonial Indian empires of power-sharing, regional autonomy and accommodation and rigidly united geographically, culturally and socially diverse regions and people into a centralized state of so far unknown persistence.

This development naturally did not proceed unchallenged. The problems and doubts connected with the realization of the utilitarian state model were expressed by some British administrators as well as by Indians themselves. In the course of the debate Thomas Munro, for instance, criticized the extension of such direct political rule over India and rejected the notion that the best ways of rule were British or European ones. He envisaged the future of the subcontinent as a British-dominated federation of 'various and perhaps differently constituted regimes experimenting with government in their diverse social, economic and historic settings, and all learning from the improvement of any'.[29] The partners for such a federation should have been the indirectly ruled princely states with their more or less unbroken tradition of indigenous rule.

As a matter of fact, there existed alongside the directly ruled part of India the so-called indirectly ruled India. The EIC, on her way to acquire political power over the South Asian sub-continent, decided not to conquer all its territories but to leave some parts of it under the rule of the former kings and princes. The reasons were manifold, reaching from strategical (use of such states as buffers in the frontier regions) to economic (attempts to keep administrative and military expenses low). The company created so-called subsidiary treaties with the princely states, in which they assured them of their military aid and protection in case of armed conflicts with neighbours or internal insurrections. In return the states accepted the EIC as their mediator in foreign affairs and conflicts in general. In some cases the states were obliged to pay tribute or to maintain troops of the company. There was to be no interference in the internal politics of those states, though the company reserved for itself the right to take over the administration from the ruler in case of 'mismanagement'. In such a case, the representatives of the company who took over usually tried to reform the princely administration on the lines of the British–Indian example. Such a case was the princely state of Mysore. During a debate on the restoration of princely rule in Mysore held in the House of Commons on 24 May 1867,[30] the Secretary of State for India Lord Cranborne argued in favour of the restoration. In his speech he compared the political and administrative systems of British and native India and pointed out certain defects of the British system. In the first place he deplored the rigidity and the extreme centralization of the British system which made it rather inefficient under the circumstances of the sub-continental dimension of India and which had already led to catastrophes in extreme situations like famines or floods.[31] As a result of an inquiry that was started by the Indian Political Service, some of the British representatives in the princely states admitted that the new administration was too expensive and inefficient for the states concerned.[32]

A critical approach to the introduction into India of a form of government along British lines was developed step by step among English-educated Indian intellectuals. The Bengal reformer of the 1820s, Ram Mohan Roy, while judging British rule in India basically favourably and believing that India must have a modern and secular state, insisted 'that it was possible to glean from India's past experience the essential elements for the construction of a modern Indian polity'.[33] During the second half of the nineteenth century critical attitudes among Indian intellectuals strengthened in connection with their growing number and political consciousness. A landmark in this respect was the foundation of the Indian National Congress in 1885 which became a major platform for critics of British rule. In his presidential address of 1893 at the Congress session in Lahore, the prominent Indian nationalist D. Naoroji criticized the high costs of the Indian administration which India itself had to bear, although it served British interest in the first place.[34] Two years later, S. Banerji, a leading Bengali nationalist of that time, deplored the high expenditure on administration and defence with no possibility for the Indians to participate in the decisions.[35] Subsequent critics note that the missing participation in political decision-making was deplored.

In connection with a growing amount of interference in their inner politics and administration, there were critical remarks on the type of administration introduced in the princely states. The destruction of existing indigenous political and administrative structures in these states and their uncritical substitution by British ones was mentioned by the *dewan* (Prime Minister) of Mysore, C.V. Rangacharlu. He remarked: 'Real progress came to an end with the introduction of ... first elements of regular government. All ideas of further improvement took the form of a continued introduction of new departments ... without any comprehensive attempt to adapt them to the circumstances of the province'.[36] Years later, in 1922, a non-official scheme for political and administrative reforms was published by one Krishna Rao, a native of the princely state of Mysore. In the introduction to his proposal he recorded for Mysore a 'growing popular feeling that its present administrative machinery can no longer be allowed to continue without creating much unnecessary discontent'.[37] He further decried that a bureaucratic government – though benevolent – still had serious defects: it depended on the ability and goodwill of the administrator. Therefore, he concluded, such a government had to be amended by a strong element of democratic control. In this connection he referred to the representative assembly introduced in 1882 in Mysore and to legislative assemblies established in the course of time in different princely states after the British–Indian model. He concluded, however, that the authority and power of these institutions had to be extended and reshaped in accordance with traditional Indian political conduct, because 'the con-stitutional advance of the people of Mysore need not necessarily follow the same lines as obtaining in the countries of the West or in India'.[38] Indian traditions should be remembered and reintroduced according to the demands of modern times.

Despite a critical attitude on behalf of quite a number of people – Indian as well as British – one has to realize that the political and admini-strative practice of British India as well as of the princely states was not altered. Although (after the mentioned debate in 1867) the ruling house of Mysore was reinstated in 1880, the political and administrative structures introduced by the British remained untouched. The importance and influence of the Indian Civil Service in British India and of the Indian Political Service in the princely states remained unchanged. Both continued to be promising fields of employment and career for a considerable number of British people. The notion of the 'civilizing mission' of their engagement added above all a moral halo to British rule. During the second half of the nineteenth century, with the end of British supremacy in the world and growing demands for a redistribution of spheres of influence, British hold over India gained an additional strategic importance which made the loosening of Britain's grip improbable.

Yet, there were some new developments during the second half of the nineteenth century in India. Under the impact of the Indian uprising of 1857 that shed British rule heavily, and under the pressure of the demands of a growing number of nationalist Indian intellectuals, the British realized that in order to secure their rule in India they had to find support among a greater number of Indians. By the means of introducing elements of representation they tried to secure the support of the upper layers of Indian society. This decision, however, was not taken unchallenged. It ran counter to the conviction of many British politicians – conservatives and liberals as well – who held that Indians were not able to represent themselves because of the backwardness of their society and their 'despotic' inheritance. For instance, John Stuart Mill argued in his *Considerations on Representative Government* that there were 'dependencies whose population was in a sufficiently advanced state to be fitted for representative govern-ment',[39] having in mind Britain's white colonies. With regard to India and the 'Black Colonies' he observes 'But there are others which have not attained that state, and which, if held at all, must be governed by the dominant country ... ' Further examples of this opinion are many, among them the viceroy of India Lord Curzon who insisted that 'never in the wildest dreams' could India become a self-governing dominion like Canada or Australia.[40] His successor in the post of the viceroy, Lord Minto, was convinced of 'the hard fact that Western forms of government were unsuited to India' and 'could never be akin to the instincts of the many races composing the population of the Indian Empire'.[41] Therefore, the introduction of elements of representation was a very slow and hesitant process that did not really alter the power structures. They remained firmly in the hands of the British.

The decision to introduce even a limited version of British democracy into India, while welcomed by English-educated moderate intellectuals, was criticized by radical nationalists who, under the influence of the revivalist movement, demanded observance of the indigenous traditions of political conduct in India and, thus, an amendment of British democracy. One of them was Sri Aurobindo Ghose, one of the leading figures of the radical wing of the INC. He formulated his critique of European democracy in 1903. He wrote: 'Asia is not Europe and never will be Europe. The political ideals of the West are not the mainspring of the political movement in the East, and those who do not realise this great truth are mistaken'. Explaining the major difference between Asian and European models of democracy, he pointed to the weakness of European democracy in an Asian society: 'It [European democracy] takes as its motive the rights of men and not the dharma of humanity'. The individual man with his rights and aspirations stands in the centre of European concept of democracy, while in an Asian society the community and *dharma* – the duty to serve the community – is the base of society. Criticizing the notion that there was no democratic tradition in India Aurobindo points out: 'Democracy has travelled from the East to the West in the shape of Christianity... But when Asia takes back democracy into herself she will first transmute it in her own temperament'.[42] In his view the East takes back what originally had been her own and what by the way of exchanging ideas comes back now. In treating democracy this way Aurobindo did not reject it, but insisted on the amendment of the European version according to Asian contexts.

Another problem arose with the introduction of the elective element into the councils of British India. In Britain the constituencies for election were based on the territorial principle, i.e. all people living in a certain area together elect their representatives. In India, however, under the circumstances – illiteracy, missing communicational links and political awareness, it was to be feared that traditional social linking like caste and community would dominate the voting behaviour of the uneducated masses. Especially by the representatives of the minority community of Indian Muslims the selection of representatives by majority vote was regarded as a danger. At the end of the nineteenth century Sir Sayyid Ahmad Khan, one of the leading members of the Muslim community, expressed his critique and rejection of the British territorial system. He remarked that under the existing conditions, with the Muslims lagging behind the Hindus in matters of English education and economic strength and numbering only about one quarter of the Indian population, elected representation would be a disaster for the Muslims. Under the given social conditions everyone would vote for candidates of their own community with the consequence that the Hindus would dominate the councils and safeguard their interests, while Muslims would have no such opportunity. 'It would be like a game of dice, in which one man had four dice and the other only one'.[43]

The fears of S. A. Khan and later Muslim politicians of a lasting political domination of the majority community over the minorities dominated the confrontation inside the national movement for the years to come. While the goal of achieving independence from British rule was never a point of disagreement, the distribution of political power between the Hindu and the Muslim communities in a future, free India became a continuous 'apple of discord'. Muslims tried to secure their share in power by demanding seat reservation and separate electorates. The Hindu-dominated Indian National Congress declined all such demands by arguing that secularism was their ideology and would be the ideology of free India and that there was no need of community-based safeguards. The growing tension between the two main communities of India was explained by the Indian Statutory Commission in 1930:

> So long as people had no part in the conduct of their own government, there was little for members of one community to fear from the predominance of the other. The gradual introduction of constitutional reforms, however, had greatly stimulated communal tension as it aroused anxieties and ambitions among many communities by the prospect of their place in India's future political set-up.[44]

Religious affiliation had been made the decisive distinction by which the inhabitants of India were grouped together as 'Hindus' and 'Muslims' from the very beginning of their rule by the British. In the accounts of early travellers of the seventeenth and eighteenth centuries this distinction of religious groups is clearly visible. Later on, it was utilized by the East India Company for administrative convenience. As Th. R. Metcalf puts it: 'The British came to believe that adherence to one or the other of these two religions was not merely a matter of belief, but defined membership more generally in a larger community.'[45] In the course of time this understanding was made the base of British politics in India. At the turn of the nineteenth century, membership in one or the other community largely decided the character of a man and his social and political behaviour. Therefore, British administrators reacted positively when, in 1906, a delegation of Indian Muslims asked for communal rather than territorial representation. This decision suited both the British understanding of the political interests the Muslim community would have (as opposed to those of the Hindu community) and their practical aim – to divide and rule, creating greater fragmentation through having as many different interests as possible represented. The introduction of communal electorates is widely understood to be a decisive factor in the emergence and expansion of communalism in Indian politics.[46] The well-known Indian historian K. N. Panikkar, for instance, in his introduction to *Communalism in Indian History, Politics and Culture* comes to the conclusion that the introduction of the principle of elected representation in public institutions actively promoted the rising of communalism in India.[47]

As a matter of fact, the importance of British politics and institutions in this process has to be acknowledged and should not be underestimated or belittled. There seem to be some more reasons for this development. First of all, unlike in Great Britain, the process of secularization in the society did not take place in India or was at least limited to an extremely small number of English-educated intellectuals. Therefore, religion played a decisive part in the daily life of the people – it influenced their identity basically. Although with the growth of nationalism provincial identities such as 'Bengali' and 'Punjabi' began to develop, the issue of belonging to one or the other religious community remained important in most cases. A secularized all-Indian identity standing above religious affiliation was claimed as its ideology by the Indian National Congress, but could materialize only in parts of the movement and its leaders. Politically conscious Muslims continued to feel uneasy and demanded safeguards for their share in political representation in the form of separate electorates or seat reservation. In underestimating the force of these demands rather insensibly, the INC failed to find a compromise with the Muslim demands. The Pakistan plan and its subsequent realization was the result of this failure.

Elements of representation and election were introduced into quite a number of princely states by English-educated princes and *dewans*. As has been mentioned, in Mysore a representative assembly was introduced as early as 1882. In 1922 the South Indian state of Cochin had a legislative assembly of over 60 members with an elected majority. The Rana of Jhalwar ruled his state with the help of a legislative assembly consisting of an upper and a lower house with an elected majority in the lower one. In Travancore, a legislative council operated with a non-official majority. The authority of these assemblies was often restricted to debates of certain issues and to recommendations to the prince and his *dewan*. They did not have legislative power nor the power to decide the budget of the state. The electorate was restricted by an educational and property census; in some of the states community or caste affiliation was important. Not even in princely states like Travancore, where no separate electorate on caste or community affiliation was introduced, did selecting representatives by elections result in communal animosities among the population and in the government service.[48] This illustrates well that the development of communalism was not exclusively linked to separate electorates, as it is often understood, but to the introduction of the elective element into representation in general.

Indian society in princely states as well as in British India was highly divided and political affiliation developed mostly on caste and communal lines. This phenomenon seems to have been even more strongly developed in the princely states, where the unifying impact of direct British rule and all-Indian nationalism was rather weak. Nevertheless, the suitability of representation and election and of democracy as a political principle was never rejected by the Indians. From the time of its introduction it was hailed as progress bringing India nearer to self-government. All the cited critical remarks by Indians do not question the parliamentary democracy as such but demand an adoption of this European system to the different social and political conditions of India. Even in those princely states that were often seen as backward, the principle of representation on the basis of election was widely accepted – of course with the inclusion of the princes as constitutional heads of the proposed government. After the attainment of freedom in 1947 the princely states of the Indian sub-continent were advised by the departing British to join either of the two newly independent states of India or Pakistan. This advice was backed by political pressure carried out by the Indian successor government on the princes. In exchange for generous privy purses and posts in India's political and diplomatic service, the ruling princes had to sign documents of accession thus merging their states with the surrounding territories. In case of states that did not submit to these pressures (as for instance the princely state of Hyderabad) the army ensured integration and thereby the realization of the unitary state concept of the INC.

It was only a relatively small number of Indians, highly educated, financially independent, secularized and Anglicized in their behaviour and thinking, that held the opinion that the British system could be introduced and that India and its people should adopt themselves to the British system and its underlying ideology. These people were, however, influential and took the lead of the Indian national movement. Most of the critics, in closer touch with the masses of the Indian population, pleaded for an adoption of the British system to Indian circumstances, with an orientation towards traditional Indian political conduct. Unfortunately, their voices were not heard. The fact remains that not much of an adoption or 'Indianization' of parliamentary democracy has so far been achieved.

Conclusions

The structure of the contemporary Indian state and its parliamentary democracy is mainly an inheritance of the colonial past. Elements of parliamentary democracy introduced into British India under the predominance of a highly centralized bureaucratic state came to form a special type of 'colonial democracy'.

The impact of that colonial democracy was reflected in the perceptions of the leading nationalist politicians of India. After independence, when they formed the government of India, they retained the main structures of the highly centralized state, amended by a parliamentary system that did not really control the bureaucratic state structures and thus ensure a firm political grip of the centre over the federal states. A critical reversion of the inherited political structures as a whole did not take place. Though on the surface India succeeded in maintaining the parliamentary system, the above-mentioned problems in centre–state relations as the most visible ones, growing Hindu communalism and ongoing regionalization of parties and politics illustrate the sharpening of the inherited imbalance.

Under today's circumstances – a fast-changing world and the growing weight of Asian countries in international economics and politics – greater self-consciousness among the same countries and an increasing orientation towards traditional political and social values can be observed. This development should be kept in mind in considering the Indian situation. A reorientation towards the pre-colonial traditions of loosely connected states with wide political, cultural and economic autonomy and the political practice of accommodating political structures to changing political realities could result in a revision of the inherited 'democratic authoritarianism'[49] and bring about an overdue decolonization of the Indian democratic system. Such a revised democracy would be a step towards finding a solution not only to the intra-Indian problems of centre–state relations, communalism and strengthening of parliamentary control, but could provide a solution to much more comprehensive and urgent problems such as Indo–Pakistani relations and the Kashmir question , as well as a first real chance to solve the pressing economic and social problems of the South Asian region.

Notes

1   M. Mitta and S. Koppikar, 'Changing Equations', *India Today*, 30 June 1996, pp.42–45.

2   A. Jalal, *Democracy and Authoritarianism in South Asia*, Cambridge: Cambridge University Press, 1995, p. 12.

3   A.L. Basham, 'Ideas of kingship in Hinduism and Buddhism' in A.L. Basham (ed.), *Kingship in Asia and Early America*. 30th International Congress of Human Sciences in Asia and North Africa. Seminars. Mexico City: El Colegio de Mexico, 1981, p.115.

4   Basham, 'Ideas of kingship', p. 119.

5   Ibid., p. 125.

6   B.K. Sarkar, 'Democratic ideals and republican institutions in India', *The American Political Science Review*, Vol. 12, No. 4, 1918, p. 585.

7   Basham , 'Ideas of kingship', p. 129.

8   L. Rudolph and S. Hoeber Rudolph, 'The subcontinental Empire and the regional Kingdom in Indian state formation', in: P. Wallace (ed.), *Region and Nation in India*, New Delhi: Oxford IBH Publishing Co., 1985, p.50.

9   The following account is based on B.S. Cohn, 'Political systems in 18th century India: the Banares region', *Journal of the American Oriental Society*, Vol. 82, No. 3, 1962, pp. 312-320.

10 The East India Company operated in parts of India since the seventeenth century.

11 Eric M.C. Stokes, *English Utilitarians and India*, Oxford: Clarendon Press, 1959.

12 R.S. Sharma, 'The socio-economic basis of Oriental despotism in India', in A.L. Basham (ed.), *Kingship in Asia*, p. 133.

13 K.A. Wittfogel, *Oriental Despotism: a Comprehensive Study of Total Power*, New Haven: Yale University Press, 1957.

14 Ch. Grant, 'Observation on the State of Society among Asiatic Subjects of Great Britian, Particularly with Respect to Morals and on the Means of Improving It', (privately printed, 1797), quoted from Stokes 1959, p. 31.

15 Mill never visited India; he was even of the opinion that personal experience would prevent an objective judgement.

16 J. Mill, *History of India*, London: Baldwin, Cradock and Joy, Vol. 2, 1817, p. 195.

17 Ibid., p. 166.

18 Stokes, *English Utilitarians*, p. 53.

19 A. Dow, *History of Hindostan*, Vol. 3, 'Dissertation on Despotism', London: n.p., 1770, pp. 7–27, quoted in Th. R. Metcalf, *Ideologies of the Raj: The New Cambridge History of India III. 4.*, Cambridge: Cambridge University Press, 1994, p. 7.

20 B. Stein, *Thomas Munro: The Origins of the Colonial State and His Vision of Empire*, Delhi: Oxford University Press, 1989, pp. 352–53.

21 Stokes, *English Utilitarians*, pp. 63–64.

22 Ibid., p. 73.

23 At the centre a council advising the governor general/viceroy did already exist. It consisted of official members only. Indians had no access.

24 Named after the secretary of state for India, Montague, and the viceroy of India, Lord Chelmesford.

25 Because of the partition, parts of the establishment were transferred to Pakistan where a new centre with provincial sub-structures had to be created.

26 This is also true for Pakistan, Bangladesh (former East-Pakistan) and Sri Lanka (Ceylon, however, did not have an ICS and the Ceylon Civil Service had been reformed by 1963).

27 *Diwani* rights were conferred by the Moghul emperor upon his trustees – and in this case, upon the East India Company. In addition to trading rights, *diwani* rights included tax collection and administration of justice in the territory concerned.

28 Jalal, *Democracy and Authoritarianism*, p. 10.

29 Stein ,*Thomas Munro*, p. 349.

30 Princely rule in the South Indian state of Mysore had been abandoned in 1832.

31 L/P&S/20/H44. 'Correspondence regarding the comparative merits of British and Native Administration in India', Calcutta, 1867, India Office Library, London.

32 L/P&S/20/H44. 'Letters of the Agent to the Governor-General of North-East Frontier and Commissioner of Assam H. Hopkinson and Commissioner of Mysore, F. Clerk', Calcutta, 1867, India Office Library, London.

33 B.N. Ganguli, 'Political and Economic Thought of Ram Mohan Roy', in N.R. Ray (ed.), *Ram Mohan Roy. A Bi-Centenary Tribute*, New Delhi: National Book Trust, 1974, p. 56.

34 A.M. Zaidi, *The Encyclopaedia of the Indian National Congress*, New Delhi: Chand Pubications, 1977, p. 387.

35 Ibid., p. 625.

36 *Fifty Years of British Administration*, by a native of Mysore,London: n.p., 1874, quoted from: R. Ramakrishnan, 'British policies in princely Mysore (1831–81)', in N.R. Ray (ed.), *Western Colonial Policy – a Study of Its Impact on Indian Society*, Vol. 1, Calcutta: Institute of Historical Studies, 1981, pp.275–76.

37 Krishna Rao, 'Mysore reforms: a non-official scheme', typewritten manuscript written in Mysore, India Office Library London, V 15447, 1922, p. 2.

38 Ibid., p. 21.

39 J.S. Mill, *Considerations on Representative Government*, quoted in J.M. Robson (ed.), *Collected Works of John Stuart Mill*, Vol. XIX, Toronto: University of Toronto Press, 1977, p. 567.

40 Metcalf, *Ideologies of the Raj*, p. 225.

41 Lord Minto is quoted here from Metcalf, *Ideologies of the Raj*, p. 223.

42 Aurobindo Ghose, 'Asiatic Democracy', in *Sri Aurobindo`s Birth Centenary Library, Vol. 1, Bande Mataram. Early political writings*, Pondicherry: Sri Aurobindo Ashram, 1972, pp. 757–58.

43 Shan Muhammad (ed.), *Writings and Speeches of Sir Sayyid Ahmad Khan*, Bombay: Nachiketa Publishers, 1972, p. 210.

44 *Report of the Indian Statutory Commission*, Vol. 1, London: Stationary Office, 1930, p. 29.

45 Metcalf, *Ideologies of the Raj*, p. 133.

46 Communalism is a term that describes the understanding that political interests are dominated by the religious affiliation of the concerned people.

47 K.N. Panikkar (ed.), *Communalism in India: History, Politics and Culture*, New Delhi: Manohar, 1991, p. 8.

48 D. Kooiman, 'Separate electorates: experiences from colonial India'. Paper presented at the symposium on 'Changing identities under colonialism', Berlin, 1993.

49 Jalal, *Democracy and Authoritarianism*, p. 249.

8 GOOD GOVERNANCE – DEMOCRACY OR *MINZHU*?

Geir Helgesen and Li Xing

Introduction

This chapter is a contribution to the current debate on democracy and human rights in East Asia with a focus on the differences between Western notions of 'good governance and democracy' versus the East Asian concept of *minzhu*.[1] The notion of East Asia in our context mainly comprises the Confucian cultures of China, Taiwan, Korea, and Japan, while the notion of 'the West' in the following comprises the liberal aspects of North America and Western Europe.

Democracy has in recent years been elevated to the position of good government on a global scale, even though the underlying conditions for democratic success are much disputed. After the end of the Cold War the issue of human rights and democracy has become a hot topic in the Western media, and it is placed on the agenda of foreign policy formulations in the West and bestowed conditionality in international relations. This imposition of conditionalities for democracy and human rights has polarized the discourse on this issue. The causes of this are various, but they are obviously the outcome of the end of the Cold War. It is only since the end of Cold War that democracy and human rights have reached a high international salience. In conjunction with new demand and emphasis from the West on liberal democracy and Western-oriented rights, the developing countries in the Third Word have been under economic and political pressure to privatize their economies and adopt liberal democratic principles and procedures for governance. 'Good governance' has replaced the Cold War anti-communism alliance to become the central feature of Western development assistance. The definition of 'good governance' is in the West largely equated with a system of democracy based on parliamentary institutions, coupled with a free market system in the area of economic production. An important aspect of the above context is the collapse of the socialist regimes in Eastern Europe and China's switch to market economy. The West, especially the United States, took the opportunity to develop a brand new post-Cold War 'world order' centring around democracy and human rights. A link was established between democracy and the network of international aid agencies, particularly the IMF, the World Bank and the United States Agency for International Development (USAID). This was likewise the thinking behind the establishment of the new European Bank for Reconstruction and Development (EBRD) in 1991 to help restructure the Eastern European and former Soviet economies. It was also the guideline for American linkage of MFN (Most Favored Nation) trading status to China's human rights record.

Notwithstanding the fact that democracy and human rights are used as trump cards in the political and economic strategies of the West against 'the Rest', there are indeed signs supporting the claim that the world is about to become a global community. Revolutionary developments in communication and transportation technology strongly support this idea, just as a vast variety of problems fundamental to the survival of human life on earth prove to be of a global kind. These problems are often a combination of man-made and natural disasters of which environmental threats are the most visible and most widely publicized. They can obviously only be solved in world-wide cooperation. There is therefore no doubt that the present – for better or worse – is an era of globalization.

The 'globalization wave' represents a tide of privatization and structural adjustment policies that were either adopted by or imposed on various states in the Third World so as to lessen or diminish the role of state in the national economic development. The forced marketization of domestic economies was, as a consequence, paralleled by the globalization of capital, technology, markets and services, as various barriers to foreign investment and trade were removed under pressure from international economic institutions. It is obvious that the thrust of globalization has been pushed forward largely by the West and that it serves to keep or increase its economic influence and hegemony over the rest of the world.

At the same time, we are also witnessing a growing awareness of local and regional characteristics. Not least the absence of the one dominating confrontation on the international political scene, mentioned above as among the reasons behind the alleged global drive for democracy, has probably also had the opposite effect of giving room for more local and regional oriented political considerations. These two trends, the global and the local orientations, are often seen as mutually exclusive; the former being open-minded, outward reaching, as well as modernization and development oriented; the latter on the contrary narrow-minded, inward-looking, oriented towards status-quo and even being retrogressive, longing for 'the good old days'. This either/or thinking may be a Western affliction, but it seems nevertheless to have affected the political discourse outside the Western hemisphere as well, not least in East Asia where post-war politics has been strictly divided according to the Cold-War East–West dichotomy. It seems to be about time to realize both the consequences and the new possibilities in the present world, now that the old order has been abandoned and a new one not yet firmly established. An important first step is to do away with faults and misrepresentations.

The present chapter, thus, will present some discussions and viewpoints in light of the East–West differences in both concept and practice of democracy expressed in the form of good governance.

Politics and Culture: East and West

The impact of culture on politics is obviously multifarious. As politics basically have to do with social relations, with ways and means of achieving power to influence decisions concerning societal matters, it is hard to envisage any element of politics to be 'culture-free'. Lucian W. Pye has described how political power is extraordinarily sensitive to cultural nuances. Therefore cultural variations are decisive in determining the course of political development.[2] Samuel Huntington goes even further in describing cultural differences as possible or even probable sources of fundamental conflicts:

> Different civilizations have different views on the relations between God and man, the individual and the group, the citizen and the state, parents and children, husband and wife, as well as differing views of the relative importance of rights and responsibilities, liberty and authority, equality and hierarchy. These differences are the product of centuries. They will not soon disappear.[3]

It has long been accepted that political culture and cultural orientations play a significant role in the economic behaviour of individuals and nations. As early as the beginning of this century Max Weber maintained that despite favourable conditions for rationality in traditional China, Confucian humanism, as opposed to Protestant Calvinism, was inimical to the development of the spirit of capitalism. However, the rapid industrialization of the Japanese, South Korean and Taiwanese economies, and not least the advancements of Chinese economy in the past 15 years, have forced a reassessment of this viewpoint. In recent years, many studies have focused on the behaviour and interactions among individuals, families and companies in the economic development of these states. The Weberian argument was turned upside down and East Asian development patterns were identified with, for instance, enterprising paternalism, lifetime employment, organized recruitment from schools and communities, company spirit, seniority wages, and enterprise unions.[4]

This culturalist approach has all along been contested by self-declared Western universalists who see values as rather irrelevant for the economic and political process. In recent years the culturalists gained some territory, but at the time of writing, yet another somersault is being performed in the field of Asian studies. The financial crises in Southeast and East Asia are taken as definitive proof against notions claiming a positive causal effect of certain values on economic development. Cosy relationships between political leaders and economic entrepreneurs are again seen solely in the light of corruption and a strong work ethic is once again seen as a disguise for class repression – as is the notion of a special Asian leadership style. To us these spontaneous reactions to current problems in the economic sphere make little sense. To exploit the current crisis as evidence against the validity of a cultural relativist position in social studies is an unneccessary vulgarization of the debate. In the following, we shall state our position concerning the links between politics and culture and then trace some of the sources of the East–West differences.

Political culture may be a fairly recent construct,[5] but political powerholders have always been well aware of the political importance of culture, in the sense that any political system establishes its own interpretation of the past to serve present needs, in order to establish a *culture* as a common point of reference in the political process. Thus the cultural context may to some extent be based on a constructed tradition, and mainly established to serve the needs of the elite layers of society holding political power. But power elites cannot pick and choose any cultural context they like, simply so as to remain in power. If the cultural construction contradicts basic values and norms recognized among people as genuine, sound, and true aspects of their tradition, they will sooner or later rebel against such 'false images'. The relationship between culture and politics is thus reciprocal and dialectical; each phenomenon affects the other in a continuous process. Absolute determinants are fortunately out of fashion in social sciences at present. But in assessing each of the two phenomena being discussed here, the one in relation to the other, it is important to understand *culture* in the role of context, and *politics* as the more fluctuating dimension of the two. This imply that basic social and moral values and norms are seen as a given condition, not un-changeable, but difficult to direct at will. Political systems, no matter their ideological leanings, are affected by this given condition stemming primarily from the impact of parents on their children. The continuity of social and moral values and norms between generations are seldom included as an important factor in determining the way political systems work. In the political culture approach to politics, however, the basic point of departure is that every political system is a unique socially constructed creation within the confines of a cultural context, which to a greater or lesser degree shapes the pattern of human interaction in the system. Culture is here defined as the values held and the norms followed by a distinct group of people. Culture has also been described as 'the software of the mind'[6] and as 'unstated assumptions, standard operating procedures, ways of doing things that have been internalized to such an extent that people do not argue about them'[7] or 'obviously valid' ideas and behavioural patterns that do not need to be debated.[8]

In the political culture approach, where 'attitudes, beliefs and rules that guide a political system'[9] make up the main sphere of interests, an a priori definition of democracy is irrelevant. Child-rearing and internalization of values and norms in the various agencies of socialization such as the family, education, and newsmedia on the other hand become highly relevant. Based on this perspective, it is not very difficult to find some of the key East–West differences regarding issues such as democracy and human rights. The most important differences relate to areas like: stability vs. rapid change; order vs. authority; and traditional values vs. modernization. Differences within these areas indicate East–West gaps between political cultures in their conceptualizations of the human being, society, change, development and values.

Sources of East–West Differences

Before entering a debate concerning conceptual differences between East Asia and the West with regard to democracy it is important to point at some of the sources of these differences. In contrast to Western culture, that has been predominantly occupied with scientific development, the East Asian culture has been preoccupied with social relations. A result of this has been that while the Western world-view became future-oriented, putting emphasis on being progressive and up-to-date, the East Asian world-view became oriented towards the past, cultivating social relationships based on imitations of great models. This links directly with the different mode of expression in Eastern and Western humanism. While humanism in the West denoted a break with religious mysticism, making a clear distinction between God and man, the East Asian humanism did not engage in a showdown with religious beliefs. In East Asia, many of the gods originally came from the human world. They became gods exactly because they possessed exceptional virtues and spiritual powers. The supernatural in East Asian philosophy is an objectification of the spirit of humanism. This is probably a difference of great importance when relating to the relationship between people in the political sphere. This seems obvious in a historical context, but even when relating to modern systems this must be brought in mind.[10]

Discussing democracy, freedom, liberalism, authoritarianism, dictatorship, etc., one is obviously inserting oneself into a Western historical context. These concepts emanate from a Western political and theoretical discourse reaching 25 centuries back to Athens, the dominating *polis* among other Greek city states at that time. Political thinkers like Thucydides, Plato, Aristoteles and Pericles were among the theorists (and practitioners as well) of this democracy, and part of their writing is still considered among the classics in theories of democracy. This tradition connects directly with the more recent contributions of Machiavelli, Hobbes, Locke, Montesquieu, Rousseau, Paine, Jefferson, Madison, Bentham and the Mills (both James and John Stuart), not to forget Tocqueville. There are several others that deserve mention in a list pretending to be anything close to complete. The number of central contributors to the theory of democracy is obviously increasing as we approach the nineteenth and twentieth centuries, and not least the divergence between proponents of different kinds of democracy is dramatically increasing.

Furthermore, historical milestones such as the Glorious Revolution in England (1688), the American Declaration of Independence (1776) and the French Revolution (1789) play decisive roles in the political discourse we briefly relate to here. This rather provocatively long list of names connected with the above-mentioned moments of condensed history serves one main purpose: to underline the simple fact that the history of democracy – in theory and practice – is a Western experience, created out of the specific needs and aims of shifting relevance in a long period of time and in a specific part of the world, namely the one commonly labelled the West. It can thus be argued that liberal democracy, in its full-fledged form, is primarily a characteristic of the economically advanced Western societies and is more a product of social-economic development than its cause.[11]

A transfer of these traditions, their experiences and vocabularies, to East Asia has hitherto been the norm. Some countries, of which China is the most notable, turned socialist and initially adopted the ideas and vocabulary of 'international' i.e. Western Communism. In other countries Western 'missionaries' of liberal democracy played together with segments of the local elite to establish the West as the only acceptable and civilized model in politics. Both 'Communism' and 'liberal democracy' were simply presented as systems to emulate, and it was eventually expected that these East Asian copies should turn out as true realizations of the original Western models. Disregarding different basic ideas and perceptions of man and society, political institutions were set up and governments were established according to foreign blueprints. Due to the international balance of power and the strong economic and political-ideological interests that were invested in this 'world-system', there was no real interest in or opening for local experiences, not to mention experiments.

However, in any part of the world historical events with tractable effects on the political discourse can be traced, and of course there have been political thinkers outside the Western hemisphere. Although *minzhu* is a modern concept, it does not mean that political thinking and dis-course have not existed in East Asia. In China Confucius stands out, but also Lao Tse, Mencius, Chu Hsün Tse, Chuang Tse, Mo Tse, and Han Fei can be mentioned among ancient philosophers relating to politics. Later Wang Yang-ming and Chu Hsi both were influential, while Kang Yu-wei and Fung Yu-lan were among the modern philosophers who have affected not only Chinese, but certainly the East Asian political thinking in general.[12] In Korea Yi Hwang (T'oegye) and Yi I (Yulgok), two prominent neo-Confucianists, are ascribed special roles in the indigenous political tradition.[13] In order to identify the basic aspects of East Asian political tradition with relevance for the modern political project in that region, the focus should be on the shift of dynasties, of dominating philosophies and religious creeds, wars, occupation and colonization, unequal trade and other direct foreign influences, etc. and especially on the intellectual representation and articulation of such phenomena and events. It is not a single value or a specific, easily identifiable way of thinking and living that characterizes East Asia compared to the West. In both parts of the world there are internal differences, tendencies pointing in the opposite direction from mainstream or official thinking. Traditionally legalism made up a strong political and philosophical counter-tradition in East Asia, at times even occupying the position of an official state ideology. And communitarianism has been and is still a potent political ideology in several Western countries, often constituting mainstream thinking about society and politics. This does not, however, alter the above argument pointing at basic similarities between the East Asian countries, similarities which often are exactly those aspects where East Asia differs from the West. To address these complicated problems one needs adequate tools.

According to what could be termed political ethnomethodology – a position relevant in the political culture approach – it is the politics that make sense to the people under study, and how they make sense, that is relevant. Such cross-cultural research demands a perspective based on reliable knowledge about basic tenets of people's world-view. In the case of East Asian legalism and the Western communitarianism mentioned above, it is important to realize that both ideologies in the 'local' versions are subordinated to the dominating world-view. Thus, Western communitarianism does not run counter to individualism; from the communitarian position it is on the contrary argued that only its principles can secure an environment that makes it possible for the individual to fulfil its personal desires. East Asian legalism – or democracy for that matter – on the other hand does not contradict a collective world-view, but bases its considerations on such a view. The way a system operates depends to a large degree on how people – who populate the institutions of the system – view themselves in relation to other people and the world in general.

Thus, in this chapter it will be argued that as much as the world truly needs a growing global awareness, there is an equally strong need for a better understanding and for mutual acceptance of existing local and regional distinctive marks. Instead of treating globalism and localism or regionalism as mutually exclusive phenomena, they should rather be seen as mutually dependent aspects of a comprehensive development process.

An encounter with Western-centrism seems to us to be a necessary point of departure for a proper cross-cultural discussion concerning political processes. The more so as this is linked to a basic prerequisite in cross-cultural studies of politics, maintaining that the political sphere is virtually interlocked with the dominant socio-cultural patterns in the given society. This realization has developed as it has become increasingly clear that differences other than political and ideological ones exist and play a crucial role in forming political systems and practices. A subtle but apparently persistent difference is the cultural characteristics of people living in different parts of the world. Beliefs, values and norms transfused from generation to generation in the socialization process are most likely of greater importance to politics than has hitherto been acknowledged.

Therefore, in this era of globalization where national and international elites establish world-wide networks and build bridges interconnecting the global 'community', these same elites run the risk of losing contact with their immediate support bases: their own people. If that happens, globalization will remain a 'virtual reality' only, and democracy will crumble where it is supposed to work and fail to develop where it is supposed to do so. This is not to argue for a localist approach, viewing the world in terms of 'us' and 'them', in which 'we are the good ones' and those outside are people of lesser quality and importance. Seen from our perspective, East Asia as well as the West are both in the process of meeting two interdependent challenges. The first is to revitalize the relationship between the governments and those governed. This could be termed: to make democracy work. The second challenge is to take part more actively in a multi-cultural world community. In both cases the necessary point of departure is one's own cultural background. Our concern here is especially East Asia, and in the following the development in China and South Korea will serve as examples of a political modernization process in a non-Western cultural sphere.

Minzhu or **Democracy?**

Today, China is no exception from the chain-structure of globalization – a new stage in world capitalist development – a movement which no single superpower or block of powers in the world system can control or resist. From the day China decided to open its market to the whole world, it began simultaneously to be dragged into the net of global capitalism. From that day on, China began to be truly vulnerable to the influence of external forces. In the recent past China has been bound up with the more general debate – which now has re-emerged – as to how far it should rely upon its own cultural and scientific traditions in order to catch up to the advanced countries, and how far it should import ideas and technology from the outside. Seen in this light, debates over democracy cannot be divorced from broader cultural questions and from the issue of how far China could, or should, allow itself to become dependent upon the external world.[14]

Traditionally Korea was as seclusive as China in relation to the West, and for some reason Koreans managed to seal off their country longer than both China and Japan. Since the Second World War, however, South Korea has been part and parcel of the capitalist world market, allegedly governed by liberal democratic governments following the Western lead. Currently the democratically elected government in South Korea is implementing political and institutional reforms to restructure its economy and consolidate democracy. In South Korea, democracy has gone from playing a role as a major disguise for authoritarian military governments to becoming a widely acclaimed institutionalized form of government. From the first post-war government to the present one, the conventional wisdom has been that democracy as a political system is a phenomenon with universal characteristics.[15] Recently efforts have been made to uproot illegitimate and undemocratic practices of former regimes, past misdeeds have been sought to be mended, and more – or more genuine – democracy has been the goal. There is nothing to indicate that these efforts are hypocritical and much has been achieved. But there are still open questions related to the desired political development. Among them a growing awareness of the problematic link between structure and culture contributes to making concerned Korean scholars search for new pathways towards a socially acceptable political system.[16]

Discussion of good government, political representation and consent are basic problems in any political system above the village level all over the world. A basic question is: Which individuals should be entitled to act as true representatives and as such receive authorization to command general decision-making power? Essentially this question centres around the nature of political leadership. In Western political thinking this is often dealt with as the problem of legitimacy, and it is moreover closely linked to institutional practices and considerations. Key features in liberal democracy that attempt to meet the criteria of political legitimacy include legal guarantees of citizenship rights, first and foremost the right to vote, as well as freedom of expression and organization. Linked to these rights is a competitive electoral system with political parties. And finally – on the institutional level – there is a system of checks and balances between the legislature, executive, judiciary and administrative powers.[17]

All the above-mentioned institutions, rules and regulations are developed to make the political system workable in an individualistic society. Not just any individualistic society, but a society characterized by individualism based on Christianity that, in Francis Fukuyama's words:

> ... provides the concept of a transcendent God whose Word is the highest source of right. In modern liberalism, the Christian concept of a universal God is replaced with the concept of an underlying human nature that becomes the universal basis of right. Liberal rights apply to all human beings as such, just as God's law did in Christianity, transcending any particular set of real-world social obligations.[18]

This transcendent source of morality enables the Western individual to ignore personal social obligations from the sphere of the family to that of the state. Accordingly, the individual is the point of departure in Western political thinking. Concepts of freedom, rights, and legal guarantees are all 'contracts' developed to secure the individual in relation to the collective. Collective bodies in the political system ultimately have the same ideal goal: to protect and defend the individual human being. This 'social contract' theory was first formulated by Thomas Hobbes in his main work on the modern state, *Leviathan* (1651), where he argued that in the pre-social history of humankind people enjoyed absolute freedom. Total freedom, however, involved a risk for the individual of being harmed or molested by the actions of others. In order to avoid this individuals living in societies had to agree on certain social rules and thus to surrender some of the personal freedom to a third party, the state, which became the authority to secure that the rules were followed by all.[19] The idea of a social contract based on a realization of the true human nature was undercutting the role and authority of religion. In Hobbes', Locke's, and Montesquieu's version of the good society individual happiness was the ultimate goal of a community and liberty meant freedom to dispose of one's own property.[20]

Another significant but not so often discussed trait in Western political thinking is that the whole construction is based on a notion of *distrust*. In the West this is called realism, and as reality seems to prove that power corrupts, the whole system revolves around mutual checks and balances. This distrust is possibly unavoidable in highly developed Western commercial societies, but even the above-mentioned twentieth century philosophers tended to believe that power needed to be controlled and managed, otherwise it would become a tool to seek personal profit. In Western thinking this has remained a basic axiom, and here it is held to be true in any country of any kind. It is hardly believed that power can be restrained by morality, therefore, legal means are employed to stipulate systems of supervision and control in order to avoid power running amuck. And therefore, in modern Western democracies the whole political system has been divided into a myriad of interest groups, each of which legitimately fights for its own rights, and – ideally – accepts the best possible compromise in the end.

This struggle and compromise, which is controlled by checks and balances, based on a negative perception of power as well as on the mutual distrust called realism, is thought to provide the best possible political system. It carries the label democracy, and is often referred to as government *of* the people, *by* the people, and *for* the people. In the West it is sacrosanct, and because the language of political discourse throughout the world has become Westernized, it almost amounts to heresy to question this as a universally valid understanding of democracy. But this general approach of Western political culture, which focuses on individual freedom and rights and protects individuals from coercion of the state, is too simple and too narrow. This is a concept of liberal politics that only relate to state institutions, whereas economic and cultural factors are regarded as separate and irrelevant spheres. The liberal model considers individual freedom to be more important than equality, and material scarcity is not seen as an obstacle for individuals to enjoy freedom. The flaw of liberal democracy is that it ignores the fact that in order to feel free, individuals must enjoy a certain degree of political and economical equality. If basic material needs of the individual citizen are ignored, political freedom remains irrelevant. Therefore, to distinguish between democratic and authoritarian regimes solely based on the narrow concept of liberal democracy is improper and misleading.

Contrary to the Western political heritage, East Asian political traditions encourage people to trust the moral example and goodwill of public officials, and it emphasizes moral and ideological education. This is only possible because of a radically different theory of man, who is seen as an 'intersubjective being, a being who cannot be determined independent of other human beings'.[21] Focusing on relationship rather than the individual makes hierarchy and authority inescapable basic phenomena in political thinking. And it makes the collective a primary process in relation to each individual member of the group. The patriarchal family is the ideal which this way of thinking takes as its point of departure and all other social relations are based on this ideal.

Western observers look upon this tradition with deep-seated scepticism. In the West, one prefers to trust an institutionalized system of checks and balances. Not least the current crisis in East Asia reaffirms Western criticism. Though it is an economic crisis, the political scene is not left untouched. To take South Korea as an example, a lot of unhealthy economic transactions have been possible solely because of personal connections. Unrealistic economic activities have taken place and been kept alive due to brotherly relations between political powerholders and financial tycoons.

Are East Asians too naive and their traditions therefore dysfunctional? In tracing the origins of East Asian philosophical ideas and moral systems, it is not difficult to find that they were all products of a non-commercial world. Thus, many East–West differences are the products of a different background of social development and transformation. The familialistic view of society is not without a control-and-check system though, but Confucian teachings provide us with a system based on a certain kind of social morality. Confucianism sees the ruler as a boat and people as water. Following the logic of Confucianism: water can hold the boat, and water can also overturn it. If the ruler loses the 'mandate' it is considered natural that people eventually stand up in revolt.

In comparison with the relationship discussed above between Christianity and Liberalism, the one acting as the transcendent source of morality for the other, the political ideology stemming from Confucianism is characterized by benevolent authoritarianism. When using the Confucianist concept, it is important to see Confucianism as both philosophy and state orthodoxy. As a philosophy, it is in the simplest terms an interpretation of ideal social praxis as the perfect complementarity of roles in which each individual conducts himself or herself in an exemplary way that befits that individual's position relative to others within society. As a state orthodoxy, Confucianism regards the government or the highest political authority as the true instrument in guiding the conduct of the society. The aim of Confucian orthodoxy was the well-organized society provided by the moral guidance of a Confucian-informed government. It is important to bear in mind that this moral philosophy traditionally made up the basis of the leading state ideology throughout East Asia, as well as the ethics of daily life for the majority of the people in the region. The social relevance and political strength of Confucianism, not to mention its longevity, are due to this coexistence of political philosophy with social morality, making the state appear as the natural extension of one's family.[22]

It is a widely accepted fact that China is the cradle and core representative of East Asian civilization in which Confucianism was the basic moral philosophy and social doctrine. This Confucian world-view has always been the antithesis of individualism. It was fiercely against the pursuit of self-interest, considering any one who demands individual rights as a selfish 'small man'. Even when the imperial system broke down in the early twentieth century, releasing a great deal of cultural iconoclasm among Chinese intellectuals, it was still very rare to find consistent defenders of self-interested individualism. It was commonly accepted that the state granted rights and determined their limits.[23] Approaching the end of the century, under quite another political system Chinese students during the 1989 mass demonstrations, while calling for democracy, were actually demanding the right to be heard and the removal of corrupt officials. It can thus be argued that what they really wanted was non-corrupt, clean, good and honest government, not the formal 'democracy' in the Western version.

Confucianism is naturally associated with China. It is less known that the traditional political culture of Korea probably was more imbued with Confucianism than was the case even in China, where it originated. In modern South Korea 'the formal state ideology of Confucianism has long since disappeared'.[24] In addition, as a philosophy that people claim to support, or as a moral teaching they consciously adhere to, Confucianism is almost non-existent in South Korea. But over the years the values and norms of this philosophy have permeated the Korean society possibly to a larger extent than in any other East Asian country.[25] Even more important, as Yang and Henderson pointed out in 1958, 'No other tradition of thought and government which can be closely associated with Korea's past was to leave so permanent an influence into the present day'.[26] More recent studies suggest that this still is a valid judgement.[27] Based upon a 1990 sample survey from South Korea directed by Godwin Chu,[28] Chu and the other authors of the book presenting and analysing the survey results conclude that 'the Confucian tradition is alive and well'.[29] This was also confirmed in two surveys focusing on the political culture of intellectuals in South Korean urban settings conducted in 1990 and replicated in 1995.[30] The response pattern to questions related to moral-philosophical matters are, for an exceptionally strong majority of the respondents in the above mentioned surveys, totally in accordance with Confucianism.[31]

As noted above, Francis Fukuyama has pointed out that the most striking incompatibility between democracy and Confucianism is the latter's lack of support for individualism or a transcendent law that would stand above existing social relationships and provide the ground for individual conscience as the ultimate source of authority.[32] From the view of (Christian) liberalism, (Confucian) authoritarianism is a negative phenomenon, whether benevolent or not. But this judgement is obviously based on an awkward approach, as neither of the two ideologies can reasonably be judged by each other's basic values, if the aim is to understand the apparent differences between East and West, differences that indeed include perceptions of self and society. If the point of departure in Confucianism is social relationships rather than individual human beings, and if there is nothing above humanity, i.e. no transcendent source of morality, the nature of political leadership must be seen in relation to this fact. If East Asians, as Fukuyama claims, do not command 'a source of legitimate authority on the basis of which they can revolt against their families and the web of social ties into which they are born', why should such an authority then be introduced into their society? No doubt this, from a liberal point of view, would be considered a great developmental breakthrough towards modernity. But it would also without doubt effect the destruction of the indigenous cultural pattern on which the society as well as the state now stands. Ultimately the social fabric – as it is known in East Asia today – would evaporate. To see this as progress demands a strong conviction in the Western liberal cultural superiority and universal validity.

Authoritarian government in East Asia has been seen as an integral part of a development strategy which had the strength not only for consolidating societies in developmental flux but also for creating entrepreneurial classes to compete on the world market. East Asian elites have seen authoritarian government as a useful expedient for effective policy-making in the face of political instability. Most East Asian policy-makers did not regard Western democracy on its own as a political system that necessarily would lead to development. From their point of view, what a country needed at its initial developmental stage was discipline more than democracy.[33]

Of course it ought to be pointed out that this corollary is not per definition true. Authoritarian and anti-democratic regimes did not automatically lead to economic development. But without the devotion to development as found in the East Asian states, whether democratic or not, developing countries are not likely to achieve a real breakthrough, not to mention modernization. Not only East Asian politicians and intellectuals hold this view. In a special focus on *Culture: the Neglected Dimension of Development*, Ismaïl Serageldin, then director of the World Bank's Africa Department, wrote that a relevant framework for effective institutions is a prerequisite for development. He traced the failure in Africa to the absence of such institutions, and said that 'the lack of a viable cultural framework erodes national self-confidence and leads to social fragmentation with westernized elites and poor, alienated majorities'.[34]

The situation in Taiwan and South Korea during the past three decades demanded authoritarian regimes in order to achieve political stability and long-term predictability of the system. They are examples of gradual evolution from political dictatorship to limited pluralism. But neither of them reformed their political system until their economic development was well advanced.

We have sought to substantiate that the formation of East Asian people's governments cannot but be different from their Western counterparts. They can hardly be based on individualism, and concepts of freedom, rights, and legal guaranties must necessarily be translated because the East Asian context differs substantially from the one where these ideas have developed. In the long run it could possibly even be more realistic if the whole political apparatus be based on trust rather than on distrust, knowing that social relationships are fundamental in the underlying collectivistic world-view.

East Asian Political Perspectives on Man and Society

Social institutions such as the family, the lineage, local social networks, school and workplace networks, etc. all of whom subordinate individual drives and aspirations in favour of the group, play a critical role in generating order and continuity, and are in East Asia valued accordingly. The importance attached to order and the overall interest of society as a living entity leads East Asian leaders to attribute moral superiority to the community over the individual. The Chinese one-child policy may serve as an example. From a Western perspective the one-child policy is considered to be a severe violation of human rights.[35] This viewpoint is challenged in a recent survey, where data indicate that the population policy of the Chinese state is accepted by urban citizens even when the fertility requirement goes contrary to family norms.[36]

The survey focused on urban women and dealt with, among other issues, the placement of fertility decisions at national or individual level. To the statement *The number of children is the choice of the individual*, 42 per cent agreed, 46 per cent disagreed, and 12 per cent did not answer. Shifting the focus from the individual to the family brought a change in the response pattern. The statement *The nation has to adopt a policy to control population*, is met with 83 per cent acceptance, while 7 per cent disagreed and 10 per cent did not answer. Comparing the individual with the national perspective in the statement *The individual must voluntarily submit to the policy of the nation*, 85 per cent agreed, 6 per cent disagreed, while 9 per cent did not answer.[37] This response pattern implies that although Chinese women might wish to have more children, they accept a policy of population control. In a liberal context this seems contradictory, but it might only be an illustration of the problems attached to cross-cultural judgements without cross-cultural considerations. If the Chinese population in the post-liberation period has been taught core virtues rooted in the Confucian tradition in a kind of 'proletarianized' Confucianism,[38] the above-mentioned response pattern may reflect the extent to which this teaching has succeeded.

The close linkage between perceptions of family and state is not confined to the Chinese mainland. Recently Singaporean Prime Minister Goh Chok Tong rejected the Western demand for fundamental political reforms by saying:

> Our institutions and basic policies are in place to sustain high economic growth. But if we lose our traditional values, our family strengths and our social cohesion, we will lose our vibrancy and decline. This is the intangible factor in the success of the East Asian economies.[39]

This view is also shared by other Asian leaders. Thailand's King Bhumibol has expressed the essence of this perspective by placing emphasis on duties rather than rights. He encapsulates the Asian societies:

> A nation is made up of various institutions in the same way as all the organs which make up a live body. Life in a body can endure, because the organs, large or small, function normally. Likewise, a nation can endure, because its various institutions are firm and are fully discharging their respective duties. You must all realize that the nation is the life, the blood and the property of everyone ... To uphold and safeguard the nation is the duty ... of every party. Each and everyone must work together ..., sharing common aims and objectives. Should any group fail in its duty ... the entire nation may collapse and be destroyed.[40]

This organic perception of society using biological terms to describe not only how society is understood, but also how it is felt, is very 'Asian'. Social science in the West has great difficulty in accepting this style and its implications. But to most East Asians the parallel between the human body, the family and society is not only acceptable, but in fact very natural. Let us quote a few authoritative examples to substantiate our claim.

Not much similarity may be found between the King of Thailand and a North Korean *Juche*-ideologue, but in explaining the importance of leadership, the North Korean terminology is parallel to that of the royal Thai. The leader is described as nothing less than

> [T]he highest brain of the people. This means that the leader occupies the same place as the brain in the human body. The brain regulates and controls all functions of the organism of the man ... Likewise, it is the leader that regulates and controls the functions of the enormous organism called the masses of the people.[41]

Such a blatant description justifying strong leadership may not be easily found outside East Asian communist systems. But other varieties of this biological, blood-based political morality exist, and among them the field of moral education is dominant.

Chinese philosophy has always emphasized moral education to an extent where this might be seen in the place of formal religion.[42] The moral and spiritual foundation of the West was established on Judaeo-Christian religious doctrines, and religion in the West, whether Protestant or Catholic, has been pervasive and dominant in Western culture. In East Asia, it was not religion but moral philosophy that provided the spiritual basis for culture. It can be said that ethics and morality have a religious quality in East Asia.

Moral education is a standard and compulsory curriculum subject in the educational system in all the East Asian and several other Asian countries. Looking for fields where the moral and ideological ideas of the governing elites are revealed, this one is suitable. Here the world-view of the political authorities, or at least the world-view which the authorities wish to imbue in the populace, is clearly revealed. In the 1991 edition of South Korean moral education textbooks, commissioned by the Ministry of Education, the family is presented as the nucleus of the nation, and the nation as an extended family. The idea of ancestor worship and filial piety is explained as a blood-based relationship characterized by a feeling of being *one and the same*. Generations are not only linked by sharing a name and a common history and destiny, they are considered as being the same flesh and blood. The textbook explanation is that:

> the relationship between parents and children is an inseparable physical one in which they share bones, flesh, and blood. It is a relationship in which both parents and children feel inside each other.[43]

This description of ancestor worship and filial piety, the mainstay of Confucianism, is extended to a moral and blood-based nationalism. As the whole people can be divided in children, parents and ancestors, the

> ancestral worship, which is only a part of our unique tradition, has great vitality that enable us to belong and depend on our family as well as our people, nation, and race.[44]

In *The Third Wave*, Huntington claims that Confucianism as an obstacle to democracy in the 1980s was weakened in Korea by urbanization, education, the development of a substantial middle class, and the impressive spread of Christianity. His assertion is modified, though, by the following: 'Yet it remained unclear whether the struggle between the old culture and the new prosperity had been definitively resolved in favor of the latter'.[45] The problem with this scenario is that some values, here the indigenous ones, are perceived as belonging to the past, blocking change and growth, while other values, the imported ones, are future-oriented, and obviously linked to development and progress. This scenario would be understandable if the analysis were based on the idea that democracy, exactly as it evolved in the West, was the natural goal of societal development everywhere. It would then be an understandable, but undoubtedly still a Eurocentric view. A more open-minded approach to non-Western democratization would be to avoid the distinction between traditional and modern, and instead use concepts like indigenous and imported.

The two surveys mentioned earlier, conducted among South Korean intellectuals in 1990 and 1995, substantiate our critique of Huntington's approach.[46] The target groups in the two surveys can generally be characterized as: modern, urban, educated, articulated, politically aware and concerned, and well-informed and experienced in international matters, among other things by acquiring parts of their education from Western universities. More than 75 per cent of the respondents in both surveys agreed to the following five statements:

- Respect for one's ancestors will surely survive modernization in Korea.
- Good morals and a humane attitude are the most important qualities in politics.
- Only a morally strong society without political and economic corruption can shape a better future for all its members.
- The objective of democracy is harmonious social relations.
- Korean democracy must take the traditional culture as its point of departure.

Based on the near-consensus agreement upon the statements above, a distinction between traditional and modern seems obsolete to us – no longer relevant in this post-cold-war era. And, moreover, such a distinction automatically rates basic values as being more or less modern, if not more or less civilized. Seen in a culture-relativistic perspective, leaving the scene open for other forms of social practices including other forms of good governance, it is more reasonable to perceive the values as being on different levels, some more basic and others more superficial, when it comes to their power as guidelines for political views.

East Asian 'Values Democracy'?

Modernization and democratization has for long been a Western-oriented project in East Asia, a project where the elites have been busy dissociating themselves from the past, seeing the indigenous culture as a conglomeration of outdated ideas and philosophies linked with stagnating peasant societies. This trend is now challenged. Notwithstanding current problems, as East Asia reaches a higher level of economic development and status in the global community, the magnetism of the Western/American model gradually loses power. At present the dividing line between countries adhering to state 'socialism' as opposed to countries following the Western model of 'free market economies' with 'liberal' political systems is in the process of being erased. In East Asia, where state socialism formally still exists as a political alternative, there seems nevertheless to be a growing awareness of the common cultural traits that bind the region together and distinguish it from other parts of the world.

This was clearly revealed in the 1993 Bangkok Declaration signed by representatives of Asian States as a regional preparation for the World Conference on Human Rights in Vienna. Even though the universality and objectivity of human rights were adopted, it was also stressed that social justice and a just world economic order are seen as prerequisites for realizing these rights. And it was emphasized that the significance of national and regional peculiarities and various historical, cultural and religious backgrounds must be taken into account. This important but rather cautious and non-provocative dissent, agreed upon by all the Asian representatives in Bangkok, with Japan as the noted exception,[47] was basically ignored by Western government representatives and the Western media in the enthusiastic mode of universal agreement that marked the final documents of the Vienna conference.

In addition to the Bangkok Declaration, another indication of this trend of focusing on common features of Asian culture was the semi-official Commission for a New Asia, which after a meeting in Malaysia in 1993 released a report to encourage an Asian Values Democracy, or Benevolent Democracy.[48] The report is a product of the joint efforts of a commission of sixteen intellectuals including former government advisers. The group consists of citizens from ten Asian countries with different political systems and ideological inclinations, as well as members from two non-Asian countries.[49] It is the stated intention of the Commission to work for an Asian renaissance, in order to single out the direction for mutual economic prosperity in order for the whole continent to assume its rightful global position.

The reflections in the report on a good political system, acceptable in relation to the values and mores of Asia, and able to take root in Asian societies, are worth noting. In brief this system is characterized by a number of reciprocal relations: personal freedom that requires individual responsibility; initiative which presupposes discipline; individual rights which must be seen in relation to collective obligations; and that the condition for social welfare is individual unselfishness. This morally founded reciprocal social system emphasizes the balance between the individual and the community, between rights and duties, between personal happiness and the common welfare of society. It is the obligation of the state to secure this balance, to secure the right to social order, and to secure freedom from anarchy and chaos. Neither a weak nor a passive state is able to maintain such a system, whereas a morally strong state is. In this perspective the state is viewed as a body capable of establishing the framework to secure a balance between the rights and duties of the individual and of the collective. The East Asian tradition of central authority or hierarchical loyalty establishes a framework for concerted national action. The emphasis on the well-being of the collective as opposed to the personal interests of the individual in Confucian philosophy translates into a political demand within Confucian orthodoxy for obedience to the will of the government as the means to true social harmony.

This East Asian vision of good government challenges the liberal 'cult of the individual'. It stresses that in order to be resilient and durable the system must both relate to existing culturally conditioned values, and at the same time try to entrench the very fabric of society with a political culture facilitating appropriate relationship between the leaders and the led. Recent statements from political leaders in the region can also be listed as examples of this new cultural consciousness. Lee Kuan Yew of Singapore has been particularly outspoken on this issue, as has Prime Minister Mahathir of Malaysia. Even the prime ministers of China and Japan, Li Peng and Hosokawa, made a joint statement in 1994, warning the West against forcing their type of democracy upon others.[50]

Prospects for a Culturally Acceptable Mode of Government

In the process of globalization, the concept of democracy has to be reconsidered not only in East Asia but in the West as well. Not to find the ultimate model, but to realize the simple truth, that the divergence between ideal democracy and the existing world-wide reality seems to increase. Asian critique of Western democracy often focuses on aspects that are viewed as negative social consequences of the democratic system such as divided families, drug problems and crime. Former Singaporean Prime Minister Lee Kuan Yew is an outspoken critic of US-style 'Western democracy':

> I find parts of it totally unacceptable: guns, drugs, violent crime, vagrancy, unbecoming behavior in public – in sum the breakdown of civil society. The expansion of the right of the individual to behave or misbehave as he pleases has come at the expense of orderly society. In the East the main object is to have a well-ordered society so that everybody can have maximum enjoyment of his freedom. This can only exist in an ordered state and not in a natural state of contention and anarchy.[51]

Similar arguments are forwarded by Kishore Mahbubani, who criticizes the direction of American society. Its democracy has experienced serious problems of its own in reconciling individual rights with the interests of the larger community:

> American society, by permitting all forms of lifestyle to emerge – without any social pressures to conform to certain standards – may have wrecked the moral and social fabric that is needed to keep a society calm and well ordered. A well-ordered society needs to plant clear constraints on behavior in the minds of its citizens. In the United States it is clear that many such fundamental psychological constraints have collapsed, with the acceptance of all forms of lifestyle as legitimate.[52]

This critique, as well as the one forwarded by Lee above, reflects the fact that judgments based on fundamentals in one culture lose validity when applied to the reality in another. Whether or not one acclaims this critique, it seems clear that both Lee and Mahbubani take it for granted, that the state through the political power-holders in the last instance has responsibility for the population at large. In definitions of Western liberal democracy this responsibility has been de-linked from the political system, and the Asian critique is thus perceived as misplaced, irrelevant and even anti-democratic.

More direct political problems are threatening liberal democracy, however, problems that must be rendered culturally relevant. Democracy as government of the people, for the people, and by the people stands more and more as an illusion in most Western countries. Politics has developed from people's power into a trade for specialists. Instead of being a dialogue between leaders and the led, the discussion between advocates of alternative solutions to political problems is guided by commercial advertisement companies. Elected politicians are hunted by lobbyists, who in turn are paid by large organizations and huge private firms, and the time horizon for a politician is limited to the period between two elections. The outcome of election campaigns increasingly depends on money and public relations consultancies, which leaves little room and reason for popular political participation. Instead of providing the public with information to qualify for democratic participation the mass media have become a source of entertainment. Thus political apathy and alienation among 'the grassroots' is prevalent. Whether this situation is solely due to the intrusion of market 'rationality' into politics, or if one must look for other reasons as well, lies outside the scope of this chapter. But regardless of the reasons, Western politics seem to be steadily developing in a less and less democratic direction. The recent establishment of a European Union with supra-national political authority in central matters has not contributed to moderate political alienation among the Europeans.

East Asia has opened up remarkably in the past few years; still, no country in the region is likely to succeed in making a liberal system identical to those established in the West work in their country. Political pluralism seems to have taken root, but even if it has happened as quickly as manufacturing technology did in the 1960s and 1970s, it is not an uncontested development. Despite our disagreement with Huntington's arguments discussed above, we would like to credit him for bringing culture (he mainly applies the term 'civilization') back into the forefront of political science studies. By emphasizing that culture will play an increasingly important role in world politics, he has managed to raise an international scholarly debate concerning the terms of international political discourse.

In relation to our present discussion, another of Huntington's observations concerning Asia deserves special attention. He points to the dominant-party system as an interesting consequence of the strong trend of continuity in East Asian political culture. This system involves competition for power without alternation of power-holders, and participation in elections for all but participation in office only for the mainstream party.[53] He suggests that such a system may be seen as representing 'an adaption of Western democratic practice to serve Asian or Confucian political values. Democratic institutions work not to promote Western values of competition and change but Confucian values of consensus and stability'.[54]

From a Western point of view this may not be at all acceptable. Proponents of democracy, as it has been known hitherto, might wish to reserve the concept to political systems with more clear-cut definitions living up to some basic aspects delineated in the liberalist tradition. The problem with this is that we then shall have to continue operating with 'the West against the rest'.

The liberal model of democracy has been elevated to the position of a universal truth. This is, however, a conceptual misrepresentation. As it has been discussed above, a model developed in one part of the world, based on one particular set of conditions in one particular period of history, cannot – as a matter of course – have general validity. This would be acceptable under one fundamental condition which is, that not only is man created alike, but furthermore that people in all parts of the world have exactly the same hopes and aspirations, the same ideas about good and evil, the same emotional needs, dreams and desires. But this is hardly so. People may biologically be created equal and alike, although with different predispositions and abilities. But from the time of Creation the given circumstances have been different in different parts of the world. For this reason, people actually develop distinctly different values and norms which guide their world-views. These values and norms include the preferences of importance in relation to political viewpoints.

But if every political system is a unique, socially constructed creation within the confines of a cultural context, which to a greater or lesser degree shapes the pattern of human interaction in the system, politics in the West may currently be said to have lost some of the cultural touch. This may be connected to the weak position of religion in many Western countries, if one perceives of religion in the Durkheimian sense as a system of beliefs and rituals with reference to the sacred which binds people together into social groups. Seeing this in Fukuyama's perspective as referred above,[55] the great problems that can be observed in Western politics and society may emanate from the disappearance of the basis of the transcendent source of morality which, in Fukuyama's words, enables the Western individual to ignore any kind of social obligations from the family sphere to the state. If the sacred source has evaporated, total freedom may remain, but with this also insecurity and alienation. In the Weberian way of understanding religion, this kind of freedom implies a lack of meaning in life and with life.

The aim of stressing reciprocal relationships in the East Asian version of good government discussed above was to secure the balance between the individual and the community, between rights and duties, between personal happiness and the common welfare of society. These considerations are basic, not only in the East Asian context, but to the survival of any political system and any society, and they should therefore be brought to the forefront of the global political agenda.

Notes

1   *Minzhu* is a Chinese literal translation of the word 'democracy'. Originally there was no such term in the Chinese vocabulary or in that of other East Asian countries. The term can be found in the classical texts however, for instance in Mencius, but here with a different meaning. The modern *minzhu* is a constructed

concept gradually formed at the beginning of this century when China was in the revolutionary transition from a feudal dynasty to a republic. Then *minzhu* became an important part of Sun Yat-sen's *Three Principles*. The notion of *minzhu* implied that China had something to learn from the West; people's voice should be heard. *minzhu* being used in the title of this article in contrast to democracy aims to indicate the link with, as well as the distinction from, the Western concept of democracy. *Minzhu* in the Chinese or East Asian sense – it is also known and used in Japanese and Korean – does not necessarily embrace the definition of democracy from the Western political and theoretical discourse.

2   L.W. Pye, *Asian Power and Politics*. Cambridge, Mass: Harvard University Press, 1985, p. vii.

3   S.P. Huntington, 'The Clash of Civilizations?' *Foreign Affairs*, Vol. 72 No. 3, 1993, p.25.

4   Roy Hofheinz Jr. and Kent E. Calder, *The East Asia Edge*, New York: Basic Books, 1982.

5   The concept was coined in the late 1950s and early 1960s. See Gabriel Almond, 'Comparative Political Systems', *Journal of Politics*, Vol. 18, 1956; Gabriel A. Almond and S. Verba, *The Civic Culture: Political Attitudes and Democracy in Five Nations*, Princeton, NJ: Princeton University Press, 1963; and Lucian W. Pye and Sidney Verba (eds), *Political Culture and Political Development*, Princeton, NJ: Princeton University Press, 1965.

6   G. Hofstede, *Cultures and Organizations: Software of the Mind*, McGraw-Hill: New York, 1991.

7   H.C. Triandis, *Culture and Social Behavior*. McGraw-Hill, New York: McGraw Hill, 1994 p. 16.

8   Ibid.

9   N. Abercrombie (ed.), *Dictionary of Sociology*, London: Penguin Books, 1994 p. 315.

10   J.S. Wu, 'Western Philosophy and the search for Chinese wisdom', in Arne Naess and Alastair Hannay (eds), *Invitation to Chinese Philosophy*, Oslo: Universitetsforlaget, 1972 pp. 5–9.

11   Gordon White, 'Democratization and Economic Reform in China', *The Australian Journal of Chinese Affairs*, No. 31, 1994 p. 79.

12   W.T. Chan, *A Source Book in Chinese Philosophy*, Princeton, NJ: Princeton University Press, 1963.

13   K.B. Lee, *A New History of Korea*, Seoul: Ilchokak Publishers, 1984.

14   P. Ferdinand, 'Socialism and Democracy in China' in David McLellan and Sean Sayer (eds), *Socialism and Democracy*, London: Macmillan Academic and Profession Ltd, 1991, p. 173.

15   There was a period, coinciding with Park Chung-hee's regime from 1961 to 1979, when the official policy in South Korea was that 'full democracy', as defined in the West, did not fit the Korean situation (C.H. Park, *Our Nation's Path*, Seoul: Dong-A Publishing Company Ltd., 1962). But in this period the

intellectual elite – even stronger than before – emphasized that democracy had to be seen as a universal concept (K.S. Min, 'Personal Reflections on Democracy in Korea' Center for Korean Studies Colloquium Paper No. 3, Honolulu, 1975).

16 C. Hahm, 'The Clash of Civilizations Revisited: A Confucian Perspective'. Paper presented at La Trobe University, Australia, 1995.

17 D. Held, *Models of Democracy*, Cambridge: Polity Press, 1987, p. 204.

18 F. Fukuyama, 'Confucianism and Democracy', *Journal of Democracy*, Vol. 6, No. 2, 1995, pp. 29–30.

19 Held, *Models of Democracy*, pp. 48–50.

20 C. Hahm, 'The Confucian Political Discourse and the Politics of Reform in Korea'. Paper presented at the Annual Meeting of the American Political Science Association, New York (Copyright APSA), 1994, pp. 7–9.

21 Ibid., p. 12.

22 K.O. Kim, 'A Study on the Political Manipulation of Elite Culture: Confucian Culture in Local Level Politics.' *Korea Journal*, Vol. 28, No. 11, 1988, p. 10.

23 Ferdinand, 'Socialism and Democracy in China', p. 166.

24 M. Robinson, 'Perceptions of Confucianism in Twentieth-Century Korea', in Gilbert Rozman (ed.), *The East Asian Region: Confucian Heritage and its Modern Adaption*, New Jersey: Princeton University Press, 1991, p.224.

25 K.P. Yang and G. Henderson, 'An Outline History of Korean Confucianism', *Journal of Asian Studies*, Vol. 17, No. 1, 1958, p. 94.

26 Ibid., p. 88.

27 Y.S. Chang, 'The Urban Korean as Individual', *Korea Journal*, Vol. 17, No. 5, 1977.

28 584 randomly selected respondents were interviewed nationwide, 530 questionnaires provided complete data (Zhongdang Pan, Steven H. Chaffee, Godwin C. Chu and Yanan Ju, *To See Ourselves: Comparing Traditional Chinese and American Cultural Values*, Boulder, Colorado: Westview Press, 1994, p. 201).

29 Ibid., p. 209.

30 The target groups in the two surveys were the politically concerned and articulated urban intellectual elite. University professors and students form the majority, together with journalists, schoolteachers and civil servants. In the 1995 survey workers and housewives were also represented. The 1990 survey covered 500 respondents, the 1995 survey 838 respondents. The study is presented in G. Helgesen, *Democracy and Authority in Korea: The Cultural Dimension in Korean Politics*, Richmond: Curzon Press, New York: St.Martin's Press, 1998.

31 Ibid. See also G. Helgesen and S.R. Thomsen, *Measuring Attitude Dimensions: The Case of South Korean Democratization*. NIAS Report No. 27, 1995.

32 Fukuyama, 'Confucianism and Democracy'.

33 Li Xing, *China and East Asia vs. the West: Controversies, Clashes and Challenges*, Working Paper No. 47, Aalborg University, Denmark, 1995, p. 11.

34 *UNESCO Sources* No. 25, 1991, p. 10.

35 In the 1995 UN Women's Conference in Beijing Hillary Clinton, the US first lady, in a much-acclaimed speech advocated the woman's rights as human rights, and stressed that it is the woman's right to decide upon childbirth or abortion.

36 C.N. Milwertz, *Accepting Population Control – Urban Chinese Women and the One-Child Family Policy*, Richmond, UK: Curzon, 1997.

37 The empirical data in Milwertz' study is based on 857 questionnaires and a number of in-depth qualitative interviews with Chinese urban women.

38 G.G. Reed, 'Moral/Political Education in the People's Republic of China: learning through role models', *Journal of Moral Education*, Vol. 24 No. 2, 1995, pp. 99, 101.

39 G. Rodan, 'Ideological Convergences Across "East" and "West": The New Conservative Offensive'. Working Paper No. 41, Aalborg University, Denmark, 1995 p. 9.

40 King Bhumibol Adulyadej, as quoted in Garry Rodan and Kevin Hewson, 'The Clash of Cultures or Convergence of Political Ideologies', paper presented at: 'Looking North: Reassessing the Framework and Unravelling the Myths', held by the Asia Research Centre, Murdoch University, 18–19 November 1994.

41 C.H. Kim, *The Immortal Juche Idea*, Pyongyang: Foreign Languages Publishing House, 1984 p. 178.

42 Wu, 'Western Philosophy', p. 12.

43 Korean Ministry of Education, *Moral Education, Seventh Grade*, Seoul 1991, pp.60–61.

44 Ibid., p. 81.

45 S.P. Huntington, *The Third Wave: Democratization in the Late Twentieth Century*, Norman and London: University of Oklahoma Press, 1991, p. 304.

46 Helgesen, *Democracy and Authority*.

47 Japan's reasons for departing from the rest of Asia in this particular case was not officially voiced. If Japan had sided with the other Asian countries it might have caused a little more 'noise' on the international political scene in Vienna.

48 Noordin Sopiee, *Towards a New Asia*. A Report of the Commission for a New Asia, Kuala Lumpur, 1994.

49 The twelve countries are: Australia, Bangladesh, China, Hong Kong, India, Indonesia, Japan, Malaysia, the Philippines, Russia, Singapore, and Vietnam. The report *Towards A New Asia* received support from Sasakawa Peace Foundation.

50 M. Alagappa, *Democratic Transition in Asia: the Role of the International Community*, East–West Center Special Reports, Honolulu, 1994, p. 17.

51 F. Zakaria, 'Culture is Destiny. A Conversation with Lee Kuan Yew', *Foreign Affairs*, Vol. 73 No. 2, 1994, p. 112.

52 K. Mahbubani, 'The United State: "Go East, Young Man"', *The Washington Quarterly*, 1994 pp. 5–23.

53 Huntington, *The Third Wave*, p. 306.

54 Ibid.

55 Fukuyama, 'Confucianism and Democracy'.

9 *DEMOKRASI PANCASILA* AND THE FUTURE OF IDEOLOGY IN INDONESIA

Hans Antlöv

Indonesia has for decades been one of the most devoted agents in Asia for a political structure based on cultural ideology. Ever since nationalists prepared for the independence of their nation-of-intent two generations ago, it was clear that Indonesia was not going to be a liberal Western democracy. It was instead to be founded on its proud indigenous values and traditions. During the 1990s, this Indonesian type of political structure has been seen as a so-called Asian values polity. With Western governments increasingly pushing for a single (liberal) definition of democracy, Asian statesmen have put forward their own political alternatives. Political leaders in Indonesia have until recently remained strongly faithful to their kind of authoritarian government, the so-called *Demokrasi Pancasila*. Only recently, after the financial and political turbulence of 1997–98, and the transition to a new president, has a hesitant state-initiated policy to depart from this ideology begun.

It is important to remember, however, that the state-supported *Demokrasi Pancasila* has never been the only political discourse in Indonesia. There have always been other co-existing ideologies. This is obvious, but often forgotten in Indonesia, because the state-supported ideology has been so dominant, both nationally and as part of the wave of Asian values. What we shall do in this chapter is first to look closer at *Demokrasi Pancasila*, its ideological roots and official discourse. We shall then turn to one of several alternative cultural-political perceptions, a community-based, popular understanding of politics, and see what it promises for the future of democracy in Indonesia.

Pancasila in Nation-Building

When Indonesia declared itself independent and democratic in August 1945, already the aspiration of its leaders was not to make the new nation a regular Western democracy. The nation was based on the five moral principles of *Pancasila*: monotheism, humanitarianism, nationalism, consensus-democracy, and justice. We can hear the enchanting voice of Soekarno when, in 1945, he first declared this idea of a specific Indonesian nation-state. 'If I compress what was five [the Pancasila principles] into three, and what was three into one, then I have a genuine Indonesian term, *gotong royong*, mutual cooperation. The state of Indonesia, which we are to establish, must be a *gotong royong* state. Is that not something marvellous: a *Gotong Royong* state'. Soekarno envisaged a nation built on mutual cooperation between different classes and political parties, not on competition and opposition. He continued to declare that Indonesia shall be a democracy, but not like the democracies of the West, rather a '*socio-demokrasi*', democracy combined with prosperity.

Soekarno built his modern nation-of-intent on an existing tradition. In so doing, he both emulated and localized Western notions of democracy. He emulated democracy because it had become an important global norm, and because social democracy was an important aim for the nationalists. After World War II, socialists and capitalists alike the world over took up democracy. But Soekarno also localized democracy, just as Nehru did in India with his Asian-style democracy, and national leaders in other Asian, African and European nations. Soekarno and other leaders of newly independent countries needed to do so for people to understand the new political order. The aim was to set up a form of democratic and just rule that was in line with the local aspirations of people, while being recognized by the international community.

Indonesia based its version of democracy on nationalism and communitarianism. In the original 1945 constitution – which is anything but

Western liberal – very strong powers are invested in the president. There is no division of the *trias politica*. General elections are not mentioned. There was only room for one party, the Indonesian National Party. In Soekarno's romantic view of the nation, ideological differences were to be subsumed to national interest, with the president as the wise and sole source of ultimate power and wisdom. The new Indonesian democracy was thus positioned within an age-long political tradition based on the family (*kekeluargaan*), mutual cooperation (*gotong royong*), consent (*musyawarah*), and the unity of the ruler and ruled (*manunggaling kawula lan gusti*). The ultimate model was a romanticized image of the local community, in which the people choose their wise ruler by mutual consent.

During the war of independence against the Dutch leading up to full sovereignty in late 1949, there was not much room for any kind of democracy, community-based or not. After independence, however, a surge of democracy guided ideological discussions. Due to intense political competition, Soekarno was forced to abandon his notion of a community-based democracy and move towards parliamentary democracy. A myriad of small political parties participated in the 1955 election, the first free national election in Indonesian history. Economic mis-management and political instability led to increased domestic tensions. In 1957 Soekarno held his famous 'Bury the Parties' speech where he argued for a return to the 1945 constitution, with a single strong party and close to unlimited powers to the president. Elections were postponed. Two years later, Soekarno dissolved the parliament, leading the country by presidential decree. In this 'Guided Democracy', the president reclaimed the powers originally invested in him. Again a single ideology ruled the country, *NASAKOM*: nationalism, Islam and communism. But Soekarno did not manage to balance these incompatible forces. Frustrations and conflicts led in 1965 to a failed military coup, after which Lt. Gen. Soeharto ascended to power.

Pancasila under the New Order

With Soeharto's so-called 'New Order' came again the communitarian philosophy of *Pancasila*, and since 1968, Indonesia's political order has been *Demokrasi Pancasila*. According to official texts, *Demokrasi Pancasila* is political rule through consultation, taking into consideration belief in God, a united Indonesia, humanitarianism and justice. This 'democracy' is authoritarian; opposition is not necessary since decisions are made in consensus. Political unity and order is more important than pluralism and accountability. The leader is the paternal figure that maintains political order, economic prosperity and social harmony. It is an irony that Soekarno's original idea of 'democracy' based on *Pancasila* could only be realized when he was removed. During the New Order, *Pancasila* moved from being a common platform for different ideologies into a full-fledged ideological justification of the ruling group.

Guiding Soeharto's New Order during its more than three decades of rule was this image of Indonesian society built on community and harmony. There are in this view deep-rooted cultural differences between people. Common people are servile (*budak*), obedient (*patuh*) and ignorant (*masih bodoh*), and they need not be concerned with political issues. The official policy of a 'floating mass' (*massa mengambang)* forbade political activities of any kind below districts. Until the elections in 1999, there were not any party branches or political campaigns where the majority of the population lives, in suburbs and villages. Party-political activities were allowed only for four weeks every five years, during national elections. For the rest, peasants and workers should concentrate on building the economic and sustaining the cultural development of the country. Politics was the prerogative of the rulers. The authority of a ruler (whether headman or president) was not to be questioned.

> The Government of the Republic of Indonesia is the authority that regulates the social life of the State of the Republic of Indonesia. Because of this, we Indonesian nationals are obliged to submit and to obey all the regulations that emanate from the legitimate government. We are convinced that the purpose of the Government with all its regulations is to improve the life of its nationals. The success of this governmental task also depends on the attitude of these nationals.[1]

Indonesian researchers were encouraged to search for the roots of such a *Pancasila* democracy. The Indonesian academic Eka Darmaputera, for instance, has argued that the *Pancasila*-values of unity, harmony and balance are 'deeply rooted in the value orientation of the majority of the Indonesian people' and that *Pancasila* therefore has a natural place in Indonesian society. Darmaputera draws from Javanese cosmology and affirms that common people *(wong cilik)* 'obey their *gusti* [lord] as a part of their very nature. They do this joyfully without ever losing their dignity... To serve is not a burden but a blessing'.[2] Still in the late 1990s it is a common argument that the majority of the Indonesian population needs to be protected from the evils of democracy.

The mid-1980s onwards saw more intense ideological enquiries. This time it was Supomo's 1945 idea about an 'Integralist State' that received attention. As late as in 1994, a major conference was arranged by the official body for the promotion of *Pancasila*, BP7, and several books were published.[3] The Integralist State was expected to do for the nation-state what *Demokrasi Pancasila* had done for the politics; to conceive of a form for the nation that goes beyond the universal form by focusing on the Javanese mystic notion of *manusia seutuhnya*, the 'whole man'. An 'integrated society' is made up of all layers of society working for the common good, built on the ideas of mutual cooperation and the family. Only a few years later, this corporatist idea has been discharged. There never was any official attempt to proclaim an Integralist State. But it is an interesting example of the conscious cultural engineering of the New Order.

The ultimate aim of the Integralist State and the *Demokrasi Pancasila* was for the rulers to preserve and extend their grip over society. Civil society and the *trias politica* were given no independence, since they were an integrated part of the nation. These ideas also legitimized the civilian role of the Armed Forces, through the *dwifungsi* ideology that gave them 'Two Functions': to protect the nation and take active part in its development. The oneness with leaders made even the notion of a loyal opposition unrealizable, implying also that there is no need for any guarantees to protect basic human rights. These notions go against the very core of liberal democracy, with its separation of powers, public interest and individual rights. *Demokrasi Pancasila* fits nicely into the Asian values style of politics.

Intense courses for the *Pancasila* Promotion Programme (P4), quoted above, have since 1981 been compulsory for civil servants and community leaders. School children from kindergarten to university must each year pass the important exam in '*Pancasila* Moral Education'. Students and P4 participants are taught political science orthodoxy and Indonesian history according to *Pancasila*. They are told about the achievements of the present government and given exercises on how to practise *Pancasila* in their hamlets: mutual assistance, a paternal spirit, consensus decisions. After the P4 course, participants are encouraged to spread the message to their friends and neighbours through games, lectures and religious teachings. Former president Soeharto illustrated how Demokrasi *Pancasila* should be achieved: through the continuous effort of 'making the ideology of *Pancasila* a part of the culture' (*membudayakan ideologi Pancasila*). Apparently, the contradiction was not noticed: on the one hand the government argues that *Pancasila* is based on Indonesian culture, on the other hand it must actively be promoted. It is a rather significant inconsistency, highlighting the active cultural engineering and the possibility of alternative world-views.

The official body for the promotion of *Pancasila* was until recently the BP7. This was a state-run institute that provided information about *Pancasila* and that organized the P4 courses. The BP7 trained senior P4 teachers, of whom there were some 2,300 so-called *manggala*, the highest level of teachers. The *manggala* were top civil servants and civic leaders, who provided training for university lecturers and senior ministerial staff, who in turn trained their staff, etc. all the way down to the village and primary school levels. At one time, the BP7 operated as a cultural think-tank for the government, and as a main inspiration for the ideological engineering. Under recent leadership, however, it had become slightly more independent, until it was finally disbanded in late 1998. The *Pancasila* Promotion Programme was discontinued a few months earlier. But even though these ideological programmes have been discarded, *Pancasila* remains the national ideology and is used as a common rallying point for nationalists.

Genuine Ethic or Manipulated Doctrine?

To what extent does *Pancasila* actually reflect the culture and lived experiences of people in Indonesia? How much is propaganda and engineering from above, and how much is reflection of experiences from within? Now that the political ideology is being challenged, will the values of mutual assistance and family morality also disappear? Or are the norms, as the elite claims, 'High Tradition' and the nation's cultural foundation, that will change only over a long period of time? These are not easy questions to answer. But they are crucial for us to understand the relationship between culture and politics, and between discourse and practice.

Some researchers have argued that the debate about a particular Asian political order, such as *Demokrasi Pancasila*, is phoney and that the ideology provoked by Asian rulers is nothing but a cultural disguise of authoritarian rule. This is indeed one important aspect of it, but I hesitate to dismiss the debate as easily. There are realms within which the communitarian *Demokrasi Pancasila* norms exist and make sense. They have become politicized and used by the government as political ideologies, conferring upon the audience the ideal relationship between state and citizens. To ask whether they are age-old or invented is beside the point. Culture and its textual representations are always open for fabrications and modifications. *Pancasila* values are used in Indonesia as part of a political ideology, and we cannot dismiss them simply as false consciousness or phoney. They must be examined and compared with other political programmes.

One should not underestimate the sentiments that can be evoked through ideology and engineering. I observed in a village the training ahead of the Independence Day parade in August 1996. The village headman held a speech about the achievements of the New Order, Golkar and President Soeharto. Half way through the speech – under the blazing sun – his voice broke and he started to cry. The audience, a grade ten high-school class, also cried when they were blessed with holy water by the headman. The sentiments thus evoked – of unity with the nation and the New Order – are hard to forget. Although they were obviously manipulated symbols, the show of feelings was genuine and long-lasting; the high school students were now good *Pancasila*ists.

Many of the values of the *Demokrasi Pancasila* are mirrored by local elites. During fieldwork among Sundanese villagers in West Java in periods from 1986 to 1998, I identified very similar sets of beliefs among the village elite.[4] There is within Sundanese tradition – codified in indigenous historiography – a set of norms for interaction between social classes. One morality is prescribed for the powerful and another for those without power. It is thus said among the elite that if a person in Java has power it is because he has a divine right to be in that position, not because of anything he has done. Ordinary people must respond to that power with respect and obedience. The ruler and the ruled are united by a supernatural bond (*manunggaling kawula lan gusti,* the unification of servant and master). Loyalty and gratitude are key concepts. Because of the norm of gratitude, powerful people should not need to use physical authority or give orders. Village officials should handle village affairs in a disinterested manner, detached from the shuffling of everyday politics, just like that of the *devaraja* ruler, the personification of the exemplary and potent figure of authority. This ideal, sometimes called *perintah halus* ('rule through gentle commands'), is codified in a proverb hanging in many government offices: *Sepi ing pamrih, rame ing gawe, mangayu-ayu buwana*: 'Be disinterested, work hard, perfect the world'. The Republic of Indonesia is conceived as one large integral family with *Bapak* [Father] Soeharto as the paternal figure (and, more recently, Habibie, although he has been far less successful in promoting this idea). This metaphor builds on the notion of community and its solidarity. In the family and in the nation, social harmony prevails, conflicts are solved by consensus, and family members work in mutual assistance for the common benefit of the community. In a large corporate family, the father has a legitimate right to interfere in the affairs of his ignorant children. In this, the best of worlds, the authority of superior persons, whether teachers, senior kinsmen, or politicians, should be taken for granted. Their knowledge is divine and not to be questioned or interpreted, much like the text of the Qur'an.

The Cultural Narrative of Rule and Power

Significantly, notions of Indonesia having a particular cultural form have been supported by foreign academics. I have elsewhere[5] in more detail argued that the way that politics in Indonesia was perceived during the Soeharto era has been heavily influenced by cultural considerations. Because of the personalized rule under Soeharto and the hegemonic *Pancasila* ideology, most commentators have understood politics in Indonesia as based on patron–client relations. One of the recent books on politics in Southeast Asia (drawing heavily on dynastic Java and Thailand) concludes that

> the primary pattern of social exchange in Southeast Asia is between unequals. And although these transactions are between a superior and a subordinate, dealings are personal, face-to-face, reciprocal, and mutually beneficial. Patron-client ties are the very foundation of society and politics all over Asia.[6]

This has led to conceptualizations of the Indonesian polity using terms such as neo-patrimonial, bureaucratic, *beamtenstaat*, or Asian-style democracy. These terms have in common the basic tenet that the conceptualization of power in Indonesia makes it wise and natural to attach oneself to powerful individuals. It is, at least, something very different from liberal democracy.

But I believe that it is important to see that these dynastic and divine political notions are very much the way that the Indonesian elite wants its power to be perceived. The cultural and historical origin of these values is found among the aristocracy of Java, with its highly refined literature and code of behaviour. Most of the historical works that these norms relate to were articulated by the eighteenth- and nineteenth-century aristocracy. They display history and society from the perspective of the ruling classes, presenting a narrative of the birth, rise, development and problems of a district and its rulers. These historical works functioned as an instrument for the central state to strengthen the claims by aristocratic families on the respective regencies. I believe that in the same way that eighteenth-century historiography strengthened the bonds of dependence between ruler and ruled, studies portraying *Demokrasi Pancasila* also build on folk-models of the justification of the elite's rule, the kind of enchant-ment of power discussed above. 'Culture' is part of a discursive struggle. The elite is in search of a peaceful and just society, and *Pancasila* constitutes such a model.

But there are other political models as well. We must challenge the view of a singular political ideology in Indonesia. There is never a single value system within a society. There might be dominant ideologies and cultural hegemonies, but there are also junctures where subaltern transcripts exist. We can thus find alternative cultural realms besides, beyond and beneath the dominant *Pancasila*. There are a few other such alternative world-views, such as the Islamic discourse and the more liberal alternative put forward by pro-democracy actors. Since these views have been discussed at length in a number of excellent studies[7], I would wish momentarily to focus on the subaltern view of common people less well-known.

The View from Below

In the communities, far from the royal traditions, we find the popular culture of peasants, workers and other so-called *wong cilik*, 'little people'. To them the most important quality of leaders is not their divine powers. Authority and political might are rather achieved through correct morals and the ability to yield results in terms of protection, order, and good harvests. A leader should be close to his community, lower himself to people, understand people's conditions, and put the community's interest before his own. This is true even in the highly centralized power structure of a village on Java.[8]

While a person's social rank may be determined by wealth, spiritual excellence or seniority, prestige is to a large extent based on impressions and ideological morals of what a refined figure should be like. Prestige lies in the eyes of the beholder. Since it is based on inner qualities, it can never be demanded. Persons with wealth or fine descent who do not maintain an appearance of social order might possess a high social rank but are not able to elicit deference from the community. Wealth is one thing, social worth another. This is different from traditional authority in Weber's sense of the 'sanctity of the moral order and the attendant powers of control as they have been handed down from the past'. Leaders should instead show their worth through *jasa*, 'service-mindedness'. This instrumental notion is close to the idea of accountability within democratic theory: that leaders should face the constituency and be responsible for their policies and acts. The *jasa* of the *wong cilik* is an opportunity to criticize unwanted leaders. Common people might not have a very distinct and articulate opinion about the government's *Demokrasi Pancasila*, but this does not mean that they automatically accept it. From their point of view, the legitimacy of the centre depends on whether leaders are able to maintain order, provide protection, and afford the services that people deem important. Soekarno derived much of his initial popularity by being the 'mouthpiece of the people' (*lidah rakyat*). Such a mouthpiece, the *wong cilik* argue, must show their worth before they are given any authority. If a headman or community leader does not maintain the image of a beneficial paternal figure, there are in the village a range of sanctions to put on the unwanted leader: not inviting people to ritual meals, withholding the daily gestures of neighbourly respect, condemning people for being un-Islamic, voting against his candidate in village elections, etc. The 'community democracy' works very directly, and is often rather crude and vulgar, but it is perhaps in its operation not all that far from the effects of the electoral system within democracy. If you do not have the support of your constituency, you will not become a leader. The *jasa* system puts pressures and sanctions on unpopular leaders, and not seldom are they forced to resign, or at least change their attitude.

The importance of these norms can perhaps best be found at the intense rivalry and sentiments that surround the election of the village headman, held in Indonesia every eight years. During campaigning, candidates are excepted to provide services and goods to the constituency. Large sums of money flow from the candidates to the village; every village abounds with stories of candidates who have ruined themselves. This relates to the *jasa* that a legitimate leader should display: during the campaign, the candidates are constantly put under pressures to distribute their wealth, and thus to prove that they are worthy leaders. It is not so much vote-buying as a 'traditional' display of generosity. The candidates must be charitable and unselfish, hand out cigarettes and sweets, organize ritual meals, and even throw coins to children when they walk through village. The idea is to provide villagers with something extra and to show goodwill and *jasa*.

Much of the mobilization of votes is done through personal contact. To mobilize voters a candidate must therefore recruit sponsors. A sponsor is a local notable, with a substantial support in his or her community. Because it is impossible for a single candidate to have a network encompassing a whole village, candidates rely on these hamlet chairmen, religious teachers, village elders and other leaders with a local authority. A headman's ability to be elected is often a function of his influence with these local notables. Before the campaign starts, even before the drafting procedure, the candidates must ensure that they have the support of a sufficient number of local notables. People draw maps of the village on the ground, discussing how many sponsors each candidate could recruit, and how many voters each sponsor could mobilize. These estimates are often surprisingly accurate. When the sponsors have been recruited, they in turn put pressure on their own clients to support their candidate. They meet almost every evening in the home of their candidate, to discuss campaign tactics and measures to be taken. Sponsors take every opportunity to speak for their candidate; at councils, at the mosque, when people visit the village office, and during casual conversations. The only formal campaigning element is a few days before the election, when the village office organizes for the candidates to read the compulsory 'Work Programmes' they have submitted. There are large numbers of spectators, each supporting his or her candidate. These are often very tense meetings, and they sometimes degenerate into physical violence between groups of young men. The actual voting is done by secret ballot. A number of voting stations are arranged in the village, and voters are free to come between eight in the morning and two in the afternoon, generally on a Sunday. Votes are counted in the village office, under supervision of the sub-district office and district army command. The result is announced the same day.

Everyday Practices and the Subaltern Alternative

The popular *jasa* version challenges the *Demokrasi Pancasila* by not accepting the one-to-one relationship between power and authority. The *jasa* ideology constitute popular and practical checks and balances on the exercise of power/authority within the reciprocity of patron–client relations. To be sure, this notion of an original democracy need not in many ways be very democratic, according to Western standards. It is, however, an alternative political understanding that must be taken into the picture when talking about Indonesian political culture. It builds to a certain extent upon the same values which exist within the *Pancasila* realm, but is more instrumental and less authoritarian. The family and community are still important social entities, but rather than interpreting it as integralistic and totalitarian (as does the government), the focus is on accountability and respectability. I believe that there is something in, for instance, the village elections that constitute a basis by which a kind of representative democracy could be constituted in Indonesia. At least the notion that citizens of Indonesia are not used to elections must be dispensed with.

The co-existence of a great (*Pancasila*) and a small (*jasa*) tradition is not only related to differences between elite and peasant views, but has also something to do with different levels of analysis and discourse. First, there is the ideal or normative level of harmony and solidarity. This level is used for analytical purposes, transmitting ideal values and norms with a high degree of generalization, related to the great tradition of the courts and elite. The other level is the everyday practices – with a low degree of conceptualization, reflecting the daily realities of tensions and conflicts – in which common events are discussed; slander, quarrels or just idle chatting. This small tradition is articulated among the subaltern, sometimes as a voice of resistance, but often as an alternative to the great tradition. Discourse, also political discourse, has thus a normative and a pragmatic side, a public and private face, an on-stage/off-stage distinction.

The on-stage/off-stage metaphor is appropriate in Java with its historical character of a 'theatre state'. The fact that conduct and beliefs do not correspond in public and private spheres is obviously a universal phenomenon. In Java, conflict avoidance and inequalities have further strengthened this bias. The appearance of social harmony is precious. To publicly scold your landlord would probably mean that you are out of a job tomorrow. To criticize village leaders might mean that your hamlet will be left out of next year's development plan. Up until 1998, to question the New Order might have brought you to jail. The appearance of social harmony thus implies that public opinions can be inconsistent with inner attitudes: better to withdraw in private and, if you like, sabotage whatever if possible. Public consent and private dissent make for two levels of discourse and behaviour, one public (the ideals of harmony and solidarity) and one private (the daily realities of tensions and conflicts).

If the powerless therefore at times seem to accept the dominant ideology, it might be on the high, ideal, level. But since even *Pancasila* power tends to corrupt, common people are in private often very critical of the leadership styles that developed under the Soeharto regime. They cannot always say so in public, but they have many ways of expressing it. One way for the powerless to react against the elite is to use the dominant values and turn them upside down, something that James Scott has called 'symbolic jujitsu'.[9] The example that Scott uses for Malaysia is highly relevant also for contemporary Indonesia. There is a very powerful myth among peasants in the Malay–Indonesian world of the return of the just king (*ratu adil*), a saviour-like Messiah figure who after the Age of Madness will bring final order to the world. Messianistic *ratu adil* movements have through history challenged political stability. This myth, in the words of Scott, is 'a striking example of how an erstwhile conservative myth of divine kingship can, in the hands of the peasantry, be turned into a revolutionary myth'. When the powerful ruler has lost his divine mandate, there will be a natural transition in the form of a new ruler coming. During Soeharto's rule, several semi-messianistic movements have emerged and been crushed, such as in Tanjung Priok in 1974 and the small rebellion in South Sumatra in 1984.

In this way, if the dominant ideology fails to live up to the implicit promises that it necessarily makes, there are many ways that the hegemony can be turned into critique. The *Pancasila* principles have thus been used to re-evaluate New Order policies, deployed to resist what is perceived as improperly constituted or executed authority. The need to reinforce the fifth *Pancasila* principle, social justice, has thus been used by critics in a conscious manipulation of New Order symbols, to the effect that the New Order has not been able to create a just society. Using the concept of *Pancasila* Economy, critics of the New Order's large-scale development efforts could reiterate the emphasis on cooperation and equity found in the 1945 constitution. Other reform groups were criticizing ministers and other top civil servant, including the president, for having left the fundamental principles of consensus behind by taking decisions high-handed. *Pancasila* can also be put to more local ends, such as when local notables during headman elections demand that all the candidates display their generosity and adherence to the fifth *Pancasila* principle by providing clothes, food, cigarettes, or even building material to the community. Symbols and principles of the New Order have been used in innovative ways to criticize the same ideology. Main opposition figures in Indonesia have long argued that Soeharto has deviated from *Pancasila* and the 1945 constitution. What is needed, they argue, is a return to the foundation of the nation. This 'in-house' line of critique differs in content, not form, from the New Order. It does not reject the ideological basis of the New Order, but seeks more pluralistic and democratic interpretations. Given the harsh repression of the regime, it was for a long time the only tolerable critique.

Challenging the Soeharto Order

I believe that we saw some of these 'weapons of the weak' in action during the turbulent early months of 1998. For quite some time, people had been disenchanted with Soeharto and his family. Up to the mid 1990s, many *wong cilik* in Indonesia were satisfied with what their ruler in a faraway place provided them: political stability, economic growth, education, health-care. As late as May 1997, during the national elections, many people in my village of research (Sariendah) put their votes on the state party Golkar, perhaps out of habit, perhaps due to pressures, but also because many of them believed that Soeharto had brought development and stability to the country, just as a wise and divine ruler should.[10] But already some years earlier, more and more people in villages and cities had started to criticize the first family for their excesses. It was very similar to what happened to Soekarno in 1964–1965. He became estranged from common people, and his excesses and personal style turned against him. Soeharto's corruption and nepotism, which during a period perhaps was seen by people to develop the country, simply became too visible and too blatant. It reached all corners of Indonesia. In Sariendah the enchantment with the New Order started to wane in 1994 when a company belonging to Mbak Tutut, Soeharto's oldest daughter (and recently Minister of Social Affairs), requested land in a neighbouring village to build public housing for retired civil servants. Although the population of Sariendah showed up at the grand inauguration to see Mbak Tutut arriving from Jakarta in a helicopter, they were deeply troubled by the fact that the landowners had been forced to sell the land at very low prices. Soon perhaps it would be their turn. Similar stories of New Order excesses could be heard from mini-bus drivers who had to bribe police officers, parents who had to pay teachers for their children to pass exams, and hawkers who had to pay village officials for various permits. At the end, this soaking corruption simply became too much. For our purpose, it is also important to notice that it was perceived to originate in the centre. Just as the economic development was declared to come from tireless efforts of the president, so, too, the corrupt practices of the Sariendah headman were seen to originate in the practices of the presidential family. Many said openly that Soeharto had lost his *jasa*, and that he only thought about himself and his family, not his community.

Much of the critique against the Soeharto regime was couched in the dominant discourse, using language and symbols that were easily recognized by both the rulers and the general public. During the first months of 1998, the movement became more active and daring. The issue focused largely on the lack of proper mechanisms for accountability. The Soeharto family had grown very rich, and sanctions were put on them. Without overstating the case, this is reminiscent of the kinds of sanctions you find in a small community. During my fieldwork in Sariendah, a few families were put under sanctions from neighbours for not sharing their wealth. They were accused of using black magic and people talked behind their backs. The families were not invited to community rituals, and became increasingly marginalized. Although on a very different scale, this is also what happened to the Soeharto family. It became marginal to the concerns of common people, it misused its powers, and it was seen as draining power from the larger community. The sanctions were also similar: being the butt of jokes, being talked about behind one's back, not really daring to confront the very powerful family. When in the end even Soeharto's loyal allies (such as Golkar chairman Harmoko, economic czar Ginanjar and commander-in-chief Wiranto) eventually turned their backs on him, he had to take the full consequence of his isolation and step down from power.

The corruption on all levels of society and its perceived origin in the 'exemplary centre' was perhaps the single crucial factor that brought an end to Soeharto's rule: it caused financial turbulence, student demonstrations and the withdrawal of political support from the important middle class. Political scientists soberly call it 'internal decay' and it is often quoted as one of the determinative factors in the transition from authoritarianism to democracy. For common people, the chaos was a sign that Soeharto had lost his *jasa* and divine mandate.

The Future of Ideology

We have in this chapter looked at two different political views. It is important to recognize that neither is necessarily truer or more authentic. These ideologies reside side by side, not as separate worlds, but as possible interpretations of a political order. *Demokrasi Pancasila* has long been hegemonic because of the state's privilege to interpret its meaning, not because of anything internal to the world-view. The government has cleverly used culture in explaining politics, with the argument that liberal democracy is not suited to the Indonesian national character. Democracy would cause chaos, misery and moral decay to Indonesia. The government promise was that *Pancasila* would bring political stability and community morality.

In early 1998, when the government had failed to deliver economic growth, this cultural argument became again more important. Soeharto's reaction to the demands put on him was to call for increased cultural specificity (this was also true of Mahathir in Malaysia, but less so of Lee Kuan Yew in Singapore). The culprits were 'foreign races', aiming at disturbing national sovereignty.

The Asian alternative has for the past ten years been a coherent political challenge to Western political democratic orthodoxy, based as it is on the community rather than the individual, consensus rather than opposition, and strong governments rather than political pluralism. Authors like John Naisbitt (*Megatrends Asia*) and Jim Rowher (*Asia Rising*) have even suggested that Asian governments are the first ones to have realized the implications of a new world order, of the new potential conflicts, and addressed the intellectual and moral crisis of the West. The government has, at the very least, been successful in providing attractive investment conditions, and thus forced countries in Europe to rethink their political set-ups (the welfare states in Europe, for instance, are being dismantled to meet the challenges of this new global order). Can Pacific Asia with its tremendous economic growth be used as political examples for Africa or Latin America? Or is this nothing more than disguised neo-patrimonialism?

One important question for the future of Asian values and *Pancasila* is whether Pacific Asia and Indonesia's mismanagement will be seen as a systemic failure (and thus indict also the polical ideologies) or a result of the ruler's personal excesses. At the time of writing, this is yet to be determined. The crises might just as well be blamed on international capital, liberalization and IMF as on own mistakes, the corruption of the local elite, bad government and poor judgement. Defiantly, Abdul Ghafar Baba (former deputy prime minister of Malaysia and unofficial spokesperson) has said that the only lesson that Malaysia can draw from Indonesia is that 'if you subvert the leader the economy gets worse'.[11] One reason to sack deputy prime minister Anwar Ibrahim in September 1998 was that he was 'getting help from foreign collaborators'. Better to be 'bullish on bouncing back' than change leader; that is the attitude in Malaysia.

The debate in Thailand on 'communitarian democracy' seems also relevant. A call to return to 'traditional values' such as respect for elders, tolerance, compassion, family ties and mutual assistance is heard not only from the government, but also from leading social critics, such as Chai-anan Samudvanich. Similar voices for 'Asian values' are heard in Malaysia, where for instance former government critic Chandra Muzzafar has joined Mahathir in blaming 'the West' for conspiring to bring down Malaysia. In Indonesia, former NGO activist, now minister Adi Sasono, has recently called for a strengthening of the communitarian co-operatives and small-scale enterprises as a way out of financial crises. The call to return to tradi-tional culture is an alluring way out of the present anomie and confusion.

At stake here is the fundamental proposition of some Asian leaders that Asia is not fit for an open democracy. The reasons are sometimes located in the low level of economic development, sometimes in culture. But it always ends with the suppression of political freedoms, such as the right of expression and the freedom of assembly. But there is, as I have tried to show in this chapter, nothing in cosmology or religion in itself that explains the presence or lack of democracy. I reject the statement of cultural determination that some values (e.g. North European Protestant-ism) are compatible with democracy while others (e.g. Indonesian mysti-cism) are apt for authoritarianism. Such may be the case for the texts upon which these values are established, but we must be aware that there are no 'innate' properties of cosmologies for democracy or authoritarian-ism. We must be sceptical to the kind of cultural essentializing found among some political scientists and anthropologist who claim that cultural factors make politics very different in Asia. Culture is neither static nor unchallenged. It is ever changing, in a process of re-presentation. As such, its creation becomes crucial: the distribution of cultural knowledge and the ability to impose on others a proper interpretation. The question is not only what symbols and concepts mean but what people do with them. What implications do such ideas have? Who have the means and power to press their interpretation? To what extent do people find it necessary to appeal to such concepts and values? Thus our study of politics should relate to the sociology of knowledge and become an exploration of how such normative discourses are produced, translated, and materialized in a variety of contexts.

I hope that I have made it clear in my exposition that the Indonesian version of Asian values democracy, *Demokrasi Pancasila*, quite easily can be interpreted as an authoritarian ideology that builds on elite values. It has thus only a limited reference to common people's political perception. But this is not the main point. It is a *political* discourse, a normative projection of what rulers in Indonesia deem important. It need not necessarily relate to actual perceptions and practices, since politics, after all, is the art of accomplishing the impossible. So the future of *Pancasila* in Indonesia – and of Asian values more generally in Pacific Asia – is determined not so much on what authenticity these values have, but on how well their protagonists can solve political and economic problems. Writing in mid-1999, right after national elections, it seems indeed that the claim that citizens of Indonesia are not fit for an open political system carries very little relevance. With a rise of political consciousness and the gradual disappearance of oppression, more and more people demand an accountable political order, a system that limits the powers of the executive and that respects the voices of the poor. Such a system, I have argued, would fit right into a popular political culture.

And indeed, people in Indonesia are today demanding the end of corruption, nepotism and oppression. They want to have a free and accountable political system. When I went back to Sariendah and talked to people after the fall of Soeharto, their demands were clear: an accountable local government, a clean headman, no power politics, and less interference in daily affairs of the state and its local representatives. Even village officials were involved. They were perhaps 'born-again reformists', hoping to protect their own skin. During June–August 1998, hundreds of village headmen all over Indonesia (but primarily in Java) were forced to step down. In a celebrated case, the officials of one West Java village were kidnapped by angry villagers, demanding that they denounce corruption and nepotism.

It is less clear what the national elite wants. There is not yet even a consensus among the elite that political reforms are necessary. There is no debate in Indonesia about what democracy really is, and why it is good. Elite members fight for their own good. *Public* values – shared by all Indonesian citizens, rich and poor, Chinese and Javanese, conservative and radical, are still absent. Perhaps the only public value that is available is that of the imagined political community. Nationalism is however also threatened: by its abuses during the New Order, and by people who want to rectify these abuses. In its place might come primordialism, which by nature is exclusionary and often encourages the giving of privileged treatment to a small group of believers – in its turn leading to corruption and nepotism. A solution to this is to strengthen *Pancasila*, which provides for the freedom of beliefs. But do people want to promote *Pancasila*, given its earlier context?

Indonesia is still a far cry from genuine democracy, and given some of the incompatibilities of Indonesian politics, the road to accountability and credibility will be rocky. But yet somewhere deep inside I am optimistic, especially since most people that I talk to in Indonesia see the opportunities of the present changes, and the importance of moving away from money and power to voters and programmes. And there are clearly, as I hope that I have shown, cultural values and practices to which this democracy discourse could relate. It would thus seem that the future of democracy in Indonesia depends more upon how attractive and effective a new, more participatory, democracy can be made to the people – especially the elite – and less on the prevalence of certain 'Asian' values.

Notes

1 *Pancasila* Promotion Programme (P4) quoted in Niels Mulder, 'The Ideology of Javanese-Indonesian Leadership', in Hans Antlöv and Sven Cederroth (eds), *Leadership on Java: Gentle Hints, Authoritarian Rule*, London: Curzon Press, 1994, pp. 61–62.

2 Eka Darmaputera, '*Pancasila* and the Search for Identity and Modernity in Indonesian Society: A Cultural and Ethical Analysis', PhD thesis, Boston College, 1982 [also published by Brill, Leiden, 1988], p. 371.

3 The two most important reviews of these ideas are Marsillam Simanjuntak, *Pandangan Negara Integralistik* [The views of an integralistic state], Jakarta: Grafiti Press, 1994, and David Bourchier, 'Totalitarianism and the "National Personality": Recent Controversy about the Philosophical Basis of the Indonesian State', in Jim Schiller and Barbara Martin-Schiller (eds), *Imagining Indonesia.*

Cultural Politics and Political Culture, Athens: Ohio University Center for International Studies, 1997.
4 Cf. Hans Antlöv, *Exemplary Centre, Administrative Periphery: Leadership and the New Order in Rural Java*, London: Curzon Press, 1995, Chapter 6.
5 Hans Antlöv, 'The Java That Never Was – Cultural Notions of Politics in Indonesia', paper presented at the 10th annual European Java Workshop, Amsterdam, 9–10 May 1997.
6 C. Neher and R. Marlay, *Democracy and Development in Southeast Asia: The Winds of Change*. Boulder: Westview Press, 1995, p. 15.
7 On Islam, see Douglas Ramage, *Democracy, Islam and the Ideology of Tolerance*, London: Routledge, 1995; Robert Hefner and Patricia Hovwatich (eds), *Islam in an Era of Nation-States: Politics and Religious Revivalism in Muslim Southeast Asia*, Honolulu: University of Hawaii Press, 1997; Mark Woodward (ed.), *Toward a New Paradigm. Recent Developments in Indonesian Political Thought*, Tuscon: Arizona State University Program on Southeast Asia, 1996. On pro-democracy activists, see Anders Uhlin, *Indonesia and the 'Third Wave of Democratization'. The Indonesian Pro-Democracy Movement in a Changing World*, Richmond: Curzon Press, 1997; Philip Eldridge, *Non-Government Organisations and Democratic Participation in Indonesia*. Oxford: Oxford University Press, 1995.
8 Antlöv 1995, Chapter 6.
9 James C. Scott, *Weapons of the Weak: Everyday Forms of Peasant Resistance*, New Haven and London: Yale University Press, 1985, p. 333.
10 I was in Sariendah at the time and I am obviously aware of the wide range of pressures and intimidations that the state can put on people at elections, and that there is no real ideological alternative. But during discussions with people whom I have known for ten years, many said that they put their votes on Golkar and Soeharto because they felt it to be closest to their aspirations. Golkar received 73 per cent of the votes in Sariendah. See Hans Antlöv, 'National Elections, Local Issues: the 1997 and 1999 Indonesian Elections in a Village Perspective', to be published in Hans Antlöv and Sven Cederroth (eds), *Elections in Indonesia*, London: Curzon Press, forthcoming.
11 Interview with Abdul Ghafar Baba, 'Anwar has no support', *Asiaweek*, September 18, 1998.

10 AFTERWORD

ON CULTURES AND CONTEXTS

Laurence Whitehead

On the 150th anniversary of the Communist Manifesto a spectre is haunting Asia – the spectre of Western liberal democracy. Not even Indonesia has remained immune. India, Japan, and Sri Lanka all succumbed in the aftermath of the Second World War. The Philippines, Thailand, Taiwan and South Korea gave way in the 1980s. Malaysia and Singapore have been thrown on the defensive. Bangladesh and Pakistan vacillate. The major remaining bulwarks of resistance are Burma, Vietnam, and above all China, but even there the pressures are mounting. The logic of history is unfolding.

One hundred and fifty years after the Communist Manifesto we can see how a previous spectre then haunting Europe became embodied, and unfolded its logic. Communism lasted a long time, extended itself across the whole globe and took many forms. The communism of North Korea was very different from that of Hungary, or of Cuba, and all three contrasted very sharply with key aspects of the initial Marx-Engels blueprint, which was in reality highly geared to the specific conditions of incipient revolt in the Western Europe of 1848. Assuming that Western democracy continues to haunt Asia for the foreseeable future, it too is likely to take many forms, some of which may contrast with contemporary blueprints to an equivalent degree. Currently prevalent models of democracy also contain their share of implicit assumptions drawn from recent experience (especially the disintegration of the Soviet bloc). Presumably, liberal democracy is more adaptable and responsive to social traditions than communism, but even so there is a parallel between two 'spectres'.

Over the long haul, and in the multiple and diverse settings of Asia, democracy will persist to the extent that it adjusts. Aspects of local culture and/or context that presently generate resistance to democracy will have to be modified or absorbed.

This concluding chapter is a meditation on the country studies presented in the rest of the book. It began as a closing address to the 1995 NIAS conference, under the title 'Is Asia Different?'. It offers some sympathetic but sceptical reflections on the notion that the culture (or cultures) of the region filter and reinterpret democratic ideas and practices that are presented from without, and that such cultural filters affect both the probability of successful democratization and the quality or content of the resulting political regimes. It suggests that many of the same arguments can be reformulated in a more comparative and permissive manner if we distinguish the language of 'context' from that of 'culture' and use the former as an alternative source of explanations of democratization. One key aspect of the present Asian context that is sometimes presented in an overly culturalist light concerns reluctance to internalize political models projected and in some cases even imposed from without ('the West'). The present chapter seeks to establish its distance both from a reductionist universalism and from a culturalist essentialism. It concludes with a defence of context-sensitive approaches to the comparative politics enterprise.

Heterogeneity and Hybridity in Asian Cultures

Let us begin with the issue of Asian culture(s). This volume includes discussions of Sinhalese Buddhism; the *Demokrasi Pancasila* tradition in Indonesia; perfectionism as an impediment to democracy in the Chinese tradition; and the Confucian concept of *minzhu* as an alternative frame of reference in various parts of East Asia. It also directs attention to the impact of British imperial rule in South Asia, Hong Kong, and Malaysia, and of the US occupation of Japan. In every one of these diverse instances a strong case can be made that the history of each society has been profoundly and durably affected by authoritative teachings and imposed experiences that have created a lasting legacy of attitudes and beliefs (a 'culture') which will critically affect present and future societal receptiveness to Western models of democracy. Some of these cultural attributes may be straightforwardly incompatible with basic aspects of liberal democracy (the *Pancasila* tradition seems particularly strong in this regard). Others may be at least partially and superficially supportive

(India and Japan can be read in that way). Various key elements of the experiences described are more complex and indeterminate in sign. These are cultural attributes that might, if somewhat modified, be mobilized in support of a fairly standardized Western model of democracy (although some modifications would be required from the other side as well). Such modifications might scandalize traditionalists, but viewed historically they take place all the time, and in all cultural systems. On the other hand, they could also be drawn upon as sources of resistance to insensitive Westernization and the indiscriminate embrace of European and North American fashions and assumptions.[1] Although it received little attention in this particular collection, Islam has an especially vigorous and comprehensive tradition of resistance along these lines. (Presumably Islam deserves as much space in the cultural traditions of Asia as say Buddhism, Hinduism, or Confucianism, or indeed Christianity?) In one sense, then, we can conclude that Asia *is* indeed different from other major world regions, such as Africa and the Americas. It contains a wide array of deeply rooted civilizational traditions that pre-date European conquest, and that provide potential resources for a succession of defensive sallies against the onward march of liberal democracy, if not for some full-scale counter-attacks.[2]

However, this conclusion falls far short of the minimum claims asserted by most proponents of so-called 'Asian values'. First of all the diversity of the Asian doctrines and traditions must be stressed. There is no single Promethean Asian cultural tradition. Buddhism (which comes in many forms) is not ubiquitous, nor is Confucianism, nor can the two readily be conflated. The cultural legacies of the ancient Asian civilizations have been overlaid by many subsequent layers of teaching and experience, articulated through a variety of languages, religious practices, and competing statehoods. Diversity, hybridity and the continuous remoulding of identity are the constants of 'Asian culture', if we must use such a term at all. Moreover, Asian attitudes and beliefs have long been shaped not just by indigenous processes but by global influences. Islam and even Christianity demand recognition as component parts of any overall Asian cultural tradition, as do various European languages and the conceptual equipment they incorporate.

One way to represent this reality is to stress the coercive aspects of Western imperial rule, and this should certainly not be downplayed. But when Asians seek to share their values in international organizations, they mostly do so in English, and they speak as representatives of nation-states structured along the territorial lines prescribed by the Treaty of Westphalia. Even the word 'Asia' is European in origin (the Roman designation for what is now most of Turkey).[3] Just as there is a strong British colonial tradition woven into the political infrastructure of Hong Kong, India, Malaysia and Sri Lanka, so there is also the Spanish legacy in the Philippines (with a twentieth-century overlay of American influences). So whatever we understand by Asian culture(s) it cannot refer to some homogeneous pre-Western unity either of teachings, attitudes, or experiences. But if there is not one unified Asian culture, and if the various cultural traditions that *do* exist are prone to adaptation and to hybridity, then liberal democracy (even if it originates as an external, Western, construct) will stand in no single clearly defined relationship to regional teachings, traditions and understandings. If so, then little would be lost by broadening the range of enquiry, to consider not just Asian cultures, but Asian contexts, as they influence the implementation of democracy.

Comparing Like with Like

However, even though it is obvious that there is not just one Asian 'culture', the argument has been made that the various regional cultures all share some common 'Asian values' that are under threat from the West. If Western liberal democracy privileges individualism, or emphasizes procedures of decision-taking without regard to the morality of the resulting legal outcomes, then it could violate fundamental Asian values of community, solidarity and good government. Even granting that such Asian values might be recently constructed and not entirely uniform throughout the region, this would seem to constitute a strong argument against Asia being swept along by the current 'third-wave' of global democratization. Most of the debate on this issue has focused on the question whether the self-proclaimed exponents of Asian values really are practitioners of communitarianism and collective morality, or whether they merely invoke these arguments to cloak their own authoritarian proclivities and advantages. But there may be a more fundamental weakness with this argument. If it is indeed true that (Western) liberal democracy suffers this values deficit, then presumably it is not only Asians who should be concerned. Any genuine and well-founded critique of contemporary democracy that finds a resonance in Asia should also be taken seriously in the West. Any critique which is *not* credible to Europeans and North Americans will therefore be open to the suspicion that it is probably based on poor understanding or mis-application of Western liberal democratic practices. The essential weakness in the argument can be stated as follows: whenever the Asian values perspective on Western democracy is well founded it can appeal to universal values. When this perspective does not succeed in mounting a generally persuasive case, then it is unlikely to muster enough arguments that are specific and exclusive to Asia to carry conviction there either.

In order to determine whether or not this weakness is fatal, we need to look more closely at certain specific 'core' values, and we need to ensure that when comparing Asia and the West we are comparing *like with like* (i.e. the level of analysis adopted is equivalent on both sides). There follows a closer examination of the 'universality' (or otherwise) of the fundamental human rights enshrined in the UN Declaration, and a discussion of the Confucian perspective on human rights, both of which draw heavily on the recent work of Joseph Chan. The burden of the argument is that we can speak of attributes as 'universal' when there is a *reasonable equivalence* between the meanings and understandings they elicit in different regions, or in different linguistic and cultural settings. Strict identity is neither likely nor necessary. *Reasonable equivalence* is sufficient to generate negotiations over a common and mutually acceptable standard. On this basis, all worthwhile Asian values can in fact be reclassified as universal values.

As Joseph Chan points out there is a disjunction between the very stringent conditions that a modern philosopher would require in order to classify a human right as strictly *universal* (including timeless, as well as indifferent to place) and the looser construction of the Universal Declaration of Human Rights. The latter contains a list of items, some of which may be transhistorical (freedom from torture), but others of which include elements of historicity (the right to social security benefits). Most rights in the Declaration are vague and general, and there is no clear hierarchy between them. The Declaration also acknowledges the possibility that in certain circumstances certain rights might have to be limited. Exponents of the Asian values approach tend to accept the existence of a small hard core of truly universal human rights, but to contest the scope, weight, and ranking of the full list of items in the UN Declaration. It would be consistent with the latter to accept that 'culture or ideology-based interpretations are both inevitable and sometimes legitimate. Different cultural and ideological perspectives would strike the balance between the individual's interest and the public interest in different ways'.[4] Even within Europe there are two clearly competing schools of jurisprudence which differ over the relative importance to assign to individual freedom, on the one hand, and to order, community and tradition on the other. Chan thinks that Asian societies in general 'embrace a set of attitudes towards issues of values and morals which is different from that of the West', and in particular he thinks that tolerance of the rights of minorities is a more salient human right for Western liberals than for most Asians. So he concludes that 'because of their specific political moralities and societal contexts, Asian states can claim a wide (but surely not arbitrary) margin of appreciation in interpreting the proper scope and limitation of human rights'. The text in parenthesis is crucial. There can be a margin for cultural difference, but the margin must be proportional and not arbitrary. On this basis, universality of principle can be reconciled with a reasonable diversity of practice. Asians and Westerners may have to engage in mutual negotiations over the precise lines of demarcation but in doing so they would be affirming rather than undermining their common framework of shared values.

Foundational Doctrines and Contemporary Practices

A similar strategy of negotiation seems appropriate when examining the teachings of Confucius as they relate to contemporary international thinking about human rights. The Asian values debate has frequently been marred by the inappropriate use of different levels or types of analysis to contrast Asia with the West. Thus an idealized image of one model may be contrasted with a closely observed experience of the other. At the extreme would be the mistake of comparing, for example, philosophical doctrines from Asia with contemporary political practices in Europe, or applying, say, contemporary Western political science categories and assumptions without adjustment to earlier practices somewhere in Asia. The key point of method here is to compare like with like. Just as we would make adjustments to allow for historical context when examining the human rights doctrines of the classical Greek and Roman philosophers so a similar degree of adjustment is appropriate for Confucianism. Reasoning along these lines, Chan arrives at the following three conclusions: (a) the Confucian perspective would endorse basic civil liberties or rights such as freedom of expression and religion; (b) but its understanding of the scope of these liberties would be different from some Western, rights-based perspectives; and (c) the Confucian and those rights-based perspectives differ on the grounds of civil liberties'.[5] At the theoretical level, the key difference is that whereas Western liberals are inclined to tolerate bad or debased conduct (provided it is harmless to others) the Confucian perspective seeks social perfection, and would rank that above the tolerance of individuality. From the Confucian perspective individual rights or freedoms would be derived not from personal sovereignty, but from individual interests in developing their humanity (*ren*). When it comes to applying this general perspective to contemporary human rights issues Chan asserts its relevance but expresses caution about drawing unduly precise policy inferences. For example, he is by no means confident that it would endorse Article 49 of the Chinese Constitution (which is also matched by comparable laws in Taiwan and in Singapore). This article stipulates that parents who are unable to support themselves have a right to be supported and assisted by their children who have come of age. Although at first sight this looks like a Confucian measure, it is not in fact a direct application of the principle of filial piety. From this perspective, children should not be induced to support their aged parents through fear of punishment, nor should parents be encouraged to take their unloving children to court. This example illustrates the distance separating classical Chinese thought from the legal and normative assumptions governing human rights discourse in the modern world *as a whole*. If we examined teachings on the status and rights of women the distance would be even greater.

P. D. Premasin has carried out a similar exercise with reference to the original message of the Buddha, again acknowledging the distance between classical and modern times. He recognizes that the concept of minority groups (as in 'ethnic minorities') is of very recent origin, and so was not directly discussed in orthodox Buddhist doctrine. Nevertheless he presents what may be called a Buddhist perspective that bears on the issues of minority rights, and other human rights issues which are so pressing in most contemporary attitudes by emphasizing a common humanity shared by all and a common law of righteousness. In contrast to the Vedas, Buddha taught that human beings were originally born equal and belonged to a common species. Within the spiritual community which the Buddha established, no recognition at all was given to caste, race or colour. This stress on personal merit could be applied to slaves as well as the free, and to women as well as men. As for differences over religious belief, the Buddhist doctrinal position attempted to promote non-dogmatism and tolerance conducive to the minimization of conflict. Buddhism also advocated a critical non-dogmatic attitude towards all views, even with regard to the word of the Buddha. Critical scrutiny and testing in the light of one's own experience, and free enquiry unhindered by prejudice and emotional involvement in dogmatic views were commended. Discriminatory attitudes, ethnocentricity, hostility towards and insensitivity to the interests of persons who do not belong to one's own group can be explained, according to the psychological explanation of conflict characteristic of Buddhism, as manifestations of the three basic evils greed, hatred, and delusion.[6] If this reading is correct then the original teachings of Buddha provided a remarkably promising foundation for the UN Declaration of Human Rights that was proclaimed two and a half millennia later. However, it must also be stressed that just as the history of Christianity diverges from the teachings of Christ, so too with the history of Buddhism. This divergence has been particularly evident in the recent history of what may be called Buddhist chauvinism in post-independence Sri Lanka.[7]

A similar distance also separates the classical thinkers of Greece and Rome from the modern world.[8] This underlines the need to compare like with like – *either* classical teachings of Asia and Europe; *or* contemporary adaptations of those teachings; but not one of the former with one of the latter. Even when like is compared with like, the search should be only for reasonable equivalence, and not identity.[9] Proceeding on this basis the supposed contrasts between Asian and Western approaches to human rights may well be negotiable (within a tacitly shared framework of universal first principles) rather than incommensurable.[10]

Cultures, Civilizations and Contexts

We have argued that cultures, civilizations and social values are not incommensurable, but instead can be placed within a comparative framework that is mutually intelligible, and potentially even mutually enriching. If so, then we need to develop ways of accounting for variation that are not exclusive to only one of the cultures involved. For this purpose it is helpful to broaden the discussion from the comparison of cultures to include the comparison of contexts.

How does 'context' differ from 'culture'? It obviously depends on which definition of culture one starts from. A very broad definition, such as the influential one promoted by the anthropologist Franz Boas, will include almost everything that might also be referred to as context (although the elements might be arranged according to a different logic). According to Boas 'culture may be defined as the totality of the mental and physical reactions and activities that characterise the behaviour of the individuals composing a social group collectively and individually in relation to their natural environment, to other groups, to members of the group itself, and of each individual to himself'.[11] A much narrower conception is typically deployed by contemporary political scientists who mostly refer to 'political culture'. Their discussions tend to omit the most important contextual considerations (geographical location, institutional inheritance, economic resource base, etc.) presumably because they would typically assign these to objective structure rather than to subjective 'culture'. For my part, this chapter has referred to culture as a lasting legacy of attitudes and beliefs in society, derived both from authoritative teachings and from broader socialization processes. In contrast to the anthropological perspective, this view of culture stresses the more systematic, recurrent, large-scale, and elaborated forms of socialization ('high culture'). My view implies that (i) culture is lodged in the subjective outlook of the society; (ii) culture is shaped by identifiable doctrines and initiatives promoted from above (which implies the existence of a fairly elaborated state); and (iii) culture invokes a complex and elaborated system of discourse, with its rules, boundaries, and interconnections, all of which have to be policed and maintained.[12] At least these three assumptions seem appropriate and illuminating for the purpose we have in hand (comparing Asian and Western responses to democratization). They can be adopted here, without prejudice to the broader debate about alternative conceptions of culture in abstract.

It so happens that the most influential recent contribution to our topic by a Western political scientist is fairly close to the position just outlined, although Samuel P. Huntington tends to subsume 'culture' under his still more ambitious conceptualization of 'civilization'[13] and he draws conclusions about the potential for 'clashes' between civilizations which need not be taken up.

Huntington denies the existence of a universal world civilization, and therefore analyses 'civilizations' in the plural. In contrast to the German tradition, he rejects any sharp distinction between 'culture' and 'civilization', asserting instead that 'Civilisation and culture both refer to the overall way of life of a people, and a civilisation is a culture writ large', but adding that 'to a very large degree, the major civilisations in human history have been closely identified with the world's great religions'. Thus:

> Civilisation is the broadest cultural entity. Villages, regions, ethnic groups, nationalities, religious groups, all have distinct cultures at different levels of cultural heterogeneity ... The cultures of peoples interact and overlap. The extent to which the cultures of civilisations resemble or differ from each other also varies considerably. Civilisations are nonetheless meaningful entities, and while the lines between them are seldom sharp, they are real.

Not only does he view them as real, but also as foundational, in that 'empires rise and fall, governments come and go, civilisations remain and survive political, social, economic and even ideological upheavals'. But

> since civilisations are cultural, not political entities, they do not, as such, maintain order, establish justice, fight wars, negotiate treaties, or do any of the other things which governments do . . . A civilisation may contain one or many political units.

Finally, on the basis of this discussion of major world civilizations Huntington identifies – and even maps – seven (or possibly nine, if Buddhists and African civilizations are included) of these meaningful and millennial macro-cultural entities. As far as the 'Asia' covered by this book is concerned, Huntington's map identifies five: Sinic, Japanese, Hindu, Buddhist, and Islamic.[14]

Huntington's formulation of the issues is similar to the view of culture propounded here, in that it focuses on 'high' (literate) culture, and on large scale long-term structures of belief and understanding. These are probably encoded in language and sustained by reference to authoritative texts (which could be either religious or legal), and propagated by trained specialists (monks and holy men, for example, or state bureaucrats or other teachers).[15] Individual states or political regimes may derive their strength and orientation from these underlying cultural or civilizational resources but they are more contingent, and more transient. This is a useful perspective from which to consider Asian receptivity to the current model of liberal democracy being promoted from the West. However, Huntington's approach carries with it at least two unhelpful implications. It presents non-Western civilizations as rivals and even potential threats to an over-confident West that is in actuality losing its ascendancy. And it tends to 'reify' its conception of civilization that is to say to render it rigid and immutable. These are the two features that enable Huntington to dramatize his position by reference to supposedly inherent tendencies towards 'clashes' of civilization in the contemporary world. The alternative view favoured in this chapter is that high cultures, or civilizational, traditions only frame political understanding and action, without prescribing it. A single high cultural tradition can be reconciled with widely different types of political regime; cultural differences can be negotiated without inevitably leading to irreconcilable 'clashes'; every cultural tradition is forced to adapt and reconsider its assumptions as a consequence of exposure to alternative cultures (not least in an era when traditional literacy is superseded by digital communication. Moreover, insofar as there *are* international conflicts over regime type, or variations in the receptivity to democracy of different societies, these are better analysed by reference to a wide range of contextual considerations rather than being understood necessarily in terms of cultural (or civilizational) differences. But first we need to be clear speaking how these concepts differ and can be related to each other. The point can be further illustrated by reference to the comparative study of political democratization. I am aware that this procedure could be regarded as smuggling in the assumptions of Western rationality as though they were universal and culture free. But I have stressed the scope for mutual adjustment between the various perspectives. There is no bar on the introduction of contextual considerations that are salient in Asian cultures, and are overlooked in the west. Once the principle of commensurability has been accepted it should be open to negotiation which contextual considerations best serve the shared purpose of comparison.

Non-Cultural Factors of Democratization

Asian receptivity to the post-Cold War 'wave' of democratization is shaped at least as much by non-cultural as by cultural considerations. Geo-political factors, economic variables, and inherited structures of political interest are all major features of the Asian context that require separate analysis, and that should not be subsumed within an over-generalized or reified conception of cultural difference. Huntington's 'Japanese civilization' was compatible both with militarism and imperialism before the

US occupation, and with constitutionalism, electoralism, and demilitarization thereafter. North Korea shares the same millennial cultural traditions as South Korea, but for geopolitical reasons the two halves of Korea have adopted extremely divergent models of political organization. If there is a single Sinic civilization it encompasses the imperial, republican, and communist models of politics that have been successively established in Beijing during this century. It also embraces Hong Kong, Singapore and Taiwan, each of which is very distinctive in its political arrangements, and its receptivity to the current 'Third Wave' of democratization.

Taiwan, for example, made an abrupt switch from one-party dictatorship to a remarkably convincing replica of a conventional liberal democracy in the decade after 1986. No doubt the island's culture and value system evolved somewhat during that period, as the features that had seemed inimical to democracy were softened, and the more consensual features were reinforced. But such cultural foundations change rather slowly and lag behind political developments, rather than driving them forward. In any case, they tend to adjust to regime change rather than to determine it. If one wishes to explain the democratization of Taiwan, most of the work can be done by the deployment of the standard (one might even say universal) concepts of comparative politics, with only passing concessions to cultural specificity.[16] To be specific, as the People's Republic of China emerged from Maoism and achieved increasing acceptance in the West, Taiwan's geopolitical isolation intensified. The high-level decision to convert the island into a model of Western democracy can be largely understood as a choice of strategy to counter that isolation and regain the political initiative. The rivalry with Beijing provides a more persuasive and parsimonious framework for explaining Taiwan's current receptivity to democratization than could be generated by any kind of cultural interpretation.

Although the contemporaneous democratization of South Korea is a little more complex, similar considerations were of importance there too, whereas any supposed cultural constraints proved inconclusive. President Kim Dae Jung was well known as a critic of 'Asian values' excuses for authoritarianism before he won the South Korean presidency, and once in office he has sought to highlight the features of the Korean cultural tradition that harmonize with liberal democracy as opposed to those that conflict. In a similar vein the victor in the aborted Myanmar (Burmese) elections of 1988 and Nobel Prize Winner, Daw Aung San Suu Kyi (who has been under house arrest in Rangoon since July 1989) emphasizes the compatibility between the teachings of Buddhism and the practices of constitutional democracy.

These two examples illustrate the scope for renegotiating Asian cultural traditions in order to legitimize moves towards democracy. They also confirm that non-cultural factors (such as political power considerations) play a decisive role in determining the extent to which such cultural redefinitions are allowed to prevail, and to produce institutional effects.

A different volume would be needed to specify precisely which contextual considerations of a non-cultural variety were most crucial in determining Asia's receptivity to liberal democracy. As various chapters in this volume suggest, the answer would be different in different countries. The mixed institutional and power political legacies of Western colonialism are emphasized in the chapters on India and Malaysia. (Clearly, Western colonial rule also left a variety of more strictly cultural legacies, so that it would be artificial to view colonialism solely in power politics terms; but the most direct Western influence on Asian receptivity to democracy arises from the path to decolonization followed in each case. The cultural component of this influence is usually indirect and inconclusive.) The chapter on the Japanese electoral system emphasizes an element of institutional design (the electoral system), and the chapter on Sri Lanka also draws attention to institutional variables (majoritarianism, failure to respect the division of powers, etc.). Without undertaking a comprehensive inventory, this may be sufficient to demonstrate that culturalist approaches to the analysis of Asian democratizations require considerable supplementation (to say the least) from conventional comparative politics.

Of course 'culturalist approaches' take many forms. This chapter does not attempt to lay to rest ancient debates about the meaning of 'culture'. The book as a whole is about democracy as a form of modern government in contemporary Asia, and with that focus in mind the present chapter has adopted a definition that is fairly close to what Huntington refers to as a 'civilization'. The focus has been on authoritative teachings, and large-scale systematic processes of socialization based on written texts. This highlights the importance of organized religion, and of state-sponsored education (or even indoctrination). Parochial and subaltern aspects of culture (in the sense emphasized by most anthropology) have been downplayed. The perspective adopted here is particularly relevant when examining Asian receptivity to Western models of democracy, because it is these large-scale organized structures of belief that are most directly challenged by democratization. They offer the potential for a doctrine of systematic rejection (a potential which has been actualized by various currents of fundamentalism). But my argument has been that these indigenous Asian schools of analytical teaching and doctrine may also contain considerable potential for dialogue and even convergence on basic principles that must be of universal applicability, if they are to be applicable anywhere at all. The high or literate cultures of Asia operate at a similar level of generality to Western philosophy, and so can be compared on a basis of equivalence. It is open to negotiation how far they share a common ground with liberal democracy.

Conclusion

In conclusion, therefore, this chapter must not be read as a denial of the value or significance of the insights that can be derived from studies of Asian cultural traditions. Comparativists need to be sensitized to the varied and often subtle ways in which different cultural lenses, and indeed contrasting linguistic traditions, tend to select and structure our categories of analysis. In the present era of Anglo-Saxon linguistic, and perhaps even cultural, ascendancy it may be particularly necessary to be put on guard against the adoption of unconscious assumptions into supposedly neutral and universal frameworks of comparison, or the unthinking endorsement of terms which introduce basics to understanding between regions and even 'civilizations'. There is much to be learnt from the comparative study of cultures, understood as alternative socially located angles of vision on the world, each shaped by a particular history, geography and language. But these alternatives should be understood as no more than interpretative prisms, and should not be viewed as either procrustean or immutable. They may help to shape and select inter-pretations of what liberal democracy has to offer, and where its weak-nesses may lie, but they do not provide closed verdicts on such questions. Any of the Asian 'high cultures' mentioned in this chapter can be mobilized either to accelerate and support democratization, or to obstruct it. There are non-cultural considerations that largely explain which way it may go in any particular case, and comparativists therefore need to pay great attention to this larger context.

From this standpoint it follows that the possibilities of extending and deepening liberal democracy in Asia remain extremely open. There is no inherent cultural block which preordains that Asians must turn against 'Third Wave' experiments with democratization, and reject them as alien implants from an incompatible Western culture. The outcome (or out-comes) will depend mostly on conventional political, security and resource determinants, rather than on some supposedly immanent characteristics of Asian civilization(s) or values. Nonetheless, the existence of alternative cultural lenses will affect the outcome of Asian democratization. Equally, however, where the common ground between culturally diverse democ-racies can be highlighted, Asian democrats will find it easier to legitimize their choice of regime. This also means, of course that what will count as a 'democracy' will have to be adjusted to local idiosyncracies. The spectre of democracy currently haunting Asia could be as hard to exorcize as was the spectre of communism in nineteenth-century Europe. But if so, the democracy that takes root there will be no simple 'end of history' or mere copy of a Western blueprint. The dialogue between Asia and the West, and between theory and democratic practice, is far too open-ended for that.

Notes

1   There is a venerable tradition in Western thought which seeks to counter such insensitivity to other cultures. For example, at the end of the First World War John Dewey alerted his readers against the following mistake: 'We merely forget that we think in terms of customs and traditions which habituation has ingrained; we fancy that we think in terms of mind, pure and simple. Taking our mental habits as the norm of mind, we find the ways of thinking that do not conform to it abnormal, mysterious and tricky', and he subsequently added that 'The attempt to read Chinese institutions in terms of Western ideas has resulted in failures of understanding and action' – *John Dewey: The Middle Works, 1899–1924: Vol 11: 1918-19*, Jo Ann Boydston, (ed.), Carbondale and Edwardsville: Southern Illinois U.P. 1983, pp. 210–15. For a more recent scholarly contribution in this vein, Jacques Gernet writes that 'our own philosophical traditions, which owe so much to the suggestions stemming from certain grammatical functions [are founded on] categories considered to be universal, and are concerned with abstractions and ideas that are stable'. He claims that 'Chinese thought, in contrast, recognises only functional classifications and oppositions. It is concerned not with "yes" and "no", being or non-being, but with contraries which succeed, combine with and complement one another; not with eternal realities, but with potentialities and tendencies, phases of flowering or decline. In place of the idea of law as an immutable rule, it favours that of a model or schema of development' – Jacques Gernet, *China and the Christian Impact: A Conflict of Cultures*, Cambridge: Cambridge University Press, 1985, p. 242.

2   In Latin America, by contrast, I would argue that all pre-conquest civilizational traditions have been comprehensively marginalized, so that the only effective intellectual resources available for resisting parallel tendencies are those that can be drawn from *within* the broad heritage of Western culture.

3   Obviously the then inhabitants of what we now call Asia had no need for the term, since they were not looking at themselves collectively, and from without.

4   Joseph Chan, 'The Asian Challenge to Universal Human Rights: A Philosophical Appraisal', in James T. H. Teng (ed.), *Human Rights and International Relations in the Asia-Pacific Region*, London: Pinter, 1995, p. 33. Compare Abdullahi An-N'aim (ed.) *Human Rights in Cross-Cultural Perspectives: A Quest for Consensus*, Philadelphia: University of Pennsylvania Press, 1992, especially the four chapters in Section One on general issues in a cross-cultural approach to human rights. (Chapter Three, by William P. Alford, focuses on Post-Tiananmen China, and on the one-child policy.

5   Joseph Chan, 'A Confucian Perspective on Human Rights'. Paper prepared for the second workshop on 'The Growth of East Asia and its Impact on Human Rights', Chulalongkorn University, Bangkok, March 24–27, 1996.

6   P.D. Premasiri, 'Minorities in Buddhist Doctrine' in K.M. de Silva, Pensri Duke, Ellen S. Goldberg and Nathan Katz (eds.), *Ethnic Conflict in Buddhist Societies: Sri Lanka, Thailand and Burma*, Boulder: Westview, 1988, pp. 42–51.

7   See Stanley J. Tambiah, *Buddhism Betrayed? Religion, Politics, and Violence in Sri Lanka*, Chicago: Chicago University Press, 1992.

8   This parallels Quentin Skinner's answer to the question 'what is the point of seeing ourselves … as simply one tribe among others?' His reply is 'We can hope to attain a certain kind of objectivity in appraising rival systems of thought. We can hope to attain a greater degree of understanding, and thereby a larger tolerance, for various elements of cultural diversity. And above all, we can hope to acquire a perspective from which to view our own form of life in a more self-critical way, enlarging our present horizons instead of fortifying local prejudices.' 'A Reply to my Critics', in James Tully (ed.), *Meaning and Context: Quentin Skinner and His Critics*, Cambridge: Polity Press, 1988, p. 287.

9   Anthony J. Parel defines the study of comparative political philosophy as 'nothing other than the process, first of identifying the 'equivalences', and second, of understanding their significance. Such 'equivalences', if and when they are found, would both deepen ones understanding of one's own tradition and engender understanding and respect for the tradition of others'. Anthony J. Parel and Ronald C. Keith (eds), *Comparative Political Philosophy: Studies Under the Upas Tree*, New Delhi: Sage, 1992, p. 12. This collection compares four traditions – Western, Chinese, Indian, and the Islamic. See also Cooper on equivalencies – Barry Cooper, 'Classical Western Political Philosophy', in Parel and Keith 1992, pp. 65–68.

10 For one recent attempt to anchor the indispensable elements of 'democracy', while still allowing language, history, and culture to generate differences of

emphasis over the boundaries of the concept, see Laurence Whitehead, 'The Vexed Issue of the Meaning of Democracy', *Journal of Political Ideologies*, Vol. 2, No. 2, 1997. For an attempt to specify the way contrasting non-political conceptions and assumptions shape thinking about democracy in China and the West, respectively, see Robert X. Ware, 'What Good is Democracy? The Alternatives in China and the West' in Parel and Keith, see note 9. Barry Cooper notes that for the Athenians 'there was nothing particularly Greek about political philosophy. The best regime is no more Greek than health is Greek', and 'Classical (western) political philosophy did not exist as a distinct area of study until modern political philosophy made it possible to draw a contrast between the two. Thus classical Western political philosophy was neither understood as classical nor Western but simply as political philosophy'. Similar assumptions of universality underlay classical Chinese political philosophy, thus facilitating comparison of the two, at least from a Straussian perspective. See Barry Cooper, in Parel and Keith 1992, pp. 30 and 37.

11 Franz Boas, *The Mind of Primitive Man*, New York: Free Press, 1966, p. 159.

12 Ann Swidler defines culture as 'the publicly available symbolic forms through which people experience and express meaning' and she argues that this can provide a 'tool kit' for action, which may not be about the pursuit of culturally determined ultimate ends. She also makes a helpful distinction between the encapsulating role of culture in 'settled times' and its more combative ideological form in unsettled times. Our concern here is with Asian cultural receptivity to democracy, and therefore with the more combative ideological model of culture. The 'settled' or 'unsettled' nature of the times is determined by consideration largely outside Swidler's model – our 'non cultural' factors.

13 Samuel P. Huntington, *The Clash of Civilisations and the Remaking of World Order*, New York: Touchstone, 1996.

14 Op. cit. The map is on p. 27, and the discussion of civilizations and cultures is taken from pp. 41–44. Needless to say, the world map cannot convey nuance, overlap, or syncretism. Instead it presents each civilization as a uniform territorially homogeneous block with sharp borders. Yet it is precisely these assumptions that are in question.

15 Jack Goody warns against drawing 'too strong a dividing line between 'us' and the great civilizations of the Ancient Near East (nor yet of India or China for that matter) for they possessed and utilized one critical invention of mankind in the sphere of communication, namely writing, whose use was not merely cosmetic but penetrated deeply into many areas of social life, permitting the development of new forms of social organization and new ways of 'handling information'. He stressed 'the generalising push that writing tends to give to normative structures, partly because of the relative decontextualisation of communication in the written channel, partly because of the wider social groupings within which that communication takes place'. Jack Goody, *The Logic*

of Writing and the Organisation of Society, Cambridge: Cambridge University Press, 1986, p.182, p.176.

16 For an elaboration of this argument see Laurence Whitehead, 'The Democratization of Taiwan: A Comparative Perspective', in Steve Tsang and Hung-mao Tien (eds), *Democratization in Taiwan: Implications for China*, Basingstoke: Macmillan, 1999.

BIBLIOGRAPHY

Abe, Hitoshi, Muneyuki Shindo and Sadafumi Kawato, *The Government and Politics of Japan*, Tokyo: University of Tokyo Press, 1994.

Abercrombie, N. (ed.) *Dictionary of Sociology*, London: Penguin Books, 1994.

Abeyratne, Sirimal, *Economic Change and Political Conflicts in Developing Countries with an Investigation into Sri Lanka*, Amsterdam: VU University Press, Sri Lanka Studies No. 5, 1998.

Ahmad, Zakaria, 'Malaysia: Quasi-Democracy in a Divided Society', in Larry Diamond, Juan J. Linz and Seymour Martin Lipset (eds), *Democracy in Developing Countries*, Vol. 3, Boulder: Lynne Rienner, 1989.

——, 'The Police and Political Development in Malaysia: Change, Continuity, and Institution Building of a Coercive Apparatus in a Developing, Ethnically Divided Society', PhD dissertation, Massachusetts Institute of Technology, Mass., 1977.

—— (ed.), *Government and Politics of Malaysia*, Singapore: Oxford University Press, 1987.

Alagappa, M., 'The Asian Spectrum', *Journal of Democracy*, Vol. 6, No. 1, January 1995.

——, *Democratic Transition in Asia: the Role of the International Community*, Honolulu: East-West Center Special Reports, 1994.

Alexander, Paul, 'Shared Fantasies and Elite Politics: The Sri Lankan 'Insurrection' of 1971', *Mankind* 13, Vol. 2, 1997.

Allen, Christopher S., 'The Underdevelopment of Keynesianism in the Federal Republic of Germany', in Peter A. Hall (ed.), *The Political Power of Economic Ideas: Keynesianism Across Nations*, Princeton, NJ: Princeton University Press, 1989.

Alles, A.C., *Insurgency 1971*, Colombo: The Apothecaries, 1972.

Almond, Gabriel, 'Comparative Political Systems', *Journal of Politics*, Vol. 18, 1956.

—— and Sidney Verba, *Civic Culture: Political Attitudes and Democracy in Five Nations*, Princeton, N.J.: Princeton University Press, 1963.

Ampalavanar, Rajeswary, *The Indian Minority and Political Change in Malaysia, 1945–1957*, Kuala Lumpur: Oxford University Press, 1981.

An-N'aim, Abdullahi (ed.), *Human Rights in Cross-Cultural Perspectives: A Quest for Consensus*, Philadelphia: University of Pennsylvania Press, 1992.

Anonymous ['A native of Mysore'], *Fifty Years of British Administration*, London [1874], quoted from: R. Ramakrishnan, 'British policies in princely Mysore (1831–81)', in N.R. Ray (ed.), *Western Colonial Policy – a Study of Its Impact on Indian Society*, Vol. 1, Calcutta: Institute of Historical Studies, 1981.

Antlöv, Hans, 'National Elections, Local Issues: the 1997 and 1999 Indonesian Elections in a Village Perspective', in Hans Antlöv and Sven Cederroth (eds), *Elections in Indonesia*, Richmond: Curzon Press, forthcoming.

——, 'The Java That Never Was – Cultural Notions of Politics in Indonesia', paper presented at the 10th annual European Java Workshop, Amsterdam, 9–10 May 1997.

——, *Exemplary Centre, Administrative Periphery: Leadership and the New Order in Rural Java*, Richmond: Curzon Press, 1995.

Bailey, F.G., *Stratagems and Spoils. A Social Anthropology of Politics*, Oxford: B. Blackwell, 1969.

Bakken, Børge, *The Exemplary Society, Human Improvement, Social Control and the Dangers of Modernity in China*, Oxford: Oxford University Press, forthcoming.

Basham, A.L. (ed.), *Kingship in Asia and Early America*. 30th International Congress of Human Sciences in Asia and North Africa. Seminars. Mexico City: El Colegio de Mexico, 1981.

Bellah, Robert (ed.), *Religion and Progress in Modern Asia*, New York: Free Press, 1965.

Binder, Leonard *et. al.*, *Crises and Sequences in Political Development*, Princeton, N.J.: Princeton University Press, 1971.

Boas, Franz, *The Mind of Primitive Man*, New York: Free Press, 1966.

Bourchier, David, 'Totalitarianism and the "National Personality" Recent Controversy about the Philosophical Basis of the Indonesian State', in Jim Schiller and Barbara Martin-Schiller (eds), *Imagining Indonesia. Cultural Politics and Political Culture*, Athens: Ohio University Center for International Studies, 1997.

Boydston, Jo Ann (ed.), *John Dewey: The Middle Works, 1899–1924: Vol 11: 1918–19*, Carbondale and Edwardsville: Southern Illinois U.P., 1983.

Brokaw, Cynthia, *The Ledgers of Merit and Demerit. Social Change and Moral Order in Late Imperial China*, Princeton, NJ: Princeton University Press, 1991.

——, 'Guidebooks to Social and Moral Success: the Morality Books in 16th and 17th Century China', *Transactions of the International Conference of Orientalists in Japan*, No. 27, 1982.

Butanaziba, Yunus Lubega, 'The Making of Administrative and Economic Development plans for Malaysia, 1945–65: the International Hand', MA thesis, Faculty of Arts and Social Sciences, Universiti Malaysia, 1997.

Case, William, 'Semi-Democracy in Malaysia: Withstanding the Pressures for Regime Change', *Pacific Affairs*, 66(2), 1993.

de Cecco, Marcello, 'Keynes and Italian Economics', in Peter A. Hall (ed.), *The Political Power of Economic Ideas: Keynesianism Across Nations*, Princeton, NJ: Princeton University Press, 1989.

Chan, Joseph, 'A Confucian Perspective on Human Rights'. Paper prepared for the second workshop on 'The Growth of East Asia and Its Impact on Human Rights', Chulalongkorn University, Bangkok, March 24–27, 1996.

——, 'The Asian Challenge to Universal Human Rights: A Philosophical Appraisal', in James T. H. Teng (ed.), *Human Rights and International Relations in the Asia-Pacific Region*, London: Pinter, 1995.

Chan, W.T., *A Source Book in Chinese Philosophy*, New Jersey: Princeton University Press, 1963.

Chang, Y.S., 'The Urban Korean as Individual', *Korea Journal*, Vol. 17, No. 5, 1977.

Cheah, Boon Keng, *Red Star Over Malaya: Resistance and Social Conflict during and after the Japanese Occupation 1941–1946*, Singapore: Singapore University Press, 1983.

——, *The Masked Comrades: A Study of the Communist United Front in Malaya, 1945–1948*, Singapore: Times Books International, 1979.

Cheung, Anthony Bing-leung and Kin-sheun Louie, 'Social Conflicts in Hong Kong, 1975–1986: Trends and Implication'. Hong Kong Institute of Asia-Pacific Studies Occasional Paper No. 3, Hong Kong: Chinese University of Hong Kong, 1991.

Chiu, Stephen, 'The Politics of Laissez-faire: Hong Kong's Strategy of Industrialization in Historical Perspective'. Hong Kong Institute of Asia-Pacific Studies Occasional Paper No. 40, Hong Kong: Chinese University of Hong Kong, 1994.

Choate, Allen, 'Local Governance in China', paper presented at the seminar Asian Perspectives: Focus on China, held in Washington, D.C. March 20, 1997.

Chow, Tse-tsung, *The May Fourth Movement: Intellectual Revolution in Modern China*, Cambridge, Mass.: Harvard University Press, 1960.

Chu, Godwin C., 'The Emergence of the New Chinese Culture', in Wen-Shing Tseng and David Y.H. Wu (eds), *Chinese Culture and Mental Health*, London: Academic Press, 1985.

Chua, Beng-Huat, *Communitarian Ideology and Democracy in Singapore*, London: Routledge, 1995.

Coates, John, *Supressing Insurgency: An Analysis of the Malayan Emergency, 1948–1954*, Boulder, Colorado: Westview, 1992.

Cohn, B.S., 'Political systems in 18th century India: the Banares region', *Journal of the American Oriental Society*, Vol. 82, No. 3, 1962.

Commission for a New Asia, *Towards a New Asia*, Kuala Lumpur: Commission for a New Asia, 1994.

Cooper, Barry, 'Classical Western Political Philosophy', in Anthony J. Parel and Ronald C. Keith (eds), *Comparative Political Philosophy: Studies under the Upas Tree*, New Delhi: Sage, 1992.

Crespo, José Antonio, 'The Liberal Democratic Party in Japan: Conservative Domination', *International Political Science Review*, Vol. 16, No. 2, 1995.

Crouch, Harold, 'Malaysia: Neither Authoritarian nor Democratic?', in Kevin Hewson, Richard Robisan and Gary Rodan (eds), *Southeast Asia in the 1990s: Authoritarianism, Democracy and Capitalism*, Sydney: Allen and Unwin, 1993.

Curtis, Gerald, 'Japan', in David Butler and Austin Ranney (eds), *Electioneering: A Comparative Study of Continuity and Change*, Oxford: Clarendon Press, 1992.

——, *The Japanese Way of Politics*, New York: Columbia University Press, 1992.

Dahl, R.A., *Democracy and Its Critics*, New Haven: Yale University Press, 1989

——, *Polyarchy: Participation and Opposition*, New Haven and London: Yale University Press, 1971.

Darmaputera, Eka, Pancasila *and the Search for Identity and Modernity in Indonesian Society: A Cultural and Ethical Analysis*, Leiden: Brill, 1988.

Davies, Stephen N.G., 'The Changing Nature of Representation in Hong Kong Politics', in Kathleen Cheek-Milby and Miron Mushkat (eds), *Hong Kong: The Challenge of Transformation*, Hong Kong: Centre of Asian Studies, University of Hong Kong, 1989.

——, 'One Brand of Politics Rekindled', *Hong Kong Law Journal* 7, No. 1, 1977.

De Silva, Colin R., *Sri Lanka's New Capitalism and the Erosion of Democracy: Political writings of Dr. Colin R. de Silva in the period 1977–1988*, Batty Weerakoon (ed.), Colombo: Ceylon Federation of Labour, 1988.

De Silva, K.M., and H.Wriggins, *J.R. Jayewardene of Sri Lanka. A Political Biography. Volume 2: From 1956 to his retirement (1989)*, London: Leo Cooper and Pen and Sword Books, 1994.

——, *J.R. Jayewardene of Sri Lanka. A Political Biography. Volume 1: 1906–1956*, London: Anthony Blond, 1988.

Dennis, Peter and Jeffrey Grey, *Emergency and Confrontation: Australian Military Operations in Malaya and Borneo 1950–1966*, Sydney: Allen and Unwin, 1996.

Dewaraja, Lorna S., *The Kandyan Kingdom of Sri Lanka 1707–1782*, Colombo: Lake House Investments, 1988.

Deyo, Frederic C. (ed.), *The Political Economy of the New Asian Industrialism*, Ithaca: Cornell University Press, 1987.

Dharmadasa, K.N.O., *Language, Religion, and Ethnic Assertiveness. The Growth of Sinhalese Nationalism in Sri Lanka*, Ann Arbor: The University of Michigan Press, 1992.

Diamond, Larry, 'Three Paradoxes of Democracy', *Journal of Democracy*, Vol. 1, No. 3, 1990.

——, Juan J. Linz and Seymour Martin Lipset, 'Preface', in *idem* (eds) *Democracy in Developing Countries*, 4 volumes, Boulder, Colorado: Lynne Rienner Publishers, 1989.

——, Marc F. Plattner, Yun-han Chu, and Hung-mao Tien (eds), *Consolidating the Third Wave Democracies: Regional Challenges*, Baltimore: Johns Hopkins University Press, 1997.

Dow, A., *History of Hindostan*, Vol. 3, 'Dissertation on Despotism', London [1770], pp. 7–27, quoted in Th. R. Metcalf, *Ideologies of the Raj: The New Cambridge History of India III. 4.*, Cambridge: Cambridge University Press, 1994.

Dunleavy, Patrick and Helen Margetts, 'Understanding the Dynamics of Electoral Reform', *International Political Science Review*, Vol. 16, No. 1, 1995.

Eldridge, Philip, *Non-Government Organisations and Democratic Participation in Indonesia*. Oxford: Oxford University Press, 1995.

Emmerson, Donald, 'Region and Recalcitrance: Rethinking Democracy Through Southeast Asia', *Pacific Review*, Vol. 8, No. 2, 1995.

——, 'Singapore and the "Asian Values" Debate', *Journal of Democracy* Vol. 6, No. 4, October 1995.

Ferdinand, P., 'Socialism and Democracy in China', in David McLellan and Sean Sayer (eds), *Socialism and Democracy*, London: Macmillan Academic and Profession LTD, 1991.

Flanagan, Scott C., 'Mechanisms of Social Network Influence in Japanese Voting Behavior,' in Scott C. Flanagan *et al.*, *The Japanese Voter*, New Haven: Yale University Press, 1991.

——, 'Electoral Change in Japan: A Study of Secular Realignment', in Russell J. Dalton, Scott C. Flanagan and Paul Allen Beck (eds), *Electoral Change in Advanced Industrial Democracies: Realignment or Dealignment?*, Princeton, N.J.: Princeton University Press, 1984.

Friedman, Edward (ed.), *The Politics of Democratization: Generalizing East Asian Experiences*, Boulder: Westview Press, 1994.

Friedman, Milton, *Capitalism and Freedom*, London: University of Chicago Press, 1962.

Fukuyama, F., 'Confucianism and Democracy', *Journal of Democracy*, Vol. 6, No. 2, 1995.

——, 'The Primacy of Culture', *Journal of Democracy*, Vol. 6, No. 1, January 1995.

——, 'Asia's Soft-Authoritarian Alternative', *New Perspectives Quarterly*, Vol. 9, No. 2, Spring 1992.

——, *The End of History and the Last Man*, London: Hamish Hamilton, 1992.

Fuller, G., 'The Next Ideology' *Foreign Policy*, No. 98, Spring 1995.

Funston, John, *Malay Politics in Malaysia: A Study of the United Malays National Organisation and Party Islam*, Kuala Lumpur: Heinemann, 1980.

Gallie, W.B., *Philosophy and the Historical Understanding*, London: Chatto and Windus, 1964.

Ganguli, B.N., 'Political and Economic Thought of Ram Mohan Roy', in N.R. Ray (ed.), *Ram Mohan Roy. A Bi-Centenary Tribute*, New Delhi: National Book Trust, 1974.

'Gaoxiao "san hao" xuesheng pingding gongzuo you dai wanshan' [The evaluation work of 'three-good students' in universities must be handled well], editorial article, *Gaodeng jiaoyu yanjiu*, No. 3, 1986.

Gernet, Jacques, *China and the Christian Impact: A Conflict of Cultures*, Cambridge: Cambridge University Press, 1985.

Gerschenkron, Alexander, *Economic Backwardness in Historical Perspective*, Cambridge: Cambridge University Press, 1962.

Ghose, Aurobindo, 'Asiatic Democracy', in *Sri Aurobindo's Birth Centenary Library, Vol. 1, Bande Mataram. Early political writings*, Pondicherry: Sri Aurobindo Ashram, 1972.

Giddens, A., *Sociology*, Cambridge: Polity Press, 1989.

Gladdish, Ken, 'The Primacy of the Particulars', *Journal of Democracy*, Vol. 4, No. 1, January 1993.

Goody, Jack, *The Logic of Writing and the Organisation of Society*, Cambridge: Cambridge University Press, 1986.

Grant, Ch., 'Observation on the State of Society among Asiatic Subjects of Great Britian, Particularly with Respect to Morals and on the Means of Improving It', [privately printed, 1797], quoted from E.M.C. Stokes, *English Utilitarians and India*, Oxford: Clarendon Press, 1959.

Guo, Luoji, 'A Human Rights Critique of the Chinese Legal System', *Harvard Human Rights Journal*, Vol. 9, Spring 1996.

Ha'erbin shi shangye xuexiao guanli zhidu [The administrative system of Harbin business school], Harbin (Internal school document), 1987.

Haggard, Stephan, *Pathways from the Periphery: The Politics of Growth in the Newly Industrializing Countries*, Ithaca: Cornell University Press, 1990.

Hahm, C., 'The Clash of Civilizations Revisited: A Confucian Perspective'. Paper presented at La Trobe University, Australia, 1995.

——, 'The Confucian Political Discourse and the Politics of Reform in Korea'. Paper presented at the Annual Meeting of the American Political Science Association, New York, 1994.

Hall, Peter A., 'Conclusion: The Politics of Keynesian Ideas', in Peter A. Hall (ed.), *The Political Power of Economic Ideas: Keynesianism Across Nations*, Princeton, NJ: Princeton University Press, 1989.

Harris, Peter, *Hong Kong: A Study in Bureaucracy and Politics*, Hong Kong: Macmillan, 1988.

Hastrup, K., *Det antropologiske projekt. Om forbløffelse* [The Anthropological Project. On Amazement], Copenhagen: Gyldendal, 1992.

Hefner, Robert and Patricia Hovwatich (eds), *Islam in an Era of Nation-States: Politics and Religious Revivalism in Muslim Southeast Asia*, Honolulu: University of Hawaii Press, 1997.

Held, D., *Models of Democracy*, Cambridge: Polity Press, 1987.

Helgesen, G., *Democracy and Authority in Korea: the Cultural Dimension in Korean Politics*, Richmond: Curzon Press, New York: St. Martin's Press, 1998.

——, *Democracy in South Korea*, NIAS Report No. 18, Copenhagen: Nordic Institute of Asian Studies, 1994.

—— and S.R. Thomsen, *Measuring Attitude Dimensions: the Case of South Korean Democratization*, NIAS Report No. 27, Copenhagen: Nordic Institute of Asian Studies, 1995.

Hill, Michael and Lim Kwen Fee, *The Politics of Nation Building and Citizenship in Singapore*, London: Routledge, 1995.

Hobbes, Thomas, *Leviathan*, [1651], Harmondsworth: Penguin Books, 1968.

Hofstede, G., *Cultures and Organizations: Software of the Mind*, New York: McGraw-Hill, 1991.

Hong Kong, Legislative Council, *Hong Kong Hansard 1967*.

——, *Hong Kong Hansard 1968*.

——, *Hong Kong Hansard 1970/71*.

——, *Hong Kong Hansard 1977/78*.

——, *Hong Kong Hansard 1981/82*.

Hrebenar, Ronald J., 'The Changing Postwar Party System', in R.J. Hrebenar (ed.), *The Japanese Party System: From One-Party Rule to Coalition Government*, Boulder: Westview Press, 1986.

——, 'Political Party Proliferation, the New Liberal Club and the Mini-Parties', in R.J. Hrebenar (ed.), *The Japanese Party System: From One-Party Rule to Coalition Government*, Boulder: Westview Press, 1986.

Human Rights Task Force, *Annual Report*, 1993.

Hu, Ping, *Zai lixiang yu xianshi zhijian* [Between ideal and reality], Hong Kong: Tianyuan shuwu, 1990.

——, *Gei wo yige zhidian* [Give me a fulcrum], Taibei: Lianjing chuban gong-shi, 1988.

Hu, Shoufen, *Deyu yuanli* [Principles of moral education], revised edition, Beijing: Beijing shifan daxue chubanshe, 1989.

Hu, Wei, 'Xiandai deyu pingjia de tedian ji gongneng' [The characteristics and functions of modern moral evaluation], *Shanghai jiaoyu*, No. 7–8, 1987.

——, Tang Yuan and Ouyang Hongsen, 'Guanyu pinde pingding zhibiao tixi de yanjiu' [On the study of moral quality index systems], (Part 1), *Shanghai jiaoyu*, No. 9, 1986.

——, 'Guanyu pinde pingding zhibiao tixi de yanjiu' [On the study of moral quality index systems], (Part 2), *Shanghai jiaoyu*, No. 10, 1986.

——, 'Guanyu pinde pingding zhibiao tixi de yanjiu' [On the study of moral quality index systems], (Part 3), *Shanghai jiaoyu*, No. 11, 1986.

——, 'Guanyu pinde pingding zhibiao tixi de yanjiu [On the study of moral quality index systems], (Part 4), *Shanghai jiaoyu*, No. 12, 1986.

Huntington, Samuel P., *The Clash of Civilisations and the Remaking of World Order*, New York: Touchstone, 1996.

——, 'The Clash of Civilizations?' *Foreign Affairs*, Vol. 72, No. 3, 1993.

——, 'Democracy's Third Wave', *Journal of Democracy* No. 2, Spring 1991.

——, *The Third Wave: Democratization in the Late Twentieth Century*, Norman and London: University of Oklahoma Press, 1991.

——, 'The United States', in Michel Crozier, Samuel P. Huntington and Joji Watanuki, *Crisis in Democracy*, New York: Columbia University Press, 1975.

Hyndman, Patricia, 'Democracy in Peril. Sri Lanka: A Country in Crisis'. Report of the LAWASIA Human Rights Standing Committee, 1985.

India Office Library, London, L/P&S/20/H44. 'Letters of the Agent to the Governor-General of North-East Frontier and Commissioner of Assam H. Hopkinson and Commissioner of Mysore, F. Clerk', Calcutta, 1867.

——, L/P&S/20/H44. 'Correspondence regarding the comparative merits of British and Native Administration in India', Calcutta, 1867.

Inglehart, Ronald, *The Silent Revolution*, Princeton, N.J.: Princeton University Press, 1977.

Ivan, Victor, *Sri Lanka in Crisis. Road to Conflict*, Ratmalana: Sarvodaya Book Publishing Services, 1989.

Iwanaga, Kazuki, 'Women in Japanese Politics: A Comparative Politics', Occasional Paper 37. Stockholm: Center for Pacific Asia Studies, Stockholm University, June 1998.

——, 'Transition in Japanese Electoral Politics: Democratic Consequences of the 1996 Lower House Election,' *The Stockholm Journal of East Asian Studies*, Vol. 8, 1997.

Jackson, Robert, *The Malayan Emergency: The Commonwealth's War 1948–1966*, London: Routledge, 1991.

Jakobson, Linda, *A Million Truths: Ten Years in China*, New York: M. Evans, 1998.

Jalal, A., *Democracy and Authoritarianism in South Asia*, Cambridge: Cambridge University Press, 1995.

Jayatilleka, Dayan, *Sri Lanka. The Travails of a Democracy, Unfinished War, Protracted Crisis*, New Delhi: Vikas, 1995.

Jin, Rong, 'Yi "xuan" dai "ping" bu kequ' [Substituting 'evaluations' with 'elections' is not to be recommended], *Renshi yu rencai*, No. 3, 1989.

Johnson, Chalmers, *MITI and the Japanese Miracle*, Stanford: Stanford University Press, 1981.

Kavanagh, Dennis and Peter Morris, *Consensus Politics from Attlee to Thatcher*, Oxford: Basil Blackwell, 1989.

Kemper, Steven, *The Presence of the Past. Chronicles, Politics, and Culture in Sinhala Life*, Ithaca: Cornell University Press, 1991.

Keyes, Charles, Laurel Kendall and Helen Hardacre (eds), *Asian Visions of Authority: Religion and the Modern States of East and Southeast Asia*, Honolulu: University of Hawaii Press, 1994.

Kim C.H. *The Immortal Juche Idea*. Pyongyang: Foreign Languages Publishing House, 1984.

Kim, K.O., 'A study on the political manipulation of elite culture: Confucian culture in local level politics', *Korea Journal*, Vol. 28, No. 11, 1988.

King, Ambrose Y.C., 'Administrative Absorption of Politics in Hong Kong: Emphasis on the Grass Roots Level', in Ambrose Y.C. King and Rance P.L. Lee (eds), *Social Life and Development in Hong Kong*, Hong Kong: Chinese University Press, 1981.

Kloos, Peter, 'The Struggle Between the Lion and the Tiger', in Cora Govers and Hans Vermeulen (eds), *The Politics of Ethnic Consciousness*, London: Macmillan, 1997.

——, 'Publish and Perish: Nationalism and Social Research in Sri Lanka', *Social Anthropology*, Vol. 3, No 2, 1995.

——, '"Past Political Identities, Present Political Interests". An Indigenous Political Model in Sri Lanka', in M. van Bakel, Renée Hagesteijn, Pieter van de Velde (eds), *Pivot Politics, Changing Cultural Identities in Early State Formation Processes*, Amsterdam: Het Spinhuis, 1994.

——, 'Changing Resources, Changing Entrepreneurs', in M. van Bakel, R.R. Hagesteijn and P. van de Velde (eds), *Private Politics, A Multidisciplinary Approach to 'Big-Man' Systems*, Leiden: Brill, 1986.

Koo, Hagen, 'The Interplay of State, Class and World System in East Asian Development: The Cases of South Korea and Taiwan', in Frederic C. Deyo (ed.), 1987.

Kooiman, D., 'Separate electorates: experiences from colonial India'. Paper presented at the symposium on 'Changing identities under colonialism', Berlin, 1993.

Koon, Heng Pek, *Chinese Politics in Malaysia: A History of the Malaysian Chinese Association*. Singapore: Oxford University Press, 1988.

Korean Ministry of Education, *Moral Education, Seventh Grade*, Seoul, 1991.

Krauss, Ellis S., 'Conflict in the Diet: Toward Conflict Management in Parliamentary Politics', in Ellis S. Krauss, Thomas P. Rohlen and Patricia G. Steinhoff (eds), *Conflict in Japan*, Honolulu: University of Hawaii Press, 1984.

Lane, John C., 'The Election of Women under Proportional Representation: The Case of Malta', *Democratization*, Vol. 2, No. 2, Summer 1995.

LaPalombara, Joseph, *Bureaucracy and Political Development*, Princeton, N.J.: Princeton University Press, 1963.

Lardeyret, Guy, 'The Problem with PR', *Journal of Democracy*, Vol. 2, No. 3, Summer 1991.

Lau, Albert, *The Malayan Union Controversy 1942–1948*, Singapore: Oxford University Press, 1991.

Lau, Siu-kai, 'Basic Law and the New Political Order of Hong Kong'. Centre for Hong Kong Studies Occasional Paper No. 26, Hong Kong: Chinese University of Hong Kong, 1988.

——, *Society and Politics in Hong Kong*, Hong Kong: Chinese University Press, 1982.

——, *Utilitarianistic Familism: The Basis of Political Stability in Hong Kong*, Social Research Centre Occasional Paper No. 74, Hong Kong: Chinese University of Hong Kong, 1978.

—— and Kuan Hsin-chi, 'Public Attitude Toward Laissez-Faire in Hong Kong', *Asian Survey*, 30, No. 8, August 1990.

——, *The Ethos of the Hong Kong Chinese*, Hong Kong: Chinese University Press, 1988.

Lee, K.B., *A New History of Korea*, Seoul: Ilchokak Publishers, 1984.

Lethbridge, Henry J., 'Hong Kong Under Japanese Occupation: Changes in Social Structure', in I.C. Jarvie (ed.), *Hong Kong: A Society in Transition*, London: Routledge and Kegan Paul, 1969.

Li, Yuqi and Xie Yupu, 'Sheji laodong kepian shanghao laodong ke' [Planning a good labour class by using a labour card], *Hebei jiaoyu*, No. 10, 1989.

Lijphart, Arend, *Electoral Systems and Party Systems: A Study of Twenty-Seven Democracies, 1945–1990*, Oxford: Oxford University Press, 1994.

——, 'Constitutional Choices for New Democracies', *Journal of Democracy*, Vol. 2, No. 1, Winter 1991.

——, *Democracies. Patterns of Majoritarian and Consensus Government in Twenty-One Countries*, New Haven: Yale University Press, 1984.

Lindblom, Charles E., *Politics and Markets: The World's Political Economic Systems*, New York: Basic Books, 1977.

Linz, Juan J. and Alfred Stepan (eds,) *The Breakdown of Democratic Regimes*, 4 volumes, Baltimore: Johns Hopkins University Press, 1978.

Lipset, Seymour Martin, 'The Social Requisites of Democracy Revisited', *American Sociological Review* Vol. 59, No. 1, February 1994.

Liu, Jun and Li Lin (eds.), *Xinquanwei zhuyi* [Neo-authoritarianism], Beijing: Beijing jingji xueyuan chubanshe, 1989.

Longstreth, Frank, 'The City, Industry and the State', in Colin Crouch (ed.), *State and Economy in Contemporary Capitalism*, London: Croom Helm, 1979.

Lu, Zhou, Yang Ruohe and Hu Ruyong, *Qingshaonian fanzui zonghe zhili duice xue* [Studies in how to deal with comprehensive control of juvenile crime], Beijing: Qunzhong chubanshe, 1986.

Machiavelli, Niccoló, *The Prince* [1513], Toronto, Bantam Books, 1981.

Mahbubani, K., 'The United State: "Go East, Young Man"', *The Washington Quarterly*, 1994.

——, 'The West and the Rest', *The National Interest*, No. 19, Spring 1992.

Manor, James, *The Expedient Utopian: Bandaranaike and Ceylon*, Cambridge: Cambridge University Press, 1989.

McMichael, Philip, *Development and Social Change: A Global Perspective*, Thousand Oaks, California: Pine Forge, 1996.

Means, G.P., *The Constitution of Malaysia, Further Perspectives and Development, Essays in Honour of Tun Mohamed Suffian*, Kuala Lumpur: Oxford University Press, 1986.

——, *Malaysian Politics,* London: University of London Press, 1970.

Mickleburgh, Rod, 'Rare freedom thrives in Chinese villages', *Globe Post*, Toronto, 30 January 1995.

Mill, J., *History of India*, London: Baldwin, Cradock and Joy, Vol. 2, 1817.

Mill, J.S., *Considerations on Representative Government*, in J.M. Robson (ed.), *Collected Works of John Stuart Mill*, Vol. XIX, Toronto: University of Toronto Press, 1977.

Milwertz, C.N., *Accepting Population Control – Urban Chinese Women and the One-Child Family Policy*, Richmond: Curzon Press, 1997.

Min, K.S., 'Personal Reflections on Democracy in Korea', Center for Korean Studies Colloquium Paper No. 3, Honolulu, 1975.

Miners, Norman J., 'Plans for Constitutional Reform in Hong Kong, 1946–52', *The China Quarterly*, No. 107, September 1986.

——, *The Government and Politics of Hong Kong*, 3rd ed., Hong Kong: Oxford University Press, 1981.

Mitta, M. and S. Koppikar, 'Changing Equations', *India Today*, 30 June 1996.

Miyake, Ichiro, 'Type of Partisanship, Partisan Attitude, and Voting Choices', in Flanagan *et al., The Japanese Voter.*

Montesquieu, Baron de la Brède et de, *De l'esprit des lois*, 2 vols., [1748] Paris: Editions Garnier Frèyes, 1969.

Moore, Mick, 'Thoroughly Modern Revolutionaries: The JVP in Sri Lanka'. *Modern Asia Studies*, Vol 27, No. 3, 1993.

——, 'Retreat from Democracy in Sri Lanka?' *Journal of Commonwealth and Comparative Politics*, No. 30, Vol. 1, 1992.

Morley, James W. (ed.), *Driven by Growth: Political Change in the Asia-Pacific Region*, Armonk, N.Y.: M.E. Sharpe, 1993.

Mu, Guanzhong, 'Renkou suzhi xinlun' [New discussion on human quality], *Renkou yanjiu*, No. 3, 1989.

Muhammad, Shan (ed.), *Writings and Speeches of Sir Sayyid Ahmad Khan*, Bombay: Nachiketa Publishers, 1972.

Mulder, Niels, 'The Ideology of Javanese-Indonesian Leadership', in Hans Antlöv and Sven Cederroth (eds), *Leadership on Java: Gentle Hints, Authoritarian Rule*, Richmond: Curzon Press, 1994.

Muramatsu, Michio and Ellis S. Krauss, 'The Dominant Party and Social Coalitions in Japan', in T. J. Pempel (ed.), *Uncommon Democracies: The One-Party Dominant Regimes*, Ithaca: Cornell University Press, 1990.

Murray, Geoffrey and Audrey Perera, *Singapore: The Global City*, Folkestone: China Library, 1996.

Naisbitt, John, *Megatrends Asia. The Eight Asian Megatrends That Are Changing the World*, London: Nicholas Brealey, 1995.

Neher C. and R. Marlay, *Democracy and Development in Southeast Asia: The Winds of Change*. Boulder: Westview Press, 1995.

Ngo, Tak-Wing, 'Changing Government-Business Relations and the Governance of Hong Kong', in Robert Ash, Peter Ferdinand, Brian Hook and Robin Porter (eds), *Hong Kong in Transition*, London: Macmillan, forthcoming.

——, 'Hong Kong under Colonial Rule: An Introduction', *China Information* Vol. 12, Nos. 1/2, Summer/Autumn 1997.

——, 'Business Encirclement of Politics: Government-Business Relations Across the Taiwan Strait', *China Information* Vol. 10, No. 2, Autumn 1995.

——, 'Civil Society and Political Liberalization in Taiwan', *Bulletin of Concerned Asian Scholars*, Vol. 25, No. 1, January–March 1993.

Nizami, Z.A. and Devika Paul (eds.), *Human Rights in the Third World Countries*, Delhi: KIRS Publications, 1994.

Noordin S., *Towards a New Asia. A Report of the Commission for a New Asia.* Kuala Lumpur, 1994.

Norris, Pippa, 'Introduction: The Politics of Electoral Reform', *International Political Science Review*, Vol. 16, No. 1, 1995.

O'Donnell, Guillermo, Philippe C. Schmitter and Laurence Whitehead (eds), *Transitions from Authoritarian Rule: Tentative Conclusions about Uncertain Democracies*, 4 volumes, Baltimore: Johns Hopkins University Press, 1986.

Obeyesekere, Gananath, 'Some Comments on the Social Backgrounds of the April 1971 Insurgency in Sri Lanka (Ceylon)', *Journal of Asian Studies*, Vol. 33 No. 3, 1974.

Pan, Zhongdang, Steven H. Chaffee, Godwin C. Chu and Yanan Ju, *To See Ourselves. Comparing Traditional Chinese and American Cultural Values*, Boulder: Westview Press, 1994.

Panikkar, K.N. (ed.), *Communalism in India: History, Politics and Culture*, New Delhi: Manohar, 1991

Parel, Anthony J. and Ronald C. Keith (eds), *Comparative Political Philosophy: Studies under the Upas Tree*, New Delhi: Sage, 1992.

Park, C.H., *Our Nation's Path*, Seoul: Dong-A Publishing Company Ltd., 1962.

Pempel, T. J., 'Democracy in Japan,' in Craig C. Garby and Mary Brown Bullock (eds), *Japan: A New Kind of Superpower*, Washington, D.C.: The Woodrow Wilson Press, 1994.

——, 'Conclusion. One-Party Dominance and the Creation of Regimes', in T. J. Pempel (ed.), *Uncommon Democracies: The One-Party Dominant Regimes*, Ithaca: Cornell University Press, 1990.

——, 'The Unbounding of Japan, "Japan, Inc.": The Changing Dynamics of Japanese Policy Formulation', *Journal of Japanese Studies*, Vol. 13, No. 2, Summer 1987.

——, *Policy and Politics in Japan: Creative Conservatism*, Philadelphia: Temple University Press, 1982.

Perera, N.M., *Critical Analysis of the New Constitution of the Sri Lankan Government*, Colombo: N.M. Perera Memorial Trust, 1979.

Phadnis, Urmila, 'Sri Lanka: Crises of Legitimacy and Integration'. In: L. Diamond, J.J. Linz and S.M. Lipset (eds.), *Democracy in Developing Countries. Volume 3: Asia.* Boulder, Colorado: Lynne Rienner Publishers, 1989.

Powell, G. Bingham, *Contemporary Democracies: Participation, Stability, and Violence*, Cambridge: Harvard University Press, 1982.

Premasiri, P.D., 'Minorities in Buddhist Doctrine', in K.M. de Silva, Pensri Duke, Ellen S. Goldberg and Nathan Katz (eds.), *Ethnic Conflict in Buddhist Societies: Sri Lanka, Thailand and Burma*, Boulder: Westview, 1988.

——, *Democracy and the Market: Political and Economic Reforms in East Europe and Latin America*, Cambridge: Cambridge University Press, 1991.

Przeworski, Adam, 'Some Problems in the Study of the Transition to Democracy', in Guillermo O'Donnell, Philippe C. Schmitter, and Laurence Whitehead (eds), *Transition from Authoritarian Rule: Comparative Perspectives*, Baltimore: Johns Hopkins University Press, 1986.

Puthucheary, James, *Ownership and Control in the Malaysian Economy*, Singapore: Eastern Universities Press, 1960.

Pye, Lucian W., *Asian Power and Politics: The Cultural Dimensions of Authority*, Cambridge, Mass.: Harvard University Press, 1985.

—— and Mary W. Pye, *Asian Power and politics: The Cultural Dimensions of Authority*, Cambridge, Mass.: Harvard University Press, 1985

—— and Sidney Verba (eds), *Political Culture and Political Development*, Princeton, NJ: Princeton University Press, 1965.

Quarterly Newsletter of the South-Asian Human Rights Action Programme, 1992–93.

Ramage, Douglas, *Democracy, Islam and the Ideology of Tolerance*, London: Routledge, 1995.

Rao, Krishna, 'Mysore reforms: a non-official scheme', typewritten manuscript written in Mysore, India Office Library London, V 15447, 1922.

Rear, John, 'One Brand of Politics', in Keith Hopkins (ed.), *Hong Kong: The Industrial Colony*, Hong Kong: Oxford University Press, 1971.

Reed, G.G., 'Moral/political education in the People's Republic of China: learning through role models', *Journal of Moral Education*, Vol. 24, No. 2, 1995.

Reed, Steven R., 'The 1996 Japanese General Election', *Electoral Studies*, Vol. 16, No. 1, 1997.

——, 'The 1990 General Election: Explaining the Historic Socialist Victory', *Electoral Studies*, Vol. 10, 1991.

Ren, Xiao'ai, 'Jianli tuanjie, minzhu, pingheng, hexie de shisheng guanxi. Xin shiqi banzhuren gongzuo chuyi zhi yi' [Build a united, democratic, balanced, and harmonious relation between teachers and students. My humble opinion on class teacher work in a new era]. (Part one), *Beijing jiaoyu*, No. 9, 1988, and (Part four), *Beijing jiaoyu*, No. 12, 1988.

Report of the Commission on Constitutional Reform. Colombo: Ceylon Government Press, 1969.

Report of the Indian Statutory Commission, Vol. 1, London: Stationary Office, 1930.

Review of Emergency Regulations, Colombo: Centre for the Study of Human Rights, University of Colombo (in association with Nadesan Centre), 1993.

Richardson, Bradley M. and Scott C. Flanagan, *Politics in Japan*, Boston: Little, Brown and Company, 1984.

Robinson, M., 'Perceptions of Confucianism in Twentieth-Century Korea' in Gilbert Rozman (ed.), *The East Asian Region. Confucian Heritage and its Modern Adaption*, Princeton, NJ: Princeton University Press, 1991.

Rodan, Garry, *Ideological Convergences Across 'East' and 'West': The New Conservative Offensive*, Working Paper No. 41, Aalborg University, Denmark, 1995.

—— and Kevin Hewson, 'The Clash of Cultures or Convergence of Political Ideologies', paper presented at a conference entitled 'Looking North: Reassessing the Framework and Unravelling the Myths', held by the Asia Research Centre, Murdoch University, 18–19 November, 1994.

Ronan, Colin A. and Joseph Needham, *The Shorter Science and Civilization in China*, Cambridge: Cambridge University Press, 1978.

Rudner, Martin, *Nationalism, Planning and Economic Modernization: The Politics of Beginning Development*, London: Sage, 1975.

Rudolph, L. and S. Hoeber Rudolph, 'The subcontinental Empire and the regional Kingdom in Indian state formation', in P. Wallace (ed.), *Region and Nation in India*, New Delhi: Oxford IBH Publishing Co., 1985.

Rule, Wilma, 'Women's Underrepresentation and Electoral Systems', *PS: Political Science and Politics*, Vol. 37, No. 4, 1994.

Samaraweera, Vijaya, 'The Administration and the Judicial System', in K.M. de Silva (ed.), *Sri Lanka, A Survey*. London: Hurst and Company, 1977.

Saravanamuttu, Johan, 'The State, Authoritarianism and Industrialization: Reflections on the Malaysian Case', *Kajian Malaysia*, 5(2), 1987.

Sarkar, B.K., 'Democratic ideals and republican institutions in India', *The American Political Science Review*, Vol. 12, No. 4, 1918

Särlvik, Bo, 'Valsystemet i Storbritannien' [The electoral system in Great Britain], *Statsvetenskaplig Tidskrift* 1994.

Sartori, Giovanni, *Parties and Political Systems*, Cambridge: Cambridge University Press, 1976.

Scalapino, Robert A., 'Democratizing Dragons: South Korea and Taiwan', *Journal of Democracy*, Vol. 4, No. 3, July 1993.

Schmitter, Philippe C., 'Reflections on Where the Theory of Neo-Corporatism Has Gone and Where the Praxis of Neo-Corporatism May Be Going', in Gerhard Lehmbruch and Philippe C. Schmitter (eds), *Patterns of Corporatist Policy-Making*, London: Sage Publications, 1982.

Schumpeter, Joseph A., *Capitalism, Socialism and Democracy*, 3rd. ed., London: George Allen and Unwin, 1950.

Scott, James C., *Weapons of the Weak: Everyday Forms of Peasant Resistance*, New Haven and London: Yale University Press, 1985.

Senaratne, Jagath P., *Political Conflict in Sri Lanka, 1977–1990*, Amsterdam: VU University Press, Sri Lanka Studies, no 4, 1997.

Shamsul A.B., 'Economic Dimension of Malay Nationalism', *Developing Economies*, September 1997.

Sharma, R.S., 'The socio-economic basis of Oriental despotism in India', in A.L. Basham (ed.), *Kingship in Asia and Early America*. 30th International Congress of Human Sciences in Asia and North Africa. Seminars. Mexico City: El Colegio de Mexico, 1981.

Shi, Jun, 'Mangmu "panbi" bu keqi' [Blind 'climbing' is not desirable], *Renshi yu rencai*, No. 8, 1990.

Shiratori, Rei, 'The Politics of Electoral Reform in Japan,' *International Political Science Review*, Vol. 16, No. 1, 1995.

Shirk, Susan, *Competitive Comrades: Career Incentives and Student Strategies in China*, Los Angeles, Berkeley: University of California Press, 1982.

Short, Anthony, *The Communist Insurrection in Malaya 1948–1960*, London: Frederick Muller, 1975.

Simanjuntak, Marsillam, *Pandangan Negara Integralistik* [The views of an integralistic state], Jakarta: Grafiti Press, 1994.

Skinner, Quentin, 'A Reply to my Critics', in James Tully (ed.), *Meaning and Context: Quentin Skinner and His Critics*, Cambridge: Polity Press, 1988

Smith, T.E., 'The Malayan Elections of 1959', *Pacific Affairs* 33, 1960.

——, *Report on the First Election of Members to the Legislative Council of the Federation of Malaya*, Kuala Lumpur: Government Printer, 1955.

Stein, B., *Thomas Munro: The Origins of the Colonial State and His Vision of Empire*, Delhi: Oxford University Press, 1989.

Stenson, Michael, *Industrial Conflict in Malaya: Prelude to the Communist Revolt of 1948*, London: Oxford University Press, 1970.

Stinchcombe, Arthur L., *Constructing Social Theories*, New York: Harcourt, Brace and World, 1968.

Stockwell, Anthony J. *British Policy and Malay Politics during the Malayan Union Experiment, 1942–1948*, Kuala Lumpur: Malaysian Branch of the Royal Asiatic Society, 1979.

Stokes, E.M.C., *English Utilitarians and India*, Oxford: Clarendon Press, 1959.

Stubs, Richard, *Hearts and Minds in Guerrilla Warfare: The Malayan Emergency 1948–1960*, Singapore: Oxford University Press, 1989.

Sun, Longji, *Zhongguo wenhua de shenceng jiegou* [The deep-structure of Chinese society], Hong Kong: Jixian she, 1983.

Swamy, M.R. Narayan, *Tigers of Lanka. From Boys to Guerillas*, Delhi: Konark Publishers, 1994.

Taagepera, Rein and Matthew Soberg Shugart, *Seats and Votes: The Effects and Determinants of Electoral Systems*, New York: Yale University Press, 1989.

Tambiah, Stanley J., *Buddhism Betrayed? Religion, Politics, and Violence in Sri Lanka*, Chicago: Chicago University Press, 1992.

———, *Sri Lanka. Ethnic Fratricide and the Dismantling of Democracy*, London: I.B. Tauris and Co, 1986.

Taylor, R.H., 'Delusion and Necessity: Elections and Politics in Southeast Asia', *Items* 48, No. 4, December 1994.

Thurston, Anne F., 'Village Elections in Lishu County: An Eye Witness Account', *China Focus*, 1 May 1995.

Tilly, Charles, 'War Making and State Making as Organized Crime', in Peter B. Evans, Dietrich Rueschemeyer and Theda Skocpol (eds), *Bringing the State Back In*, Cambridge: Cambridge University Press, 1985.

——— (ed.) *The Formation of National States in Western Europe*, Princeton, N.J.: Princeton University Press, 1975.

Toffler, Alvin, *Previews and Premises*, London: Pan Books, 1984.

Tremewan, Christopher, *The Political Economy of Social Control in Singapore*, London: Macmillan, 1994.

Triandis, H.C., *Culture and Social Behavior*, New York: McGraw-Hill, 1994.

Trindade, F.A. and H.P. Lee, *The Constitution of Malaysia, Further Perspectives and Development, Essays in Honour of Tun Mohamed Suffian*, Kuala Lumpur: Oxford University Press, 1986.

———, *The Constitution of Malaysia: Its Development 1957–1977*, Kuala Lumpur: Oxford University Press, 1978.

Tsang, Steve Yui-Sang, *Democracy Shelved: Great Britain, China and Attempts at Constitutional Reform*, Hong Kong: Oxford University Press, 1988.

Uhlin, Anders, *Indonesia and the 'Third Wave of Democratization'. The Indonesian Pro-Democracy Movement in a Changing World*, Richmond: Curzon Press, 1997.

Van der Horst, Josine, *Who Is He, What Is He Doing? Religious Rhetoric and Performances in Sri Lanka during R. Premadasa's Presidency (1989–1993)*, Vol. 2, Amsterdam: VU University Press, Sri Lanka Studies, 1995.

Vittachi, Tarzie, *Emergency '58: The Study of the Ceylon Race Riots*, London: Andre Deutsch, 1958.

Wacks, Raymond (ed.), *Civil Liberties in Hong Kong*, Hong Kong: Oxford University Press, 1988.

Wade, Robert, *Governing the Market: Economic Theory and the Role of Government in East Asian Industrialization*, Princeton, NJ: Princeton University Press, 1990.

Wah, Loh Kok, 'Developmentalism in Malaysia in the 1990s: Is the shift from the politics of ethnicisms underway?', a working paper for The First Malaysian Studies Conference, Kuala Lumpur, Malaysia, 11–13 August 1997.

Wang, Huning, '"Wenge" fansi yu zhengzhi tizhi gaige' ['Cultural Revolution' and the reform of the political system], *Shijie jingji daobao*, 29 September 1986.

Wang, Keqian, 'Shilun jiazhi he pingjia' [On values and evaluations], *Shehui kexue jikan*, no.1, 1990.

Wang, Xingzhou, 'Guanyu daode pingjia de jiu ge wenti' [On some problems of moral evaluation], *Dongbei shida xuebao (zhexue shehui kexue ban)*, No. 3, 1987.

Warnapala, W.A. Wiswa, *Civil Service Administration in Ceylon. A Study in Bureaucratic Adaptation*, Colombo: Department of Cultural Affairs, 1974.

Watanuki, Toji, 'Patterns of Politics in Present-Day Japan', in Seymour M. Lipset and Stein Rokkan (eds), *Party Systems and Voter Alignments: Cross-National Perspectives*, New York: The Free Press, 1967.

White, Gordon, 'Democratization and Economic Reform in China', *The Australian Journal of Chinese Affairs*, No. 31, 1994.

Whitehead, Laurence, 'The Democratization of Taiwan: A Comparative Perspective', in Steve Tsang and Hung-mao Tien (eds), *Democratization in Taiwan: Implications for China*, Basingstoke: Macmillan, 1999.

Wildavsky, Aaron, 'Changing Forward Versus Changing Back', *Yale Law Journal* 88, 1978.

Wilson, A. Jeyaratnam, *S.J.V. Chelvanayakam and the Crisis of Sri Lankan Tamil Nationalism, 1947–1977*. London: Hurst and Co, 1994.

——, *The Break-up of Sri Lanka. The Sinhalese–Tamil Conflict*, London: C. Hurst and Company, 1988.

Wittfogel, K.A., *Oriental Despotism: a Comprehensive Study of Total Power*, New Haven: Yale University Press, 1957.

Wong, Siu-lun, 'Business and Politics in Hong Kong During the Transition', in Benjamin K.P. Leung and Teresa Y.C. Wong (eds), *25 Years of Social and Economic Development in Hong Kong*, Hong Kong: University of Hong Kong, 1994.

Woodward, Mark (ed.), *Toward a New Paradigm. Recent Developments in Indonesian Political Thought*, Tuscon: Arizona State University Program on Southeast Asia, 1996.

Wu, J.S., 'Western Philosophy and the search for Chinese wisdom', in Arne Naess and Alastair Hannay (eds), *Invitation to Chinese Philosophy*, Oslo: Universitetsforlaget, 1972.

Xia, Daoxing, 'Gaige sixiang pinde ke kaocha de changshi' [An attempt to examine the reform of ideology and morality classes], *Jiaoxue yanjiu (xiaoxue ban)*, No. 4, 1987.

Xie, Hongmao and Chen Weifeng, 'Daxuesheng suzhi zonghe ceping tansuo' [Exploring the comprehensive appraisal of university students], *Fujian gaojiao yanjiu*, No. 1, 1991.

Xing, Li, *China and East Asia vs. the West: Controversies, Clashes and Challenges*, Working Paper No. 47, Aalborg University, 1995.

Yang, K.P. and G. Henderson, 'An Outline History of Korean Confucianism', *Journal of Asian Studies*, Vol. 17, No. 1, 1958.

Yatim, Rais, *Freedom under Executive Power in Malaysia: A Study of Executive Supremacy*, Kuala Lumpur: Endowment, 1995.

Yeh, Wen-hsin, *The Alienated Academy: Culture and Politics in Republican China, 1919–1937*, Cambridge, Mass.: Council on East Asian Studies, Harvard University, 1990.

Yoshikado, Nishio, *Nihon seiji no kiki* [Japanese politics in crisis], Tokyo: Tokyo shimbun shuppankyoku, 1994.

Youngson, A.J., *Hong Kong: Economic Growth and Policy*, Hong Kong: Oxford University Press, 1982.

Yü, Chün-fang, *The Revival of Buddhism in China. Chu-hung and the Late Ming Synthesis*, New York: Columbia University Press, 1981.

Zagorin, Perez, *Ways of Lying*, Cambridge, Mass: Harvard University Press, 1990.

Zaidi, A.M., *The Encyclopaedia of the Indian National Congress*, New Delhi: Chand Pubications, 1977.

Zakaria, F., 'Culture is Destiny. A Conversation with Lee Kuan Yew', *Foreign Affairs*, Vol. 73, No. 2, 1994.

Zhang, Yutian *et al.* (eds), *Xuexiao jiaoyu pingjia* [Evaluation in school education], Beijing: Zhongying minzu xueyuan chubanshe, 1987.

Zhongguo baike nianjian 1982 [China encyclopaedic yearbook 1982] Beijing: Zhongguo dabaike quanshu chubanshe, 1982.

Zimmerman, Joseph F., 'Electoral Systems and Representative Democracy', *PS: Political Science and Politics*, Vol. 37, No. 4, 1994.

CONTRIBUTORS

Hans Antlöv is an anthropologist working in Jakarta as programme officer of the Ford Foundation's Programme on Governance and Civil Society.

Børge Bakken, a sociologist, is a senior researcher at the Nordic Institute of Asian Studies in Copenhagen.

Geir Helgesen, a cultural sociologist, is a senior research fellow at the Nordic Institute of Asian Studies in Copenhagen.

Kazuki Iwanaga is a senior lecturer in Political Science at Halmstad University, Sweden.

Peter Kloos is professor of Non-Western Sociology at the Free University in Amsterdam.

Tak-Wing Ngo, a political scientist, is a lecturer in Chinese Politics at the Sinological Institute, Leiden University.

Bettina Robotka, a historian, is a senior researcher at the Seminar of South Asian History and Society, Humboldt University, Berlin.

Shamsul A.B. is professor of Social Anthropology and dean of the Faculty of Social Sciences and Humanities at the Universiti Kebangsaan Malaysia in Bangi, Selangor.

Laurence Whitehead, a political scientist, is an official fellow in politics at Nuffield College, Oxford University.

Li Xing is a research fellow at the Research Centre for Development and International Relations, Aalborg University, Denmark.

INDEX